Records and Information Management
Fundamentals of Professional Practice
3rd Edition

William Saffady, Ph.D.

Consulting Editor: Mary L. Ginn, Ph.D.
Composition: Cole Design & Production
Cover Art: Brett Dietrich

ARMA International
11880 College Blvd., Ste 450
Overland Park, KS 66210
913.341.3808

A5026 | 978-1-936654-71-0

Contents

Chapter 2   **Preparing Retention Schedules I: Inventorying Records** **37**

Preface

Like its predecessors, this edition of *Records and Information Management: Fundamentals of Professional Practice* deals with principles and practices for systematic management of recorded information. It is intended for newly appointed records managers, for experienced professionals who want a review of specific topics, for supervisors whose oversight responsibilities include records management functions, for planners and decision-makers who develop strategies and tactics for managing their organizations' information assets, and for undergraduate and graduate students of records management or allied disciplines, such as library science, archives management, information systems, and office administration, that are concerned with the storage, organization, retrieval, retention, or protection of recorded information.

The third edition is organized into eight chapters that reflect the scope and responsibilities of records management programs in companies, government agencies, universities, cultural and philanthropic institutions, professional services firms, and other organizations:

- *Chapter 1* **examines the role of records management as a business discipline.** It begins with a summary of the conceptual foundations of systematic records management, followed by an overview of the most important components of a records management program and an evaluation of records management's contribution to organizational effectiveness.

- *Chapter 2* **is the first of two chapters about records retention.** It discusses the records inventory, a fact-finding survey that identifies and describes an organization's records. It explains inventory work steps, emphasizing important considerations for records managers who must plan and conduct inventories for retention scheduling.

- *Chapter 3* **deals with the purpose, content, and format of records retention schedules.** They are a core component in a systematic records and information management program. This chapter emphasizes legal and operational considerations that determine how long an organization must retain its records, and it provides examples of legal and regulatory retention requirements for commonly encountered types of records. The chapter also discusses the implementation of retention schedules, including secure destruction methods for confidential records and the importance of auditing retention practices for compliance with retention schedules.

- *Chapter 4* **surveys the characteristics and components of records centers.** These centers provide economical warehouse-type storage for inactive records. This chapter emphasizes factors that records managers must consider when planning, implementing, and operating in-house records centers or when evaluating the facilities and capabilities of commercial storage providers. Topics include records storage containers, shelving, fire protection requirements, environmental controls, material handling equipment, and retrieval operations.

- *Chapter 5* **examines two document imaging technologies: digital imaging (scanning) and micrographics.** It explains the distinctive characteristics and advantages of each technology for managing recorded information. It also describes image production methods as well as system requirements for retrieving, viewing, and printing document images. The chapter concludes with a discussion of imaging service companies as an alternative or supplement to in-house imaging operations.

- *Chapter 6* **deals with vital records, which contain information that is indispensable to an organization's mission-critical operations.** Vital records protection is placed into the context of an organization's business continuity and disaster preparedness initiatives. Components of a systematic program for identification and protection of vital information assets, including methods for assessing risk and reconstructing records in the event of a disaster, are discussed.

- *Chapter 7* **examines filing principles and methods for physical (paper) records and, where applicable, other media.** It begins with a discussion of centralized filing, followed by surveys of file arrangements, filing equipment, and filing supplies. Rather than explaining how to file, it presents essential concepts from an analytical and managerial perspective.

- *Chapter 8* **deals with digital documents, an important and rapidly growing category of recorded information.** It begins with an overview of document indexing concepts, including the identification of indexing parameters and selection of index values. Three computer applications that deal specifically with digital documents: document management systems, records management application software, and email archiving software are described and discussed.

In every chapter, the treatment is practical rather than theoretical. The discussion of specific topics emphasizes **best practices**, which are defined as the most advisable courses of action for particular recordkeeping problems or processes. Published standards, the embodiment of best practices, are cited where applicable.

Although terms and concepts are defined when first introduced in the text, *Appendix A* **provides a glossary of important definitions for convenient reference.** *Appendix B* **contains suggestions for further study and research about records management concepts and practices.**

Chapter 1

Records Management as a Business Discipline

Records management is a specialized discipline that is concerned with the systematic analysis and control of information created, received, maintained, or used by an organization pursuant to its mission, operations, and activities. By definition, *records management* is concerned with information that is recorded or "written down" as opposed to merely memorized or exchanged verbally. The concept of a **record** as a written instrument is well established. As defined in the 1911 edition of *Encyclopedia Britannica*, "a record is a document regularly drawn up for a legal or administrative purpose and preserved in proper custody to perpetuate the memory of the transaction described in it." The 1913 edition of *Webster's Revised Unabridged Dictionary*, published by G. & C. Merriam Company, defines a record as "a writing by which some act or event, or a number of acts or events, is recorded." More recently, the latest edition of the *American Heritage Dictionary of the English Language*, published by Houghton Mifflin, defines a record as "an account, as of information or facts, set down especially in writing as a means of preserving knowledge." *Webster's New World Collegiate Dictionary* similarly defines a record as "anything that is written down and preserved as evidence."

In this context, "written down" encompasses a variety of recording methods, including, but not limited to, handwriting, typewriting, drawing, computer data entry, computer printing, photography, audio recording, and video recording. Thus, handwritten notes and voice recordings made during a meeting are examples of **recorded information** as are any subsequent transcriptions made from them. In some cases, however, confidential information—discussed "off the record," as it were—is intentionally excluded from such voice recordings and transcriptions. The excluded information may be very important and have a decisive impact on an organization's operations and activities, but it does not come within the scope of records management authority or initiatives unless and until it is written down. As a matter of policy, an organization may also choose to exclude certain types of recorded information from the scope of records management authority. Such "nonrecords" are defined and discussed later in this chapter.

The previous edition of this book characterized records as physical objects that contain information, but the term "record" is variously used to denote an information-bearing object, the information that the object contains, or both. The ISO 15489-1 standard, *Information and Documentation—Records Management, Part 1: General,* and the ISO 30300 standard, *Information and Documentation— Management Systems for Records—Fundamentals and Vocabulary,* define records as information that is created, received, or maintained in "pursuance of legal obligations or in the transaction of business." No mention is made of the physical medium on which the information is recorded. The Oxford English Dictionary provides a similar but more general definition of a record as "a piece of evidence or information constituting an account of something that has occurred, been said, etc."

With paper documents and photographs, which are sometimes described as **physical (paper) records/documents** to distinguish them from electronic records, there is a one-to-one correspondence between an information-bearing object— one or more sheets of paper, for example—and its contents—a payment voucher, a medical test report, an employee's performance evaluation, an item of correspondence, etc. Either the physical object or its contents might be termed a record. By contrast, an electronic storage medium, such as a hard drive, typically contains information about many different matters. In such situations, the individual documents or files saved on the hard drive are considered records. The hard drive, the physical object that contains the information, is not. Exceptions are encountered, however. A DVD or videotape, for example, might contain a video recording of a meeting or other event and no additional information, in which case the term "record" might be used interchangeably to describe the storage medium and its contents. Similarly, a voluminous database might occupy an entire storage medium or multiple media.

Whether applied to physical objects or their contents, the term "record" encompasses information in any format on any medium. The Federal Records Act (44 U.S. Code 3301) provides a useful model for other organizations to follow. It defines U.S. government records as:

> "all books, papers, maps, photographs, machine-readable materials, or other documentary materials, regardless of physical form or characteristics, made or received by an agency of the U.S. Government under Federal law or in connection with the transaction of public business and preserved or appropriate for preservation by that agency or its legitimate successor as evidence of the organization, functions, policies, decisions, procedures, operations, or other activities of the Government or because of the informational value of the data in them."

Public record laws in other countries include comparably broad definitions.

- **Canada.** The Canadian Access to Information Act (R.S. 1985, c. A-1, s-1), for example, defines government records as "any documentary material, regardless of medium or form."

- **The United Kingdom.** In the United Kingdom, for example, the Public Records Act 1958 (c.51 6_and_7_Eliz_2) defines records to include "not only written records but records conveying information by any other means whatsoever."

- **Australia.** The Australian Archives Amendment Act (No. 113, 2008) defines government records to include documents or objects "in any form (including any electronic form)." Section 2B of the Australian Acts Interpretation Act (No. 2, 1901 as amended) defines a document as "anything on which there is writing; and anything on which there are marks, figures, symbols or perforations having a meaning for persons qualified to interpret them; anything from which sounds, images or writings can be reproduced with or without the aid of anything else; and a map, plan, drawing, or photograph." It also defines a record to include "information stored or recorded by means of a computer."

- **New Zealand.** The New Zealand Public Records Act 2005 defines records to include information "in written form on any material; or on film, negative, tape, or other medium so as to be capable of being reproduced; or by means of any recording device or process, computer or other electronic device or process."

The previously cited ISO 15489-1 standard recognizes the global importance of systematic recordkeeping and the international applicability of records management principles. The concepts and methods presented in this book have been successfully implemented by government agencies, corporations, and other organizations throughout the world. The global validity of records management concepts and methods is important for multinational and transnational organizations that operate in more than one country. Such organizations can adopt consistent records management principles and practices throughout their operations, subject to variations required by local laws and regulations that apply to specific types of records.

This chapter examines the purpose and scope of records management as a business discipline. Throughout the book, "business" is used as a noun or adjective to denote or describe a purposeful activity, work to be done, or matters to be attended to by any type of organization. The term is not limited to commercial and industrial enterprises that are commonly characterized as "businesses."

The following discussion begins with a summary of the conceptual foundations of systematic records management, followed by an overview of the most important

---

Concepts and methods discussed in this book apply to recorded information that is created and maintained by organizations of all types and sizes, including:

- Federal, state, and local government agencies, including public authorities, public benefit corporations, and other quasi-governmental organizations.

- Corporations, partnerships, sole proprietorships, and other for-profit entities.

- Law firms, accounting firms, consulting firms, architectural and engineering firms, and other providers of professional services.

- Schools, colleges, universities, and other educational institutions.

- Museums, libraries, and other cultural institutions.

- Scientific and technical research organizations.

- Hospitals, clinics, physicians, dentists, clinical psychologists, physical therapists, nursing homes, and other healthcare providers.

- Not-for-profit organizations such as professional associations, philanthropic foundations, religious institutions, learned societies, social service agencies, charitable organizations, community-based organizations, and trade unions.

components of a records management program and an evaluation of the contribution to organizational effectiveness that records management makes. The chapter concludes with a discussion of the role of records management as a staff function and the relationship of records management to other information management disciplines and activities. Topics introduced in this chapter are examined in detail elsewhere in the book.

Conceptual Foundations

Although corporations, government agencies, and other organizations have been creating and maintaining records for centuries, the quantity, variety, and complexity of recorded information have increased dramatically, even exponentially, in recent decades.

Contributing factors include:

- The expanded scope and increased complexity of government operations at all levels.
- The expanded scope and increased complexity of commercial and industrial enterprises, including mergers and acquisitions that have created large multinational entities with operations in dozens or even hundreds of countries.
- Increased government regulations and their associated recordkeeping requirements, which affect the regulating agency as well as the regulated entity.
- A large white-collar workforce that depends on recorded information for the completion of assigned tasks, management analysis and decision-making, project management, and other purposes.
- The increased prominence and economic significance of information-intensive service industries such as banking, insurance, management consulting, litigation support, and healthcare.
- The widespread implementation of computers, high-speed printers, photocopiers, data communications, and other technologies that can quickly generate large quantities of recorded information in a variety of formats.

Records management principles and practices have developed in response to the increased pervasiveness of information-related activities that characterize modern work environments and the corresponding need for systematic approaches to recordkeeping requirements. While early archival initiatives emphasized the need to preserve important records, most observers trace the emergence of records management as a business specialty to U.S. government concerns about recordkeeping costs during the 1940s and 1950s. When government operations were expanding, these early initiatives concentrated on timely destruction of obsolete records and offsite storage of inactive records. Since that time, records concepts and methods have been expanded and refined considerably. Today, records management is a multifaceted field with tens of thousands of professional practitioners. While records management has its own well-defined body of principles, policies, and procedures, it incorporates ideas and practices from such related fields as computing, knowledge management, information science, library science, archival administration, and industrial engineering.

The following sections review the most important principles on which a systematic records management program is based. These principles provide a firm conceptual foundation for the development and implementation of effective records management initiatives. They must be clearly articulated in an organization's records management policies.

Ownership of Records

An organization is the owner of all records created, received, and/or maintained by its employees—subject to predetermined exclusions, by contractors, temporary employees, and unpaid employees such as student interns and volunteers—in connection with the organization's mission, business operations, and other activities. Such records are sometimes described as an organization's official records, although that phrase, which has no standard definition, may have other meanings in specific situations. For example, it sometimes denotes a government record or other record with special legal status such as a birth certificate that is authenticated by an authorized public official. Alternatively, an official record may be equated with an official copy of a record, which is defined in Chapter 3.

Terminology aside, an organization's records are its property. As the owner of its records, an organization is solely empowered to make decisions about their storage, distribution, control, protection, organization, retention, destruction, or use. In the United States, this position is well articulated for government records, which are owned by the public. The following codes are among the many examples that might be cited.

- The Federal Records Act (44 U.S. Code 3106) prohibits the unauthorized removal, alteration, or destruction of agency records. According to 18 U.S. Code 2071, destruction, mutilation, or obliteration of public records is punishable by up to three years in prison.

- Under Section 175.25 of the New York State Penal Law, removing, destroying, mutilating, or altering public records is a felony.

- According to Section 40.16.010 of the Revised Code of Washington, unauthorized destruction of public records is a Class C felony punishable by imprisonment, fine, or both.

- According to Section 6200 of the California Government Code, destruction, theft, mutilation, or alteration of public records is punishable by up to four years in prison.

Similar provisions apply in other countries. In Canada, for example, the Library and Archives of Canada Act (2004, c. 11) prohibits the destruction of government or ministerial records without the written consent of the Librarian and Archivist. In the United Kingdom, Section 6 of the Public Records Act 1958 ((c.51 6_and_7_Eliz_2) specifies that destruction of public records requires approval by the Lord Chancellor and other persons who are primarily responsible for the records. In Australia, the Public Record Office Victoria Recordkeeping Standard: Disposal (PROS 10.13) states that the Keeper of Public Records must approve destruction of public records.

From an ownership perspective, an organization's authority over its records is identical to its authority over real estate, equipment, inventory, or other property. No employee has, by virtue of his or her position, any personal or property right to or property interest in an organization's records, even though he or she may be named as the creator, recipient, custodian, or principal user of them. When permitted by records management policies and procedures, so-called personal files may be established for the convenience of individual employees, but this practice is done without any connotation of personal ownership. Such personal files may be kept in employees' offices or desks, on personal computers, or in personal storage space on network file servers. They may contain unique records or copies of selected records that reside in other locations. Because they pertain to an organization's mission, operations, and activities, personal files are the organization's property and are subject to the organization's records management policies and procedures, including retention guidelines discussed in Chapter 3. When employees retire, resign, or otherwise leave an organization, they cannot take personal files with them unless they are expressly permitted to do so.

The concept of ownership of records applies to all information, but it may require elaboration or clarification in special situations. In the United States, for example, medical records are generally treated as the property of the healthcare facility or clinician that creates and maintains them, but most states have enacted laws that give patients access to their medical records. In some states, patients are said to own the information in their medical records as opposed to the actual records, but this concept of ownership confers limited authority. Patients can obtain copies of their medical records for their own use, to give to other healthcare providers, for review by attorneys, or for other purposes. Patients cannot make decisions about the storage, retention, or destruction of their medical records by healthcare agencies or providers.

Confusion sometimes arises about the status of personal papers as distinct from personal files, which were defined above as copies of an organization's records created for the convenience of individual employees pursuant to the employees' duties as permitted by policies and procedures. As previously explained, personal files are the property of the employer not the employee. True personal papers, by contrast, are unrelated to an organization's mission, goals, objectives, or business operations or to an employee's assigned duties. They are information-bearing objects of a private nature. Examples include:

- Documents or computer files created by an employee before joining an organization and that were not used subsequently for the organization's business.

- Documents or computer files relating to professional affiliations.

- Diaries, journals, and calendars that relate exclusively to personal appointments, activities, or other personal matters.

- Notes and correspondence that are not related in any way to the employer's business.

- Papers or computer files relating to volunteer work or community service that an employee may undertake without the organization's involvement.

- Family photographs.

- Diplomas, training certificates, and citations unrelated to the employer's business.

These items are the property of their creators and are consequently excluded from records management authority. As such, personal papers are considered nonrecords, which are discussed later in this chapter. If personal papers are kept in employees' offices, they should be clearly designated as such and maintained separately from the organization's records. Some organizations prohibit employees from using organizational property or organizational computer resources to create or maintain all or specific personal papers. Examples include documents, photographs, or computer files with sexist, racist, defamatory, abusive, or obscene content; documents with copyrighted content where required permissions have not been obtained; and email messages or attachments that contain or are suspected of containing viruses or other malicious software.

Records as Assets

Broadly defined, an *asset* is something of value. While recordkeeping is sometimes treated as a tedious administrative chore or, at best, a necessary evil, systematic records management takes a different view. **Recordkeeping**—broadly defined—to encompass the creation, organization, storage, retrieval, and use of recorded information—is an ordinary and necessary aspect of virtually all business operations. Records contain information that is needed by and, in some cases, is indispensable to the organization that creates and maintains them. Recorded information is an asset not a burden.

Viewed in this way, *systematic records management* is an aspect of *asset management*, a business discipline that seeks the most effective deployment of an organization's assets to support its mission, operations, and activities. The ISO 55000:2014 standard, *Asset Management—Overview, principles and terminology*, defines an asset as something that has potential or actual value to an organization. By that definition, recorded information is a significant organizational asset. It is essential for transaction processing, the development and delivery of products and services, planning, analysis, decision-making, legal and regulatory compliance, customer service, and other purposes. In government, recorded information protects the rights of citizens, property owners, taxpayers, and others. In the private sector, recorded information protects the rights of shareholders, partners, or other owners. In healthcare and social services agencies, recorded information is an essential component of patient care and client services. In academic and cultural institutions, scientific research organizations, charities, religious groups, and other not-for-profit organizations, recorded information documents activities and accomplishments that fulfill an organization's mission.

Although asset management concepts were originally developed for life cycle planning and control of physical assets, such as equipment, buildings, and infrastructure components, they are broadly applicable to intangible assets, including financial assets, human assets, and information assets. As discussed throughout this book, the principles and objectives of asset management and records management are closely aligned. According to the ISO 55000:2014 standard, asset management enables an organization to realize value by balancing costs, risks, opportunities, and performance benefits. A systematic records management program enables an organization to realize value by balancing the costs, risks, opportunities, and performance benefits of recordkeeping systems. Asset management seeks to optimize costs and benefits at all stages of an asset's lifecycle—from construction or procurement through operation, maintenance, and disposal. Records management seeks to optimize costs and benefits at all stages of recorded information's life cycle—from creation through utilization and, ultimately, destruction or preservation.

Records Formats

Records management concepts and methods apply to recorded information in all formats, including:

- **Paper documents.** Examples include office files, business forms, engineering drawings, charts, maps, plans, patient records, student records, project files, legal case files, technical or managerial reports, and computer printouts.

- **Photographic media.** Examples include photographic negatives and slides, medical or scientific imagery, motion picture films, and filmstrips, as well as microfilm, microfiche, aperture cards, and other microforms produced from paper documents or computer data.

- **Electronic records.** Examples include computer databases, word processing files, spreadsheet files, presentations, email messages, voice mail, instant messages, document images, computer-aided design (CAD) files, geographical information system (GIS) files, computer-generated graphics, digital photography, audio recordings, and video recordings.

In some cases, ordinary or unusual objects may also be considered operating records. In many localities, for example, a construction project must be preceded by an analysis of soil samples from the proposed building site for specific environmental characteristics. The analysis is embodied in a written report for which the soil samples serve as supporting material. Similarly, pharmaceutical research organizations remove tissue samples from laboratory animals when evaluating the safety of drugs under development. The tissue samples serve as supporting materials for written toxicology reports and other test documentation. In these situations, the soil samples and tissue samples—objects that are not normally considered

Figure 1-1

**Information
Life Cycle**

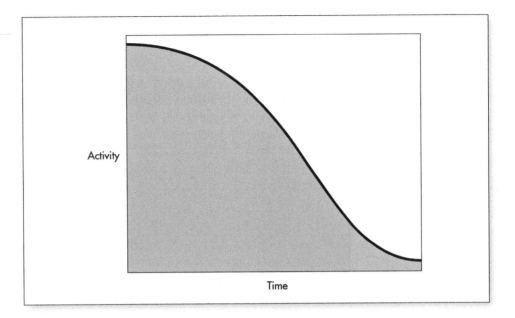

records—come within the scope of records management authority and records retention initiatives. The same treatment may apply to architectural models associated with building design projects, prototypes, and samples associated with product design projects, faunal and floral remains associated with archaeological excavation, and other objects associated with research, development, and manufacturing projects.

Information Life Cycle

As with other assets, the value of recorded information is subject to change over time. The concept of an **information life cycle** is well established in records management theory and practice. Recorded information is subject to changing requirements for timely retrieval, convenient distribution, and cost-effective storage from its creation or receipt through destruction or permanent retention. The business significance of many, if not most, records varies inversely with the age of the records. The information life cycle, showing reduced reference activity for recorded information with passage of time, is depicted in Figure 1-1. Most records maintained by corporations, government agencies, and other organizations are referenced frequently for a relatively brief period of time following their creation or receipt while transactions, projects, events, or other matters are under active consideration. As time passes and the matters to which the records pertain are resolved or cease to be of active interest, reference activity diminishes. This decrease in activity may occur gradually or abruptly.

- *Some records have short life cycles.* Notes of telephone calls, unsolicited email messages, and information generated by social media technologies, such as instant messaging, are often discarded after an initial reading. Meeting invitations, scheduled appointments, reminder notes, and other calendar items may be discarded after they are accepted and entered onto an employee's calendar. Others records, such as correspondence and email that deals with routine administrative matters, may be saved for a brief period of time then discarded.

- *Many transaction-oriented documents are referenced frequently until a transaction is completed; less often thereafter.* Purchase orders and insurance claims are referenced frequently for several weeks or months following their creation or receipt, but they are referenced only occasionally after the transactions to which they pertain are concluded. As discussed in Chapter 3, such records are typically kept for some period of time after a transaction is completed for possible use in litigation or to satisfy audit requirements.

- *Certain records retain their business value for longer periods.* Their retention parameters may be determined by the life cycles of objects or the duration of events or activities to which the records pertain. Engineering drawings of manufacturing facilities or equipment, for example, are retained at least as long as the facilities or equipment remain in service. Mortgages, deeds, surveys, leases, and other real estate records are retained as long as the properties to which they relate are owned or occupied by an organization. Records that relate to pharmaceutical products are retained as long as the products are marketed and often longer as continuing proof of safety or efficacy. Project documentation is retained as long as a project is active and for some period of time thereafter. Certain pension and trust records are retained until all beneficiaries are deceased and payment issues have been resolved. Academic transcripts are retained for a reasonable portion of a human lifetime. Hospitals, clinics, and other healthcare providers are required to retain certain medical records for a specified number of years after the last treatment of a patient.

- *Some records have continuing value that warrants long-term retention or permanent preservation.* Government agencies, for example, keep birth records, death records, marriage records, court records, property records, and certain court records permanently. Such records may be actively consulted for decades. A property title search, for example, may require access to deeds, mortgages, liens, judgments, and other documents that date back 30 years or longer. Government, corporate, and institutional archives preserve records of scholarly value, even though such records may experience limited reference activity. In fact, records of high scholarly value are often of interest to a limited audience of subject specialists. For reasons of confidentiality, some records retained for their scholarly value may not be made available to researchers for many years. Certain records— such as court records related to divorces, adoptions, juvenile offenders, and victims of sexual assaults—are retained permanently, but they may be sealed to prohibit access.

The information life cycle is divided by frequency of reference, into active and inactive (less active) stages. Each stage has distinct requirements. The active stage is concerned with the timely availability of information to support an organization's business operations. By contrast, the inactive stage is principally concerned with cost-effective, reliable retention of information, often for long periods of time. These life cycle concepts apply to recorded information in all formats—paper, photographic, and electronic. They are the basis for records retention decisions and other records management initiatives described in subsequent chapters. Many, if not most records, spend a longer portion of their life cycles in the inactive phase than in the active phase.

Records vs. Nonrecords

All records contain information, but not all information-bearing objects are considered records. Broad as they are, the definitions presented at the start of this chapter impose an important qualifier: ***Records contain information that is related to an organization's mission, operations, and activities and that come within the scope of records management authority.*** Information-bearing objects that meet this requirement are described as having *record status*. Those information-bearing objects that do not meet the requirement are categorized as *nonrecords*. Records management policies, procedures, and initiatives discussed in this book do not apply to them. Some widely cited examples of nonrecords include:

- Library materials and other publications, such as departmental copies of books or periodicals, that are acquired and maintained solely for general reference purposes rather than to support a specific business operation.

- Unsolicited brochures, catalogs, pamphlets, and other documents, usually received through the postal mail, that describe specific organizations, events, products, or services and that have no substantive business value.

- Unsolicited email, instant messages, text messages, and voice mail that have no substantive business value.

- Undistributed inventory of annual reports, bulletins, circulars, employee newsletters, brochures, posters, handbooks, publications, and other materials intended for sale or distribution.

- Blank copies of purchase requisitions, travel reimbursement requests, and other forms that, when completed for a specific business purpose, would be considered records.

- Personal papers that may be kept in an employee's work area or personal computer storage space and even filed in the same cabinets or hard drive directories as records, but that were not created or received in the course of business and do not relate in any way to the employee's duties. If information about personal matters and an organization's business is co-mingled in correspondence, email messages, or other documents, however, those information-bearing objects are considered records.

Some organizations broaden the above list to include drafts of documents once the final versions are completed, meeting notes once they are transcribed, worksheets from which data is extracted, outlines, and other records that lose their value once their contents are incorporated into other records. As discussed in Chapter 3, however, drafts, notes, working papers, and other documents of transitory value are best treated as records and made subject to retention policy guidance.

From a records management perspective, all information-bearing objects are divided into two categories: (1) records, which come within the scope of records management authority, and (2) nonrecords, which do not. The line between records and nonrecords is not sharply drawn in every case. Although lists of nonrecords are helpful, they are never conclusive. An information-bearing object may be considered a nonrecord in some circumstances and have record status in others. As an example, scientific books, journals, and other publications acquired by a pharmaceutical company's library for unspecified reference purposes or background reading by chemists, biologists, or other researchers are considered nonrecords. The same is true of photocopies of journal articles that individual scientists may keep in their work areas for general reference and professional development. On the other hand, a pharmaceutical company's intellectual property department may keep patent application files that include copies of journal articles or other publications that support the novelty of a claimed invention. A patent application may reference these publications, which are considered records because—in this context—they are directly related to a specific business activity.

Nonrecord designations exclude certain information-bearing objects from the scope of records management authority, policies, and procedures, but they do not affect the status of those objects as an organization's property. With the notable exception of personal papers, most if not all nonrecords on the previous list were paid for by the organization or acquired with the organization's resources and are the property of the organization that creates, receives, or maintains them. Thus, undistributed copies of annual reports or other publications are properly considered the organization's property and are subject to the organization's control, even though they are categorized as nonrecords from a records management perspective. An organization may have policies and procedures for distributing or disposing of excess inventory of its annual reports or other publications, but such policies and procedures would not be developed by the records management function.

Deteriorative Nature of Recordkeeping Problems

Records management is a problem-solving discipline. In the absence of systematic controls, problems with recorded information are all too familiar as the following examples illustrate.

- Large quantities of records, some of them obsolete, occupy valuable space needed for other purposes. Lack of storage space was one of the problems that brought records management to prominence as a business discipline in the 1950s, and it remains a significant concern today.

- Additional storage equipment and supplies must be purchased to accommodate the continued growth of recorded information.

- Large accumulations of recorded information are difficult to organize for effective retrieval.

- Records needed for a given purpose—be it decision-making, transaction processing, litigation support, regulatory compliance, product development, customer service, or some other activity—cannot be located in a timely manner, often with adverse consequences.

- Information handling is labor-intensive, time-consuming, and costly.

- Information that is needed to support mission-critical activities is lost or destroyed and cannot be reconstructed.

Traditionally, these problems have been closely associated with paper documents, but they apply to recorded information in all formats, including electronic formats. Storage space, regardless of record type, is not an infinitely available resource. Although hard drive capacities have increased, so have the storage demands of data-intensive computer applications, such as geographical information systems, digital asset management systems, and data mining applications that operate on voluminous data sets, so-called big data. Preparation and organization of information for computer storage and processing can be labor-intensive, time-consuming, and costly. Electronic records can be damaged or inappropriately deleted. Computerization is often viewed as a solution to the problems of paper filing systems, but the mere fact that information has been computerized is no guarantee that it can be retrieved when needed.

The previously cited records management problems are never self-limiting. As long as business activities are ongoing, records will continue to be created. Unless corrective action is taken, increasing amounts of space, equipment, supplies, and other resources will be required to store these new records. Information will never organize itself for retrieval. Essential records will be irrevocably lost. The cost of recordkeeping will continue to escalate.

The Business Case for Records Management

The need for recordkeeping is indisputable; it is an ordinary and necessary component of virtually all business operations, but there is a difference between keeping records and managing them in a planned, systematic manner.

In a section that lists the benefits of records management, the ISO 15489-1 standard cites the role of systematic recordkeeping for the orderly and efficient conduct of an organization's business. In U.S. government agencies, the benefits of systematic records management were acknowledged decades ago. The First Hoover Commission on the Organization of the Executive Branch of Government (1947-1949) included a task force that examined recordkeeping practices in U.S. government agencies and recommended legislation for the systematic management of all federal government records. The previously cited Federal Records Act specifies that heads of U.S. government agencies "shall establish and maintain an active, continuing program for the economical and efficient management of the records of the agency." In the United States, state and local government agencies are similarly obligated to implement records management policies and procedures, usually under the direction of a state archives or another designated unit. The South Carolina Public Records Act (Code of Laws of South Carolina, Section 30-1-80) is typical. It specifies that:

> "A records management program directed to the application of efficient and economical management methods and relating to the creation, utilization, maintenance, retention, preservation, and disposal of public records must be established and administered by the Archives…The head of each agency, the governing body of each subdivision, and every public records custodian shall cooperate with the Archives in complying with the provisions of this chapter and to establish and maintain an active, continuing program for the economical and efficient management of the records of the agency or subdivision."

Among the laws of other U.S. states, the California State Records Management Act (Government Code, Sections 12270-12279) requires the head of each state government agency to "establish and maintain an active, continuing program for the economical and efficient management of the records and information collection practices of the agency." The Nebraska Records Management Act (Nebraska Revised Statute 84-1207), the Oklahoma Records Management Act (67 O.S. 206), the Texas Local Government Records Act (Local Government Code, Section 203.021), and the Utah Public Records Management Act (Utah Code 63A-12-103) contain nearly identical language.

Similar mandates apply to government records in other countries. As an example, the Directive on Recordkeeping issued by the Treasury Board of Canada Secretariat in 2009 specifies that senior information management officials in federal government departments must establish and implement "key methodologies, mechanisms and tools to support the departmental recordkeeping requirements throughout the information life cycle." In the United Kingdom, the Lord Chancellor's Code of Practice on the Management of Records, which was issued in 2009, recognizes records management as a core business function and requires that public authorities implement a records management policy and a governance framework that defines roles and responsibilities for records management. According to the State Records Act 1998, every government department, agency, or other public office in New South Wales must establish and maintain a records management program. Among other Australian states with similar legislation, South Australia's State Records Act 1997 requires government agencies to maintain official records "in good order and condition," while Western Australia's State Records Act 2000 requires each government department to have a recordkeeping plan that addresses retention, disposition, and security of government records.

In nongovernmental organizations and the private sector, systematic records management is mandated by policies and executive directives rather than by law, if it is mandated at all. In such organizations, the business case for systematic records management depends on its contribution to the organization's effectiveness, for which recorded information is essential. Records management must provide demonstrable, quantifiable benefits for essential business operations or activities. These benefits include reduced operating costs, risk avoidance, and increased revenues. The following sections provide an overview of records management principles, program components, and benefits. Individual program components are examined more fully in subsequent chapters.

Programmatic Principles

As discussed in subsequent chapters, a comprehensive records management program includes policies, procedures, and processes that address significant recordkeeping issues, specifically:

- Determining how long recorded information needs to be kept to satisfy an organization's requirements.

- Ensuring compliance with recordkeeping laws and regulations in all locations where an organization has business operations.

- Managing inactive records in a cost-effective manner.

- Organizing active records for retrieval when needed.

- Protecting recorded information that supports mission-critical business operations.

These programmatic aspects are embodied in **Generally Accepted Recordkeeping Principles® (the Principles)**, which were issued by ARMA International in 2009 to foster general awareness of records management systems and standards and to assist organizations in developing effective programs for records management programs and information governance. The Principles provide a set of eight recordkeeping principles, which are paraphrased below:

1. **Accountability.** A senior executive should be in charge of the records management program. The accountable executive will delegate program responsibility to appropriate individuals, adopt records management policies and procedures to guide program personnel, and ensure that the program can be audited for compliance. A governance structure must be established for program development and implementation.

2. **Transparency.** An organization's recordkeeping processes and activities must be documented in an open and verifiable manner. Such documentation must confirm that the organization's recordkeeping policies and practices comply with applicable legal requirements and accurately and completely reflect the organization's activities. The documentation must be available to employees and appropriate interested parties.

3. **Integrity.** An organization's records must have a reasonable and suitable guarantee of authenticity and reliability. Recordkeeping processes, including audit

processes, must provide reasonable assurance that the origin, time or creation or transmission, and content of recorded information are what they are claimed to be.

4. **Protection.** An organization's records management program must protect records that are private, confidential, privileged, secret, or essential to business continuity. Recordkeeping procedures must provide appropriate protection controls from creation through final disposition of recorded information.

5. **Compliance.** An organization's records management program must comply with applicable laws, regulations, industry-specific rules of conduct, and other binding authorities related to creation, storage, retrieval, retention, disposition, dissemination, and protection of recorded information, as well as with the organization's own recordkeeping policies, procedures, and rules.

6. **Availability.** An organization's records must be organized, indexed, stored, and maintained in a manner that ensures timely, efficient, and accurate retrieval of information when needed.

7. **Retention.** An organization must retain records for an appropriate period of time to satisfy legal, regulatory, fiscal, operational, and historical requirements.

8. **Disposition.** An organization must provide secure and appropriate disposition for records that no longer need to be kept. In this context, disposition may involve destruction of records, transfer of records to another organization as part of a divestiture or other transaction, transfer of records to an archives or other scholarly repository, or transfer of records to clients or other parties who are the subjects of the records.

Records Management and Information Governance

According to the OECD *Glossary of Statistical Terms*, which was assembled by the Organization for Economic Cooperation and Development from documents issued by various international organizations, *governance* is the process by which decisions are made and implemented.

- ISO/IEC 38500, *Information Technology—Governance of IT for the Organization*, defines governance as "a system of directing and controlling."

- ISO/IEC TR 38502, *Information Technology—Governance of IT—Framework and Model*, defines a governance framework as the "strategies, policies, decision-making structures and accountabilities through which the organization's governance arrangements operate."

- Similarly broad definitions are presented in other ISO standards—such as ISO 21500, *Guidance on Project Management*, and ISO/IEC 27000, *Information Technology—Security Techniques—Information Security Management Systems—Overview and Vocabulary*—and in various other sources, including dictionaries of business terminology.

Building on these definitions, information governance can be viewed as a system for directing and controlling an organization's information assets. As such, information governance is a component or subset of organizational governance. Published definitions provide additional details.

- ARMA TR 22-2012, *Glossary of Records and Information Management Terms*, for example, defines information governance as "a strategic framework composed of standards, processes, roles and metrics that hold organizations and individuals accountable to create, organize, secure, maintain, use, and dispose of information in ways that align and contribute to the organization's goals."

- The American Health Information Management Association (AHIMA) defines information governance as "an organization-wide framework for managing information throughout its lifecycle and supporting the organization's strategy, operations, regulatory, legal, risk, and environmental requirements."

- According to the Commentary on Information Governance issued by the Sedona Conference in December 2013, information governance is "an organization's coordinated, interdisciplinary approach to satisfying information compliance requirements and managing information risks while optimizing information value."

- ISO/TS 14265, *Health Informatics—Classification of Purposes for Processing Personal Health Information*, and ISO/TR 11633-1, *Health Informatics—Information Security Management for Remote Maintenance of Medical Devices and Medical Information Systems—Part 1: Requirements and Risk Analysis*, define information governance as "processes by which an organization obtains assurance that the risks to its information, and thereby the operational capabilities and integrity of the organization, are effectively identified and managed."

An information governance framework, sometimes described as an *information governance model*, defines strategies, policies, decision-making structures, and accountabilities for creation, storage, use, analysis, distribution, disclosure, retention, disposition, and protection of information. As discussed throughout this book, records management is involved, to some degree, with all those information-related activities. Records management is an important component of an information governance program, but it is not the only component. Information governance is a collaborative initiative that requires the involvement and expertise of multiple stakeholders. Adapting a definition presented in ISO/Guide 73, *Risk Management—Vocabulary*, a *stakeholder* is a business unit or a functional area that is involved with or affected by an organization's information assets. In addition to records management, information governance stakeholders include, but are not necessarily limited to, information technology, information security, risk management, legal affairs, compliance, risk management, and the individual departments or other organizational units that have recorded information in their custody or under their supervisory control.

An information governance framework specifies roles and responsibilities that promote interaction, cooperation, and consultation among the following stakeholders, which are widely acknowledged to play key roles in defining the strategic direction for management of information assets in government agencies, companies, not-for-profit entities, and other organizations:

- *Records management develops and communicates policies, procedures, and guidelines for lifecycle management of an organization's information assets as discussed in subsequent chapters.* Information governance is not synonymous with records management, which focuses on the day-to-day execution of specific operations or activities that involve recorded information. These operations and activities are performed within the strategic framework defined by information governance.

- *Information technology creates and operates the technological infrastructure for processing, storage, retrieval, and distribution of an organization's information assets.* It optimizes the utilization of technological resources for cost-effective management of information assets, provides backup protection and disaster recovery capability for recorded information, and provides the technological expertise and support required to implement information management policies developed by other stakeholders.

- *Information security deals with issues related to confidentiality, data protection, and disclosure of an organization's information assets.* It develops and communicates data protection and privacy policies to prevent unauthorized access to recorded information, monitors and evaluates situations or events that may threaten information assets, responds to security breaches that involve recorded information, and works with other stakeholders to identify information assets that require special security arrangements.

- *Risk management identifies, analyzes, and quantifies risks that may affect, are attributable to, or are otherwise related to creation, storage, retrieval, distribution, disclosure, retention, disposition, or protection of an organization's information assets.* It develops and communicates policies and procedures to mitigate the adverse impact of specific information management policies and practices.

- *Legal affairs is concerned with legal issues and concerns that relate to recorded information.* It reviews **records retention** policies and schedules for legal acceptability. It establishes and communicates policies related to legal proceedings that involve recorded information. It provides opinions and advice to other stakeholders about legal issues related to recorded information.

- *Compliance is concerned with ensuring that an organization's practices comply with external requirements.* These requirements include laws, regulations, and industry-specific guidelines that specify retention and security requirements for recorded information, and with the organization's internal policies and directives for creation, storage, distribution, retention, disposition, and protection of information assets. Compliance will investigate suspected violations of organizational policies and present the findings with recommendations for corrective action.

- *Individual organizational units are responsible for day-to-day management of information in full compliance with applicable policies, procedures, guidelines, and directives.* They must identify and dispose of recorded information with elapsed retention periods, determine access privileges and restrictions that apply to specific information assets, organize information assets for retrieval when needed, and protect information assets from loss, damage, or improper disclosure.

In conjunction with the Principles discussed in the preceding section, ARMA International has issued an Information Governance Maturity Model that defines and describes five levels of program development—from sub-standard to transformational—for each of the eight principles. Organizations can use the maturity model for program evaluation and development, benchmarking, gap analysis, and risk assessment.

Records Retention

Companies, government agencies, educational institutions, and other organizations have long been concerned about the needless retention of obsolete records. In the United States, the Cockrell Committee (1887-1889) and the Keep Commission (1905-1909), two of the earliest bodies to examine the impact of recordkeeping practices on the cost of federal government operations, criticized the retention of unnecessary records. Early records management initiatives—such as the General Records Disposal Act of 1939, the Records Disposal Act of 1943, and the Federal Records Act of 1950—authorized the destruction of federal government records when no longer needed. Equally important, however, is the identification of records that must be kept to satisfy legal or regulatory requirements, to address operational needs, or to preserve information of enduring value.

In every organization, preservation and disposition of recorded information are critical concerns that must be governed by formalized policies and procedures rather than the discretion of individual employees. Determining how long recorded information needs to be kept to satisfy all requirements to which specific records are subject and developing effective procedures for implementing retention guidance are defining responsibilities of records management as a business discipline. Records retention policies and implementation procedures are core components of a systematic records management program. By ensuring the availability of an organization's information assets for appropriate periods of time, sound records retention policies and practices provide the foundation upon which other records management activities discussed in this book are based.

Compliance and Risk Management

As defined in the ISO 31000 standard, *Risk Management—Principles and Guidelines*, a risk management framework provides the foundation and organizational arrangements for directing and controlling an organization with regard to risk. An organization's risk management framework is embedded within its strategic and operational policies and practices. Records management is increasingly viewed as an important component of an organization's risk management framework.

In particular, a systematic records retention program can help an organization identify, evaluate, and minimize risks associated with legal matters and regulatory recordkeeping requirements.

As discussed in Chapter 3, all countries have laws and regulations that specify retention periods for recorded information associated with certain business activities and operations. These recordkeeping laws and regulations may also specify storage locations, acceptable media formats, retrieval requirements, restrictions on disclosure, and protection requirements for records associated with activities that are subject to government regulation. Some recordkeeping laws and regulations apply to commonly encountered business operations such as accounting, preparation of tax returns, and hiring of employees. Others apply to specific industries or business activities—such as financial services, utilities, healthcare, or pharmaceuticals—that are regulated by one or more government agencies.

The previously cited ISO 15489-1 standard identifies an organization's regulatory environment as a determining factor in records management initiatives. Recordkeeping laws and regulations apply to all private and public organizations that operate within a specific governmental jurisdiction. U.S. corporations, for example, are subject to recordkeeping requirements contained in federal laws and in the laws of every state or locality where they do business. Multinational organizations must comply with recordkeeping laws and regulations in all countries where they maintain business operations. Noncompliance can be costly. At a minimum, an organization will incur fines or penalties for failure to produce records when requested by government auditors, tax officials, regulatory bodies, law enforcement agencies, or other authorities. Among the many examples that might be cited:

1. The U.S. Internal Revenue Service can impose both civil and criminal penalties for failure to keep records or supply information required by the Internal Revenue Code. Deductions for which adequate documentation is not available may be disallowed with a resulting increase in taxes owed. Tax laws and regulations in other countries have similar provisions.

2. Employers that do not comply with recordkeeping requirements for Employment Eligibility Verification Form I-9 are subject to fines up to $1,100 for each form that is not retained for the minimum time period specified in 8 CFR 274a.

3. The Occupational Safety and Health Administration can impose civil penalties up to $7,000 for failure to maintain records for work-related illness and injuries as required in 29 CFR 1904. Large penalties have been imposed for willful and repeated recordkeeping violations.

4. The Customs Modernization Act provides for civil penalties of $10,000 to $100,000 per violation for failure to maintain and provide required documents to U.S. Customs and Border Protection as specified in 19 CFR 163.

5. The Bank Secrecy Act provides for civil penalties ranging from $25,000 to $100,000 for failure to comply with retention requirements for records relating to foreign financial accounts as specified in 31 CFR 1010.420.

6. Failure to comply with records retention requirements specified in Federal Motor Carrier Safety Regulations (49 CFR 379) will result in penalties up to $10,000.

In extreme cases, the failure to retain records for prescribed time periods can lead to a criminal charge of obstructing a federal audit, as defined in 18 U.S. Code 1516, while 18 U.S. Code 1812(c) specifies a fine and/or imprisonment up to 20 years for anyone who "alters, destroys, mutilates, or conceals a record, document or other object, or attempts to do so, with the intent to impair the object's integrity or availability for use in an official proceeding." Similar penalties are prescribed in 18 U.S. Code 1519.

By consulting appropriate reference tools and working with legal counsel, systematic records management initiatives identify laws and regulations that apply to specific records. To ensure compliance, legally mandated recordkeeping requirements are incorporated into records management policies and procedures.

Systematic records management can also reduce an organization's risk exposure in civil litigation, government investigations, and other legal proceedings. Recorded information plays a critical role as evidence in government audits and in product liability, personal injury, breach of contract, wrongful dismissal, and other lawsuits as the opposing parties seek to use documents, data, and other information to prove their contentions. Without clear, authoritative retention guidance, employees may unknowingly destroy records that are relevant for litigation, government investigations, or other legal matters, thereby exposing an organization to charges of destruction of evidence with intent to obstruct justice. Systematic records management initiatives can identify records that may be relevant and useful for future litigation, ensuring that those records will be available when needed. Further, in the absence of systematically developed retention policies, an organization will not be able to convincingly affirm that specific records requested during discovery by the opposing party were destroyed in the regular course of business prior to the commencement of legal proceedings.

By discarding obsolete records in a timely manner before lawsuits or government investigations are initiated, systematically developed retention policies can also reduce the logistic burdens and costs of legal discovery—the investigative phase of the pre-trial process that allows opposing parties to obtain information to help them build their claims or defenses. Discovery often involves an order for "document production," broadly defined as a request for records in paper or electronic formats. The cost of document production is directly related to the quantity of documents that must be produced, which in turn depends upon the quantity of records that the responding party has in its possession. In the absence of effective retention policies, many obsolete records, including outdated documents and drafts, will come within the scope of a document production order. These records must be identified, retrieved from their storage locations, reviewed for privilege, catalogued, copied, delivered to the requesting party, and returned to storage. If the records in question are stored offsite by a commercial provider, an organization will incur retrieval, refiling, and delivery charges to comply with a document production order. The organization must also place a **litigation hold** on these records, thereby incurring storage charges until legal issues are settled. For government agencies, retention of large quantities of obsolete records will increase the cost to comply with freedom-of-information law requests.

As the quantity of records increases, the burden of protecting personally identifiable information or other confidential records against unauthorized access will increase as well. Regulatory agencies can impose substantial penalties for the failure to protect such information. For example, banks and other financial services institutions are subject to fines up to $100,000 for failure to safeguard customer information as required by the Financial Services Modernization Act. Similarly, organizations can incur large fines for failure to safeguard and dispose of consumer credit information as prescribed by the Fair and Accurate Credit Transaction Act (FACTA).

Cost-effective Management of Inactive Records

Records management programs include a combination of elements that address both active and inactive records. In this context, active or inactive status is determined by the frequency with which records are consulted to support specific business processes or operations. The determination is admittedly imprecise: active records are consulted regularly and frequently; inactive records are not consulted regularly or frequently, but many inactive records must be retained for some period of time to meet legal or audit requirements or in anticipation of future business need, however occasional or unlikely that may be.

Distinctions between **active** and **inactive records** need not be precisely drawn to be meaningful. According to the previously discussed concept of an information life cycle, all records become less active as time passes. At any given time, some records are clearly identifiable as active or inactive, while others are at some stage in the transition from active to inactive status. Thus purchase orders and their supporting documentation are clearly active records until the ordered items are received and payment is made. A purchase order may remain active for an additional brief period of time until all questions about an ordered item and any payment issues are resolved, but it will seldom be consulted thereafter. Similarly, a special education student's individual educational program, classroom observations, health history forms, and other records will be consulted regularly and frequently while the student is enrolled. These records will become less active after the student graduates or leaves the school district.

In some cases, the transition from active to inactive status can be lengthy. Some records are consulted regularly and frequently for decades. Examples include floor plans for buildings that an organization owns or occupies, technical documentation for manufacturing equipment that remains in use for many years, and medical records for patients with chronic conditions that require continuing care. Property records, birth certificates, court records, and other records maintained by government agencies are requested unpredictably over long periods of time and must be conveniently accessible when needed.

For records in the inactive phase of the information life cycle, the principal goal is economical storage. Records storage costs are an important, if often un-recognized, component of an organization's operating costs. The earliest records management initiatives emphasized cost-effective storage and retrieval of inactive records in large corporations and government agencies. For many organizations, this remains a key motive for systematic records management. When justifying costs, money saved is the same as money earned. In corporations, partnerships, and other for-profit enterprises, economical records storage contributes to profitability by lowering the cost of doing business. In government agencies and not-for-profit organizations, cost reduction initiatives have a direct, beneficial impact on mission. Money saved through economical records storage can be directed to essential programs and services.

These considerations are particularly important where large quantities of inactive records must be retained for long periods of time. In-office storage of voluminous paper records can be costly. In the United States, for example, a typical base rent in a Class A office building, the most desirable office space in a given locality, ranges from $25 to $35 per square foot per year with some locations, such as midtown Manhattan, costing more than twice those amounts. Average office rents are even higher in London, Hong Kong, Moscow, Beijing, and Tokyo. The base rent, however, is only one component of a building's total cost of occupancy, which also includes common area charges, the cost of renovations and repairs, insurance costs, utility charges, property management fees, janitorial service charges, and the cost of grounds maintenance, among other costs. Real-estate professionals typically estimate the total cost of occupancy at two to three times the base rent for a given building. By that measure, the true annual cost of space in a Class A office building in typical U.S. locations is $50 to $105 per square foot.

A typical vertical-style filing cabinet intended for letter-size documents has a nominal footprint of three square feet, but it actually requires about nine square feet of installation space to allow for extended drawers and working room in front of the cabinet. Based on the total cost of occupancy, as calculated above, the annual cost of nine square feet of office space in a Class A building is $450 to $945. A four-drawer cabinet can store 10,000 to 12,000 letter-size pages, depending on how tightly the drawers are packed. From a cost accounting perspective, the space occupied by these records represents a direct cost or an opportunity cost to use the space for other purposes such as employee work areas or conference rooms. Based on the total cost of occupancy, the cost to store these records in a Class A office building for one year longer than necessary is 3.75 cents to 9.45 cents per page. As explained in Chapters 4 and 5, records management methodologies—such as offsite storage, microfilming, or digital imaging—can provide cost-effective, space-saving retention solutions for voluminous paper files while ensuring reasonably responsive and convenient retrieval when and if the records are needed for specific business purposes. Equally important, retention policies can ensure the timely disposal of records when their retention periods elapse.

Storage concerns are not limited to paper records. The proliferation of electronic records requires increasing quantities of computer storage devices and media. Admittedly, different economic parameters apply to paper and electronic storage. While the cost of paper records storage will continue to increase over time, the cost of computer storage has decreased steadily and significantly since the 1990s and is likely to continue to do so; but while an organization can purchase additional online storage, that practice can have adverse consequences. Computer hardware and software operate most efficiently within certain storage capacity limits. As those limits are approached or exceeded, data entry, information retrieval, data recovery, and other operations will run more slowly. Data migration and backup operations, especially full backups, will take longer to complete and require more resources as the quantity of stored data increases.

Organization and Retrieval of Active Records

For records to be useful, they must be well organized and readily retrievable by authorized persons when needed. Logical organization and reliable retrieval are the principal concerns for records in the active phase of the information life cycle. Records management initiatives for organization and retrieval of active records are broad. They include the development of filing systems and procedures for storing paper documents and the implementation of digital document management technologies that employ hierarchical file taxonomies and sophisticated indexing methods.

These initiatives can reduce labor costs and improve the accessibility of recorded information. Well-developed filing systems and procedures, for example, reduce operating costs by making efficient use of administrative labor, filing equipment, and supplies. They also improve productivity by minimizing time-consuming file searches, thereby expediting tasks that depend on the timely availability of documents. For business operations with complex retrieval and control requirements, electronic content management systems can reduce time and labor requirements to locate and retrieve records needed for decision-making, transaction processing, or other information-dependent activities, thereby expediting business operations and improving productivity. In this respect, systematic records management adds value to business initiatives.

Effective management of active records can also create business opportunities that lead to increased revenue. Well organized, readily retrievable records can have marketable, quantifiable value in certain business situations. Mailing lists and customer intelligence information, including demographic or other data about purchasing habits, preferences, and patterns, are obvious examples. In addition to being useful for an organization's own purposes, these information resources are products that can be sold to interested parties.

In other cases, recorded information is an important component of a marketable object or service. As an example, effective recordkeeping systems support the profitable exploitation of an organization's intellectual property, such as proprietary technologies, trade secrets, patents, product formulations, trademarks, and copyrights. Technology transfer agreements involving the sale or licensing of patented or unpatented inventions or manufacturing processes depend on accurate, complete records that describe the inventions or manufacturing processes in detail. The availability of thorough documentation for these highly valued knowledge assets can also be an important consideration in mergers and acquisitions.

Systematic recordkeeping practices confer also competitive advantages that can lead to increased revenues. Records management's contributions to competitive advantage are based on widely cited "value chain" concepts, which view the creation of a product or service as a series of interdependent activities, each of which adds value and costs to the final offering. The value chain model treats recorded information as a critical supporting element in business operations. From a value chain perspective, an organization with effective recordkeeping practices must enjoy a competitive advantage over an organization with less effective or ineffective ones. By organizing and expediting the retrieval of valuable information and by eliminating irrelevant information through formally-developed retention policies and procedures, systematic records management facilitates procurement, order processing, accounting, product scheduling, marketing, post-sale service, and other value chain activities. As its principal value contribution in such situations, recorded information reduces uncertainty, thereby enabling better management decisions.

Protection of Vital Records

Protection of information assets has long been recognized as an important component of records management practice. Among the earliest records management initiatives of the U.S. government, the Archives Act of 1810 provided for the construction of fireproof rooms to store the records of executive departments. The Act's underlying principle recognizes the obligations of records custodians: The public has a reasonable expectation that government agencies will safeguard essential records, but concerns about the safety of recorded information are not limited to government. Similar expectations apply to corporate shareholders, to clients of professional services firms, to customers of financial institutions, to medical patients, to students in academic institutions, and to any other persons or entities that may be affected by an organization's recordkeeping policies and practices.

In every organization, certain records contain information that is indispensable to the continuity of business processes and activities that are essential to an organization's purpose and obligations. Such records are termed **vital records**. For many organizations, the information contained in vital records is their most valuable asset. A company or government agency may place a high value on its computing equipment, for example, but compare the impact of a calamitous event that irrevocably damages a network server but leave a mission-critical database intact with the impact of a system malfunction that destroys the database but leaves the server operational. As discussed more fully in Chapter 6, a systematic records management program includes effective methods for identifying and safeguarding vital records against damage or loss as well as for recovering information contained in vital records should damage or loss occur.

The Records Management Function

In most organizations, records management is a staff function that supports the organization's primary business activities.

Other examples of staff functions include accounting, human resources, purchasing, public relations, information systems, telecommunications management, reprographic services, the legal department, and the library. Staff functions provide specialized, enterprise-wide capabilities that would otherwise have to be replicated in many departments. Presumably, those capabilities can be performed more knowledgeably, consistently, efficiently, and economically on a centralized basis. In most organizations, individual departments do not have their own attorneys, accountants, human resources specialists, or librarians. They rely on staff functions for those capabilities when needed.

Organizational Placement

In government, the records management function is often based in an archival agency. However, it may be based in other departments in not-for-profit and for-profit entities.

Country Records

The rationale for such arrangements is straightforward: through its involvement in records management policies and procedures, an archival agency can ensure the preservation of records of enduring value. The U.S. National Archives and Records Administration (NARA) is the model for archives-based records management programs. According to 44 U.S. Code 2904, NARA is to "provide guidance and assistance to federal agencies to ensure economical and effective records management." NARA is further authorized to "promulgate standards, procedures, and guidelines with respect to records management" and to conduct "inspections or surveys of the records and the records management programs and practices within and between federal agencies." Similarly, the Library and Archives of Canada Act directs the Librarian and Archivist "to advise government institutions concerning the management of information produced or used by them." In the United Kingdom, the Chief Executive of the National Archives supervises the discharge of records management duties by bodies that are subject to the Public Records Act. In Australia, the Archives Act defines the National Archives' control over Commonwealth records.

State and Provincial Records

Comparable laws define the records management authority of state and provincial archives. In New York, for example, the Arts and Cultural Affairs Law (Chapter 11-C of the Consolidated Laws) authorizes the State Archives to "review plans submitted by state agencies for management of their records" and "to provide technical assistance in records management for state agencies." Among Canadian provinces, the Archives of Ontario has approval authority over retention periods and formats for records of ministries, provincial agencies, and other public bodies.

Its authority is based on the province's Archives and Recordkeeping Act (S.O. 2006, Chapter 34, Schedule A). In Australia, the Queensland Public Records Act 2002 contains similar provisions. It empowers the state archivist to "develop and promote efficient and effective methods and procedures and systems for making, managing, keeping, storing, disposing of, preserving and using public records."

In some states and provinces, authority for managing government records resides outside of an archival agency, even where such an agency exists. The Secretary of State, for example, oversees the Records Management Division in Tennessee and the Records and Information Management Division in Montana. The records management program for the State of North Dakota is based in the Information Technology Department. In South Dakota, the records management program is based in the Bureau of Administration. In many cases, state and provincial records management programs have authority over records created and maintained by local governments and quasi-governmental agencies, including counties, cities, towns, villages, school districts, and public authorities.

Not-for-profit Records

In colleges, universities, cultural institutions, philanthropic foundations, non-governmental social service agencies, and other not-for-profit organizations, the records management function is typically based in an archives department, where such a department exists. The Harvard University Archives, for example, has responsibility for recordkeeping and retention procedures "to ensure the prudent maintenance and efficient disposition of university records." The University of Delaware's archives and records management policy clearly states the dual purpose of such archives-based records management programs: "to establish general procedures for the permanent preservation of university records of enduring value and for achieving economy and efficiency in the creation, maintenance, use, and disposition of university records."

For-profit Records

Organizational placements for the records management function are more varied in corporations, professional service firms, and other for-profit entities. The records management function may report to business services, to the legal department, to information technology, or to some other organizational unit. Each of these organizational placements has advantages and limitations:

1. **Business Services.** Early in its history, records management was categorized as an administrative support function. An organizational placement in business services recognizes the role of records management as a service-oriented support activity that contributes to corporate efficiency and effectiveness. Often, however, a corporate business service unit includes activities that have little or no relationship to recorded information. Records management may be part of the same organizational unit as photocopying, printing, graphic arts, corporate travel, conference coordination, building maintenance, parking, and the mailroom. In these situations, there is little opportunity for synergy among records management and other operations in the business services unit.

As a significant concern, a records management program based in a business services unit may have low visibility within its organization. This location, in turn, may limit potential collaborations with other departments and business services' involvement in information-related projects that other departments may initiate.

2. **Legal.** An organizational placement in a corporate legal department recognizes the importance of litigation support, regulatory compliance, environmental issues, and other legal and quasi-legal concerns as powerful motivators for systematic records management. The close association of records management and corporate legal departments makes sense, given the latter's need for reliable recordkeeping practices to support discovery and compliance initiatives and its necessary involvement in records retention decisions. An organizational placement in a legal department gives records management high visibility, a key determinant of success for an enterprise-wide records management program. The legal department is just one step below the top in many large corporations and is likely to have considerable authority, influence, and resources. On the negative side, records management programs that report to legal departments may have a narrow scope, focusing on records retention to the exclusion of other records management initiatives.

3. **Information Technology.** The importance of electronic records and technology-based content management applications underscores the complementary roles and shared interests of records management and information technology as information management disciplines. A reporting relationship to an information technology unit is increasingly viewed as a modern organizational placement that clearly distances records management from its historical association with filing and other administrative activities. As a more substantive advantage, a reporting relationship with corporate information technology, which is typically influential and well-funded, can extend a records management program's scope and impact while promoting records management's involvement in technology-based projects to which it can provide valuable input about retention issues and other matters. As a potential limitation, however, information technology personnel may have limited interest in the management of paper records, which continue to account for a significant percentage of many organizations' information assets.

4. **Other Reporting Relationships.** Other organizational placements for the records management function—reporting to a finance, internal audit, tax, or security department, for example—are less commonly encountered. These reporting arrangements have some conceptual basis, however. Some records management programs grew out of narrowly focused initiatives to define retention requirements for accounting and tax records. In some companies, the security department is responsible for information protection, disaster recovery, business continuity, and other activities related to protection of corporate assets, including information assets. Nevertheless, these organizational placements are

difficult to evaluate. Often, their success or failure depends on the personal interactions of supervisors and subordinates.

Executive Sponsorship

High-level sponsorship by a top executive of an organization is a key determinant of success for a records management program. Although not participating directly in the program's day-to-day operation, the executive sponsor will provide leadership, accountability, and advocacy for records management initiatives. Specifically, the executive sponsor will:

- Communicate with other top officials to create awareness about and advocate for records management.

- Establish and serve as the chair of a records management advisory committee as described in the next section.

- Authorize and obtain budgetary resources for specific records management initiatives and investments based on input from the steering committee and stakeholder departments.

- Delegate responsibilities for records management initiatives to appropriate individuals.

- Work with the advisory committee and stakeholder departments to foster communication, promote cooperation, and resolve differences of opinion and approach related to records management issues and activities.

- Authorize needs assessments, program evaluations, or other studies related to electronic records management as needed.

An influential member of an organization's senior management team—a "C-level" or "C-suite" official, such as a chief information officer (CIO), or the representative of such an official—is often cited as the best choice for an executive sponsor. In government, the executive sponsor may be an elected official—a secretary of state, a county clerk, or town clerk, for example. Typically, the executive sponsor will have some relationship to the organizational unit in which the records management program is based.

Advisory Committee

In some corporations, government agencies, and other organizations, an advisory committee has oversight responsibilities for the records management function. The advisory committee defines program objectives, reviews records management policies and initiatives, and is involved with records retention issues such as the review, approval, and implementation of retention schedules. Specifically, an advisory committee will:

1. Work with the executive sponsor to define and communicate strategic direction, objectives, scope, and priorities for the records management program.

2. Advise the executive sponsor about allocation of resources for records management initiatives.

3. Ensure alignment of records management initiatives with the organization's mission, strategies, and operational needs.

4. Ensure compliance of records management policies and procedures with organizational standards and best practices.

5. Receive and review reports about the status of specific records management initiatives.

6. Request and review reports and recommendations about the records management program.

7. Identify and authorize further examination of gaps, issues, and concerns related to records management.

Committee members typically represent organizational units that have a strong interest in systematic recordkeeping or have business operations that make and keep large quantities of records. Examples include the legal department, the finance or tax department, the internal audit group, regulatory affairs, risk management, information technology, and, less commonly, human resources, quality assurance, and corporate security. Departments with important collections of records—such as regulatory affairs in a pharmaceutical company, the medical records department in a hospital, the public works department in a municipal government, or the registrar in an academic institution—may also be represented.

Staffing and Duties

Generalizations about the records management function's employees and their duties are complicated by the considerable variety in staffing levels among records management programs. In most organizations, the records management function is administered by a department head who has the job title of "records manager" or some close approximation thereof. Where the head of an archival agency is nominally the records manager, as is sometimes the case in government, the records management responsibilities are typically delegated to a subordinate who functions as the head of the records management branch, division, or department. In that capacity, the records manager is responsible for representing the records management function in dealings with other organizational units, setting program priorities, developing records management policies and procedures, determining employees' work assignments and schedules, supervising staff, working with advisory committees where they exist, and performing a variety of general administrative functions, including preparation of budgets and reports.

In a one-person program, the records manager is necessarily responsible for all managerial, operational, and analytical tasks. Larger records management programs may employ one or more records analysts who work with departments or other organizational units to inventory records, determine retention requirements, and advise about the destruction of records, offsite storage, microfilming, scanning, protecting vital records, filing and retrieval methods, and other matters discussed in subsequent chapters. If a records management program has more than one records analyst, each may be assigned to work with specific departments. Alternatively, analysts may specialize in particular tasks or aspects of professional practice such as managing electronic records, document imaging applications, training, or compliance determination.

> Most records management programs have one or more employees who provide general administrative support and may perform other tasks such as data entry. Some records management programs have a part-time or full-time technology specialist for software, database, or website development.

If a records management program operates a warehouse-type records storage facility, as described in Chapter 4, it usually assigns a supervisor, one or more laborers, and administrative support to that activity. Outsourcing records storage to a commercial provider can reduce in-house staffing requirements, but it does not eliminate them. In most cases, a designated records management employee handles all business dealings with the commercial storage provider. That employee also works with departments to coordinate the transfer and retrieval of records, authorizes destruction of records stored offsite, reviews monthly charges, and performs related tasks.

Some records management programs provide document imaging services or operate central file rooms or other document repositories. Those programs employ scanner or microfilm camera operators, imaging technicians, and file clerks, as well as one or more supervisors. In some installations, these operational personnel outnumber records analysts.

In addition to the staff described above, records management programs may employ consultants, contractors, or temporary personnel to work on short-term projects or to provide specific subject knowledge, technological expertise, or other capabilities that are not available in-house. Further, some records management programs have informal working relationships with employees who perform filing, document scanning, **index** data entry, or other records-related tasks in other departments. Although those employees do not report directly to the records management program, they may take some direction from it.

Records Coordinators

As a staff function, records management develops policies, procedures, directives, and other guidance that others must implement. To succeed, the records management function requires the cooperation and assistance of knowledgeable persons in the departments, divisions, or other business units where records are kept. Many organizations have established a formal network of departmental employees—variously known as records coordinators, records facilitators, departmental records representatives, or departmental liaisons—who interact with the records management function for all matters relating to their business units. Among their responsibilities, records coordinators will:

1. Affirm that all business unit employees are informed about, understand, and accept the organization's policies and procedures related to records in their custody or under their direct supervision.

2. Work with the records management function to identify retention requirements for recorded information, to review and revise the organization's retention schedule as needed, and to identify unscheduled records.

3. Ensure that business unit records are preserved and discarded in compliance with the organization's retention schedule and any related policies, procedures, guidelines, or directives that the organization has issued or may issue in the future.

4. Work with the records management function to resolve any questions or confusion about the interpretation or implementation of records retention policies and procedures.

5. Suspend the destruction of records immediately upon notification from the organization's legal department or other authorities that such records are required for or relevant to litigation, government investigation, audits, or other legal or quasi-legal matters.

6. Work with the records management function to identify and periodically review records management requirements, problems, and concerns in their departments.

7. Identify training requirements relating to records management for departmental employees.

Records coordinators are typically designated by business unit heads. In most cases, they are administrative support personnel or other employees who are familiar with a business unit's operations and recordkeeping practices. Records coordinators report to supervisors in their own departments, but they take direction from the records management function for records-related matters.

Records Management and Related Disciplines

Records management is closely aligned with other information management disciplines and activities, including information technology, knowledge management, library science, and archival administration.

Collectively, these disciplines are involved in the systematic management of an organization's information resources, but they have nonoverlapping operational responsibilities. The information management disciplines play an important role in information governance initiatives, but information management differs from information governance, which has a strategic focus rather than an operational mission.

In some organizations, records management is part of an administrative structure that encompasses multiple information management disciplines and activities. Since the 1980s, some corporations, government agencies, and other organizations have consolidated their computing, telecommunications, records management, library, archives, and other information-related activities into a single business unit headed by a chief information officer, chief technology officer, chief knowledge officer, or similar top management official. Such consolidated business units are sometimes described as *information management directorates* or *information resource management departments*. Properly organized and administered, they promote coordination of responsibilities, encourage the exchange of ideas, and foster cooperative rather than competing relationships among information-oriented operations, while preserving the distinctive characteristics, methods, and business objectives of each.

Regardless of organizational structure, information management initiatives that support complex business operations require the coordination and collaboration of multiple disciplines and stakeholders. Information governance, as discussed earlier in this chapter, promotes such coordination and collaboration by defining stakeholder roles and responsibilities. Records management has a long history of successful interaction and cooperation with other information-related fields.

Information Technology

Records management's relationship to computing and telecommunications is clearly complementary and collaborative. Technology plays an indispensable role in systematic management of recorded information, but the various information management disciplines are involved with technology in different ways. Information technology is responsible for the selection, implementation, operation, and administration of an organization's computing and telecommunication resources, including computer hardware, computer software, and networking facilities. Records management makes use of computing and telecommunication concepts and technologies, but its focus is on recorded information rather than the equipment and software that process it.

Some records management concepts and methods, particularly those relating to active records, incorporate technological solutions, and records management responsibilities encompass information that is produced and stored by information technologies. As discussed in Chapter 8, records managers are principally interested in the application of computing and telecommunications concepts and technologies to specific information management problems such as the timely retrieval of documents or database records to support particular business operations. The records management function seldom has operational involvement with computer systems or telecommunication networks. As noted in the preceding discussion of information governance stakeholders, records management typically draws on the expertise and technology resources provided by an organization's information technology department.

Knowledge Management

Knowledge management is concerned with the systematic management, utilization, and exploitation of an organization's knowledge resources. Introduced and widely publicized as a business discipline in the early 1990s, knowledge management is a multifaceted field with wide boundaries. It encompasses the creation, storage, arrangement, retrieval, and transfer of organizational knowledge to improve performance, to promote innovation, and for continuous improvement of products and processes. Drawing on information technology, educational theory, and other disciplines, knowledge management initiatives emphasize the value of an organization's intellectual capital—its inventions, patents, trade secrets, product formulations, customer intelligence, and well-established business processes. Knowledge management deals with explicit knowledge, which is codified in documents and databases, and implicit or tacit knowledge, which is embodied in employees' education, experience, and practical skills.

Records management concepts and operations complement and promote knowledge management. Recordkeeping systems are valuable knowledge resources. Recorded information is an important embodiment of an organization's intellectual capital. It is the principal manifestation of explicit knowledge, which is externalized in databases and document repositories. By providing systematic control of recorded information throughout its life cycle, records management paves the way for knowledge management, while successful knowledge management initiatives pre-suppose and affirm the strategic and operational importance of effective records management policies and procedures.

Records management concepts and operations are less important for management of implicit knowledge, which is sometimes characterized as organizational "know how." Implicit knowledge manifests itself in the skills and experience of an organization's employees. To systematize sharing of implicit knowledge, knowledge management relies on apprenticeships, mentorships, discussion groups, hands-on training, and other initiatives that promote employee interactions that transfer knowledge among employees, thereby ensuring its wider availability. Some organizations have created knowledge maps, which catalog and index an organization's subject expertise, and knowledge bases, which document an organization's preferred practices for specific business activities.

Library Science

Records management has a close relationship to library science, on which some records management concepts are based. This relationship is most evident in document filing and indexing methodologies, which are discussed in Chapters 7 and 8. Records management and library science are equally concerned with the systematic analysis and control of recorded information, but each discipline has distinctive responsibilities that are complementary rather than competitive.

Records management is principally responsible for an organization's unpublished or proprietary information as contained in business documents, accounting records, databases, engineering drawings, and other resources. This information may be created by an organization itself or received, by physical delivery or electronic transfer, from other organizations. Often, the information is unique or exists in a limited number of copies. Libraries, by contrast, are repositories for books, periodicals, and other published information, much of which is purchased from external sources and exists in many copies. As previously discussed, these publications are generally considered to be nonrecords. As such, they are outside the scope of records management authority and are omitted from records management policies and retention schedules. Librarians are responsible for their organization, storage, retrieval, distribution, and retention.

Archival Administration

The close relationship between records management and archival administration is readily observed in government where, as previously discussed, records management authority is often based in **archival agencies**. Records management and archival responsibilities may also be in the same department in academic institutions, museums, scientific research organizations, and other not-for-profit entities; many university archives, for example, have records management responsibilities. In corporations and professional service firms where formal archival programs are less commonly encountered than in the not-for-profit sector, records managers are sometimes responsible for preserving records that reflect a company's history, products, and accomplishments.

Records may have considerable business significance but no archival value. Conversely, records may have archival value even though their business significance has elapsed. Records management and archival administration are complementary activities. Records managers concentrate on the business significance of recorded information when addressing life cycle issues and making retention decisions while relying on archivists to determine research value.

> Although records management and archival administration are allied disciplines, they have different missions. Records management is principally concerned with the usefulness of recorded information for an organization's ongoing business operations. Records management serves employees who need information to do their jobs. Archivists, by contrast, seek to preserve information of enduring value for cultural, scholarly, or other research purposes. Their clientele includes historians, social scientists, public policy analysts, and genealogists, among others.

Summary of Major Points

☑ Records management is a specialized business discipline. It is concerned with the systematic analysis and control of recorded information, which includes any and all information created, received, maintained, or used by an organization pursuant to its mission, operations, and activities. Variations of this definition are encountered in laws and regulations that define the scope and authority of records management programs.

☑ Records are information-bearing objects. By definition, they contain information that is "written down." That phrase is not limited to handwritten or typewritten records. It encompasses a variety of recording methods, including computer data entry, photography, audio recording, and video recording. Records may contain information recorded in any format on any medium by any method. This broad definition of records is well established in laws that deal with government records.

☑ An organization's records are its property. As the owner of its records, an organization is solely empowered to make decisions about their storage, distribution, control, protection, retention, destruction, or use. From an ownership perspective, an organization's authority over its records is identical to its authority over real estate, equipment, inventory, or other property.

☑ Recorded information is a strategic asset. It makes direct, significant, and indispensable contributions to an organization's objectives, efficiency, and effectiveness. Systematic records management is an aspect of asset management, which seeks the most effective deployment of an organization's assets to support its mission, operations, and activities.

☑ Systematic records management is principally concerned with development of policies and procedures that specify how long records must be kept; efficient management of inactive records; organization of active records for retrieval when needed; and protection of records that support mission-critical business operations.

☑ Records management concepts and methods have been successfully implemented by government agencies, corporations, and other organizations throughout the world. The global validity of records management concepts and methods is an important advantage for multinational companies and other organizations that operate in more than one country. Such organizations can adopt consistent records management principles and practices throughout their operations, subject to variations required by local laws and regulations that apply to certain records.

☑ The business case for systematic records management depends on its contribution to organizational effectiveness for which recorded information is essential. Systematic records management can deliver demonstrable, quantifiable benefits by reducing an organization's operating costs, by minimizing risks associated with legal matters and regulatory compliance, by reducing the time and labor to retrieve records when needed, and by protecting mission critical information.

☑ In government, academic institutions, and not-for-profit organizations, the records management function is often based in an archival agency. Organizational placements are more varied in corporations, professional service firms, and other for-profit entities. The records management function may report to business services, to the legal department, to information technology, or to some other organizational unit.

☑ Records management is closely related to other information management disciplines and activities, including information governance, information technology, knowledge management, library science, and archival administration. Collectively, these disciplines are involved in the systematic management of information resources. Records management has a long history of successful interaction and cooperation with other information-related fields.

Chapter 2

Preparing Retention Schedules I: Inventorying Records

A **records inventory** is a fact-finding survey that identifies and describes records maintained by all or part of an organization. The purpose of conducting an inventory is to gather information about the quantity, physical characteristics, storage conditions, business use, and perceived value of records that the organization maintains. As explained in Chapter 1, records management is a problem-solving activity. Recordkeeping problems cannot be successfully addressed until those problems are clearly delineated and fully understood. The characteristics of an organization's records cannot be determined by intuition or anecdotal evidence; empirical methods are necessary. As the initial step in a scientific approach to systematic control of recorded information, a thorough inventory is an essential component of an effective records management program.

Properly conducted, a records inventory provides detailed information about the nature and number of records maintained by a corporation, government agency, educational institution, professional services firm, or other organization. The inventory is a means to an end rather than an end in itself. Information collected during the inventory is used to prepare records retention schedules, which, as discussed in the next chapter, indicate the lengths of time that specific types of records are to be kept.

As an alternative to the inventory methods discussed in this chapter, retention schedules can be based on preformulated lists of generic record types that are presumably associated with commonly encountered business activities such as accounting, purchasing, human resources, engineering, or sales. That approach, which reduces the time and effort to prepare retention schedules, can be effective in some circumstances. It is best suited to straightforward business processes that are performed in more or less the same way from one organization to another and that have well-established recordkeeping requirements. A reasonable assumption, for example, is that an accounting office will have ledgers and journals; an accounts payable department will have invoices; a purchasing department will have purchase requisitions and purchase orders; a human resources department will have personnel files; an engineering department will have drawings and technical specifications; and a sales department will have customer order records. Retention requirements for these commonly encountered record types have been extensively analyzed; they are routinely included in retention schedules published by government agencies, for example. For purposes of preparing retention schedules, time-consuming empirical examination of such records contributes little, if any, new understanding about them.

As a potential shortcoming, however, retention schedules prepared in this manner are characteristically vague and incomplete. They sometimes contain highly generalized descriptions of record types that may be difficult to match against the records that a given department possesses, and they necessarily omit records associated with business processes or activities that are unusual or unique to a given organization. Only an inventory based on the empirical methods discussed in this chapter can reliably identify and describe such records. Nonetheless, lists of generic record types and predetermined retention periods are a useful starting point for inventorying records associated with commonly encountered business operations. When inventorying records in an accounting department or human resources department, for example, having a pre-formulated list of the kinds of records that are likely to be encountered is undeniably useful. In particular, pre-formulated lists of generic record types can help focus the inventory process on unique records or those with special retention requirements.

This chapter emphasizes the role of a records inventory in preparation of retention schedules, but inventory information may also be useful for other records management initiatives. In addition to confirming the existence of specific types of records held by an organization and describing their most important attributes, a records inventory can identify inactive records that might be discarded, transferred from office locations to offsite storage, or microfilmed. A comprehensive records inventory can also identify vital records and provide potentially valuable information about the quantity, arrangement, and use of an organization's **active records**.

Inventorying concepts and methods have been well-established components of records management practice for over half a century. A comprehensive records inventory consists of the following work steps:

1. Develop an inventory plan.

2. Prepare a survey instrument for collecting inventory information.

3. Conduct the inventory according to plan.

4. Tabulate or otherwise write-up the inventory results, collecting additional information and performing other follow-up tasks as necessary.

This chapter describes and discusses these work steps. It emphasizes practical considerations for records managers who must plan and conduct inventories for records retention initiatives. Once an inventory is completed, the information collected must be analyzed. That activity, which involves the formulation of retention recommendations for specific types of records, is examined in Chapter 3.

Inventory Plan

The purpose of an inventory is to identify and describe records maintained by all or part of an organization.

At a minimum, an inventory plan must address the scope of the inventory—the organizational units and types of records to be covered—and the procedures to be used to identify records. The inventory process can be time-consuming. To accomplish its intended purpose in a reasonable amount of time with usable results, an inventory must have a manageable scope. As explained in the following sections, records are inventoried at the series level in the program units where they are maintained. The records management function works with program unit coordinators to identify records and collect information about their principal characteristics.

The Records Series Concept

Inventories and retention schedules are applied to records at the series level, as opposed to the document, folder, or item level. Broadly defined, a **records series** is a group of logically-related records that support a specific business or administrative operation. A records series typically consists of multiple documents, folders, or other information-bearing items that are filed, indexed, and/or used together. Examples of records series associated with specific business functions include:

- Open purchase orders in a purchasing department
- Construction contracts in an engineering project management office
- Employee benefits records in a human resources department
- Closed claims in an insurance company
- Invoices in an accounts payable department
- Property files in a municipal building department
- Patient records in a hospital or physician's office
- Patent files in an intellectual property office
- Laboratory notebooks in a scientific research organization
- Applications pending in a college admissions department
- Incident reports in a police department
- Accident reports in an occupational health and safety department
- Litigation files in a legal department
- Work orders in a maintenance department
- Collection object files in the curatorial department of a museum
- Investigative reports in an internal audit department
- Client files in a social services agency
- Loan account records in a bank or credit union
- Tax return records in a corporate tax department
- Case files in an attorney's office or legal department
- Vehicle maintenance records in a fleet management department

A records series may exist in several different media or in multiple locations. Recent records from a given series may be kept in paper form, for example, while older records are stored on microfilm. Recent paper files may be kept in office areas, while older files are stored offsite. Recent electronic records may be kept on network drives, while older records are stored on magnetic tape. Recent email messages may be retained in users' mailboxes, while older messages are stored in an email archiving system.

Identifying Program Units

A **program unit** is a division, department, section, branch, or other administrative unit of a company, government agency, educational institution, or other organization. No standard definitions are available for these administrative units. In some organizations, departments are subordinate to divisions; in other cases, the reverse is true. As an added complication, a department or division may be divided into offices, branches, or sections. Alternatively, a section, branch, or office may be the highest level in an organization's administrative hierarchy, and departments and divisions may be subordinate to them. As a generic designation, program unit avoids confusion associated with the varying names that identify organizational units and their differing hierarchical relationships.

Within a given organization, program units vary in business functions, size, and complexity, as well as in the number and types of records they create, maintain, and use. Program units are typically distinguished by their specific missions and responsibilities, which are presumably related to and supported by the records that they create or maintain. Some program units may be large departments with hundreds of employees and several dozen records series in multiple formats; others may be small offices staffed by one or two persons who maintain a few paper files or electronic records. When planning a records inventory, the program units to be included must be identified at an early stage. This determination is typically made by consulting organization charts, directories, or administrative handbooks. In many cases, however, such documents are out-of-date, and additional program units may be discovered while an inventory is in progress or after it has been completed.

Defining the Inventory Scope

A comprehensive inventory must encompass recorded information in all formats—paper, photographic, and electronic—in every division, department, or other unit of an organization where records are kept. However, an enterprise-wide inventory plan that will cover all types of records in a single initiative may not be advisable or practical. Enterprise-wide inventories may be workable for small-to-medium size organizations—a company or government agency with fewer than 50 departments, for example—but ambitious inventory strategies pose significant logistic and analytical complications in large organizations with many business units and complex administrative structures.

Inventorying records is a labor-intensive activity that requires painstaking attention to detail. In large organizations, enterprise-wide inventories conducted in an attempt to collect information about records maintained by all program units in a single initiative can take a long time to complete; multiyear inventorying

Management, program unit participants, and even records management staff can lose enthusiasm for initiatives that fail to show results in a reasonable time frame. While information gathering can be accelerated by hiring temporary workers, forming special project teams, or otherwise augmenting a records management program's personnel resources, the collection of information is just one part of an inventory project. The inventory's findings must be synthesized and evaluated. That intellectual activity can rarely be expedited.

projects are not unheard of. The principal problem with such lengthy inventories is that preparation of retention schedules and other tasks that depend on inventory data—and are the rationale for conducting an inventory in the first place—will be correspondingly delayed. Further, some information collected during early stages of a lengthy enterprise-wide inventory may become obsolete before the inventory is completed and the findings analyzed for inclusion in a retention schedule. While an inventory is being conducted, business operations may be added or discontinued, business processes may change, and departments or other program units may merge, expand, or be dissolved. The longer the inventory time, the more likely that one or more organizational changes will affect the inventory's findings, requiring some work to be redone.

For best results, records of large organizations should be inventoried in stages, beginning with a single division or business function, then adding others as the work progresses and specific inventory tasks are completed. In a pharmaceutical company, for example, a records inventory might begin in corporate offices. When that work is completed, the inventorying initiative can proceed to research and development, marketing, manufacturing, and other organizational units in succession. In a medical center, a records inventory might be initially limited to accounting, human resources, and other administrative departments, with patient records held centrally or in clinical departments to follow in a second stage. In a multinational company, an inventory project might begin with records maintained in the headquarters country or the country with the largest, most complex accumulation of records. Alternatively, an inventory might be limited to a specific type of recorded information such as financial records in a corporation or government agency, case files in a law firm, engineering project records in a manufacturing company, property-related records in local government, or student records in an academic institution. Such records might be maintained by multiple program units. Limitations on records types can be combined with organizational limitations; as an example, an inventory might be limited to the domestic research and development division of a pharmaceutical company and, initially, to regulatory records within that division.

An inventory's scope can be limited by records format, but it is often advisable to inventory paper, photographic, and electronic records simultaneously, particularly in organizations where systematic records management is a new activity and formal records retention schedules are incomplete or nonexistent. Multiformat inventories are also recommended for organizations that need to update retention schedules prepared in the past. Among its advantages, the multiformat approach can simplify the logistics of inventorying by reducing the number of required site visits and meetings when compared to separate inventories of paper, photographic, and electronic records. Multiformat inventories can also provide useful insights into the interrelationship and redundancy of information in various formats. As an example, word processing software produces digital documents that are printed for filing or distribution and saved as computer files on hard drives, with backup copies on magnetic tapes or other media. The printed versions may be photocopied multiple times, and the originals or any of the copies may subsequently be microfilmed or even scanned for storage and retrieval.

Under the best circumstances, inventorying records is a difficult and time-consuming task. Meetings must be scheduled. Information must be collected and analyzed for completeness and usability. Follow-up discussions may be necessary to verify information or clarify specific points. Limiting an inventory's scope will make it more manageable and permit faster completion. Results and benefits will be obtained more quickly, although they will admittedly impact only a subset of the organization's records.

Management Support

An inventory initiative cannot succeed without top management support and the cooperation of knowledgeable persons in individual program units. To obtain the required support, the objectives of the inventory and its relationship to the systematic control of recorded information, must be explained to and appreciated by appropriate levels of management. To demonstrate its support, an organization's top management should send a directive to all program units that will be affected by an inventory initiative. The directive should announce that an inventory of the organization's business records has been authorized, and it should solicit the cooperation of program units to be surveyed. Presented as a management memorandum, the directive is typically drafted by the records management function for top management's review and approval. At a minimum, the memorandum should:

1. Acknowledge the value of the organization's business records as information assets.

2. Emphasize the importance of managing such records in a systematic manner.

3. Explain briefly the role of the records inventory as an essential data gathering activity and the critical first step in the systematic control of the organization's recorded information.

4. Indicate when the inventory will begin, who will conduct it, and approximately how long it will take.

5. Instruct each program unit to designate a records coordinator who will assist the records manager in identifying and understanding records that support the program unit's business operations.

Records coordinators are crucial to the success of records inventories, retention scheduling, and other records management initiatives. As discussed in Chapter 1, they are knowledgeable about the records maintained by their program units. Records coordinators are a records manager's principal contact persons for all records management activities within their program units. Records coordinators will assist the records manager in conducting inventories, arranging interviews with program unit employees who can provide detailed information about specific records series, and formulating retention and disposition recommendations for their program units. Once retention schedules are finalized, records coordinators will be responsible for implementing them in their program units.

Consultation vs. Questionnaires

Information collected during a records inventory will be used to prepare **records retention schedules**, as explained in the next chapter. An inventory's success is determined by its suitability for that purpose. Inventories must be conducted systematically and efficiently. Inventory procedures must be well planned. A formalized survey instrument will ensure the usefulness, uniformity, and completeness of information collected during the inventory process. The survey instrument delineates the descriptive information and other data that must be collected for each records series.

The survey instrument may be distributed to departmental coordinators in paper form or as a web-based questionnaire to be completed online. In either case, the survey instrument must be returned to the records manager by a specified date. The records coordinator is responsible for collecting the required information, which will typically require consultation with program unit employees who are knowledgeable about specific records series. Alternatively, a records manager can visit individual program units to conduct in-person inventories of their records. Using the survey instrument as an interview script, the records manager will meet with the records coordinator to discuss the characteristics of records series maintained by a given program unit. During the meeting, the records manager will have an opportunity, as needed, to examine paper records, view microfilm or other photographic records, and retrieve samples of electronic records for display or printing. If more detailed information about specific records series is required, the records coordinator will arrange interviews with other program unit employees. Questions related to electronic records may require consultation with information technology staff, for example.

The questionnaire and consultation methods are applicable to records in all formats. Five decades of records management theory and practice, along with extensive published research about survey methods, have identified the characteristics, advantages, and limitations of each approach:

1. **Shorter information-gathering phase.** The obvious attraction of the questionnaire method is shorter elapsed time for the information-gathering phase of a records inventory. A self-administered survey instrument distributes the inventory workload among records coordinators, allowing multiple program units to be inventoried simultaneously. The consultative method, by contrast, relies on the records management staff or, in many cases, a records analyst as a solo practitioner who must inventory program units sequentially.

2. **Limited interaction among program unit personnel.** As its principal shortcoming, the questionnaire method provides limited opportunities for direct interaction among program unit personnel who conduct the inventory and the records management staff who must prepare retention recommendations based

on inventory data. Even under the best circumstances, a self-administered survey may not yield information that is sufficiently clear and detailed to be analyzed by others. Partially completed questionnaires, misinterpretations, discrepancies in calculations, and some marginally useful responses are to be expected.

3. **Orientation sessions and written instructions.** If the questionnaire method is selected, records management staff must provide orientation sessions for records coordinators, supplemented by detailed written instructions, to explain the questionnaire's purpose and content. The orientation sessions should review the data elements to be collected and provide examples of appropriate responses to specific questions. Records management staff must also be available to answer questions or clarify issues that may arise during the inventorying process.

4. **Low response rate.** A low response rate is a problem with all self-administered surveys. Records managers rarely have the authority to demand an immediate response, and questionnaires set aside for completion at a later date are easily forgotten. Repeated telephone calls may be necessary to obtain the completed questionnaires.

5. **Greater time and resources commitment.** Although the consultation method takes longer than the questionnaire method and involves a greater commitment of time and resources by the records management function, it usually provides more accurate, reliable, and immediately usable information about a program unit's records.

6. **More detailed responses.** The consultation method yields more detailed responses and minimizes the potential for misinterpretation; confusing points can be clarified during the inventory itself. The consultation method relies on two techniques that are well established in information systems analysis: direct observation of a program unit's recordkeeping practices by the records management staff and interviews with knowledgeable persons who create, maintain, and use recorded information.

Although they are presented here as opposites, the questionnaire and consultation methods are not mutually exclusive. A mixed-mode inventory offers a potentially effective combination of the two approaches: records management staff may distribute survey instruments to individual program units for completion, then conduct site visits and interviews with departmental coordinators to review, clarify, or expand the program units' responses.

In some cases, the questionnaire method is the only practical approach to inventorying records. Due to time or economic constraints, records management staff may be unable to conduct site visits and interviews at field offices, branch locations, foreign subsidiaries, or other geographically remote program units. If an organization has multiple field offices or branch locations with similar recordkeeping practices, a site visit and interviews may be conducted at several of the locations, and the remainder surveyed by the questionnaire method, possibly with telephone interviews to clarify responses. In fact, telephone interviews should be considered as an alternative to questionnaires generally. With sufficient preparation by the records manager and a cooperative participant, a telephone interview can be an effective substitute for in-person meetings for inventorying many types of records. Inventories of electronic records, in particular, depend less on observation than on informative interaction with a knowledgeable person who can describe the characteristics and use of the records. Two examples of inventory questionnaires are shown in Figures 2-1a and 2-1b.

Figure 2-1a

Sample Records Inventory Worksheet

Records Inventory Worksheet		
Records Title / Series		
Company	Department	
Record Copy ☐ Yes ☐ No	If no, where is it?	If yes, where is it?
Description		
Dates	Retention, If Known	
Format and Size ☐ Paper _____ ☐ Electronic _____ ☐ Bound _____ ☐ Video _____ ☐ Photo _____ ☐ Microfilm _____ ☐ Other _____	Volume Cubic Feet _____ Filing Inches _____	
Reference Citation	Legal Requirement ☐ Yes ☐ No	Tax Requirement ☐ Yes ☐ No
Person Taking Inventory	Telephone / E-mail Address	Date Inventory Taken
Contact Name	Telephone No. / Ext.	E-mail Address
Remarks		

(*Source:* Sample Forms for Archival & Records Management Programs, *published by ARMA International and the Society of American Archivists*)

Figure 2-1b

**Sample Records
Inventory and
Analysis Form**

Records Inventory and Analysis			

Department / **Division/Office**

Location / **Person** / **Telephone / E-Mail** / **Date**

Record Title

Record Description

Purpose of Record

Type of Record
☐ Original – Location of Duplicate _____
☐ Duplicate – Location of Original _____

Record Format
☐ Letter	☐ Plans/Drawings	☐ Card File	☐ Printout	☐ EDP Tape
☐ Legal	☐ Video Tape	☐ Photograph	☐ Microfilm	☐ EDP Disk/Diskette
☐ Ledger	☐ Audio Tape	☐ Other _____		

Filing Method
| ☐ Alphabetic | ☐ Numeric | ☐ Chronologic | ☐ Subject | ☐ Alphanumeric |
| ☐ Geographic | ☐ Other _____ | | | |

Type of Filing Equipment
☐ Vertical   ☐ Lateral   ☐ Shelf   ☐ Other _____

Is Record Microfilmed? ☐ Yes ☐ No | If not, could microfilm be used? ☐ Yes ☐ No ☐ Unknown

Inclusive Dates of Records _____ Thru _____	Retention Period _____ Years in Office _____ Years at Records Center	Does Record Have Historical/ Archival Value? ☐ Yes ☐ No ☐ Unknown
Rate of Accumulation _____ Cubic Inches / Year _____ Cubic Feet / Year	Total Accumulation _____ Cubic Inches _____ Cubic Feet	Special Characteristics ☐ Vital Record ☐ Confidential Record Statutory Retention Period P.A. _____ Year _____
Reference Activity Rate First Year _____ Per Week in Office _____ Per Month _____ Per Year	Reference Activity Rate Subsequent _____ Per Week Years _____ Per Month in Office _____ Per Year	Reference Activity Rate Years at _____ Per Week Records _____ Per Month Center _____ Per Year

Cubic Foot Measurements   (1 cu. ft. = 1728 cu. in)
Letter-Size Drawer (Lateral) 2.0 cu. ft.......(Vertical) 1.5 cu. ft.   Microfilm, 100, 16mm Reels...........1.2 cu. ft.
Legal-Size Drawer (Lateral) 2.5 cu. ft.......(Vertical) 2.0 cu. ft.   4x6" Card File, Single Row 12"......0.2 cu. ft.
Records Center Carton..1.2 cu. ft.   5x8" Card File, Single Row 12"......0.3 cu. ft.
Shelving, 4 ft. Letter Size.....................................2.3 cu. ft.   Shelving, 4 ft. Legal Size................3.0 cu. ft.
Tab Card Drawer, Single Row 25".........................0.3 cu. ft.   Computer Tape (7 Reels).................1.2 cu. ft.

Comments

(*Source:* Sample Forms for Archival & Records Management Programs, *published by ARMA International and the Society of American Archivists*)

Inventory Timetable

Regardless of the method employed, collecting information about a program unit's records is a time-consuming process that requires painstaking attention to detail. A sense of urgency may stimulate productivity, but unrealistic deadlines are not compatible with quality work. Given the wide variety of circumstances in which records are kept, reasonable estimates of completion time can only be made in the context of specific work environments, but the following factors are broadly applicable:

1. If the consultation method is used, site visits and interviews will likely require two to three hours per program unit, including preliminary preparation, the time required to schedule the interview, and travel time to the program unit location. At an average of 15 minutes per records series, a site visit for a program unit with 10 records series will require at least 2.5 hours if everything proceeds according to plan, which is not always the case. Program units that are aware of recordkeeping problems are generally eager to participate, but some interviews and site visits may be difficult to arrange.[1] Obtaining a meeting date acceptable to all parties can require multiple telephone calls and/or email messages, especially if a records coordinator wants additional employees to participate in the interview. Some meetings will be canceled at the last minute and must be rescheduled.

2. Several days and multiple site visits may be required to complete an inventory in a large program unit with multiple business functions and complex or unusual recordkeeping requirements. Although not typical, such program units may have several dozen records series. Due to scheduling constraints, fully surveying that quantity of records in a single meeting may not be possible. A records coordinator will rarely be able to dedicate an entire day to the inventory process. The interview must be continued over two or more site visits. As a complicating factor, the records coordinator may not be familiar with all business functions of a large program unit. In such situations, the interview process must be broadened to include additional program unit employees with the requisite knowledge. The records coordinator will typically arrange these interviews, but they may not occur for several days or weeks.

3. Follow-up interviews, telephone calls, or exchanges of email messages may be needed to clarify specific points raised during interviews or to obtain additional information that was not available when the initial interview was conducted. Often, questions about the characteristics or business value of specific records series—the quantities of records in offsite storage, the size of a computer database,

---

[1]   Scheduling interviews is a potentially tedious and frustrating aspect of a records inventory. To get off to a good start, a kickoff meeting with departmental coordinators and other interested parties is helpful. Records managers can introduce the purpose of the inventory initiative, explain the interview methodology to be used during site visits, and provide an opportunity for departmental coordinators to ask questions about the interview process. Attendees should be asked to bring their calendars so that some interviews can be scheduled at the conclusion of the meeting.

or the dates covered by records that have been scanned or microfilmed, for example—cannot be answered immediately. The records coordinator may need several days to obtain this information from knowledgeable persons or other sources.

4. As discussed at the end of this chapter, additional time will be required to summarize, tabulate, or otherwise write up an inventory's findings from notes taken during interviews and site visits. Preparation of an accurate, detailed summary will take longer than the interview itself. As a useful rule, each hour of interview time will require an additional two to three hours of follow-up work.

A realistic inventory timetable must take all these factors into account. As an example, an inventorying initiative in an organization with 100 program units—including 25 large program units with more than a dozen records series each, 50 medium-size program units averaging 8 to 10 records series each, and 25 small program units with less than 6 records series each—may require 200 to 250 working days (about one calendar year), exclusive of the time required to analyze inventory results and draft retention schedules as discussed in the next chapter. That estimate may be optimistic. Follow-up requirements are unpredictable and can prove time-consuming. Large program units may have multiple divisions, each of which must be surveyed separately. A financial unit, for example, may have separately administered divisions for general accounting, accounts payable, accounts receivable, purchasing, payroll accounting, and other financial functions. Similarly, a human resources unit may have separate divisions for hiring, labor relations, employee benefits, compensation, and other personnel-related functions.

A systematic, thorough inventory cannot be expedited. Top management must understand that time spent obtaining reliable, detailed inventory findings will facilitate the preparation of appropriate retention recommendations for recorded information as well as the identification of vital records and other records management activities that depend on accurate, complete inventory data.

Special Issues for Electronic Records

Inventories of electronic records are complicated by the fact that such records are invisible and consequently difficult to identify. Record characteristics cannot be easily determined by observation as they can with paper files. Empirical methods may be useful for magnetic tapes, optical disks, and other removable media, but most electronic records are saved on hard drives.

When inventorying records in individual program units, the existence of electronic records can often be determined by inquiring about electronic counterparts when paper or photographic records are identified. That approach, however, will not identify the many electronic records—databases, statistical data files, or geographic data files, for example—that have no paper or photographic counterparts or the increasing number of records that originate in electronic form—so-called born digital records—and are never printed. To ensure comprehensive coverage, some records managers recommend that electronic records be inventoried by identifying and analyzing the specific information systems with which they are associated.

Broadly defined, an *information system* consists of hardware and/or software components that are designed to perform one or more information processing operations. To identify electronic records associated with computer-based information systems, a records manager must first identify the application software utilized by a given program unit. Both custom-developed computer programs and pre-written software packages must be considered. Data files, text files, digital images, or other electronic records series associated with such software can then be identified. This method is easiest to implement for electronic records that are created and maintained by computers installed in and operated by a given program unit. It can also be used for electronic records associated with information processing applications that run on mainframes, midrange computers, and network servers installed outside of the program unit. Such computers—which create and maintain electronic records on a program unit's behalf—may be operated by an organization's information technology department or, in the case of so-called hosted applications, by a cloud-based service provider.

The same method can be used to inventory electronic records created and/or used by audio and video recording and playback equipment, as well as by data recorders and other specialized instrumentation encountered in certain scientific, engineering, and medical applications. As with computer-based information systems, the records manager must first determine the type of devices employed by a given program unit, then identify the electronic records associated with such devices. If a program unit has camcorders or other video recording equipment, for example, the records manager should inquire about videotapes, DVDs, or other media produced by such equipment. Similarly, records managers should inquire about video recordings produced for the program unit by centralized video departments or video service companies.

As a potentially significant limitation, inventories conducted on a program unit basis may fail to identify electronic records associated with enterprise-wide information systems that serve multiple departments. Such records may support inter-departmental communications, budget preparation, and multidepartmental transaction processing, as well as such analytical activities as knowledge management, data mining, and decision support. Examples include electronic mail, web pages posted on the public Internet or organizational intranets, computerized document repositories created by content management software, and centralized databases and data warehouses that contain financial, personnel, customer, product, and other information. Although these centralized information resources serve multiple program units, they are not the property of any single program unit. The records they create and maintain usually reside on computers that are operated and administered by centralized information technology departments. Individual program units access these enterprise-wide electronic records, but they are not responsible for storing, protecting, or otherwise managing them. The records are not stored locally. Consequently, they may not be mentioned when inventorying a program unit's records.

Records coordinators and other program unit employees are presumably knowledgeable about the purpose and value of electronic records from a business perspective, but they may not be able to answer questions about media, file formats, archiving practices, data backup procedures, and other technical matters relating to creation, storage, retention, and protection of specific electronic records. Interviews with technical specialists will often be required to obtain this information. Appropriately knowledgeable interviewees must be identified for this purpose. For applications that operate on computers managed by an organization's information technology unit, the technical specialist should be the employee who is principally responsible for a given application. For applications that run on departmental servers, the technical specialist should be the departmental employee who manages the application. For hosted applications, cloud-based service providers have technical support personnel assigned to specific accounts.

The Survey Instrument

Records are inventoried at the series level, where a series is a group of logically related records that support one or more business processes or operations performed by a given program unit.

When an interview is scheduled with a given program unit, the records coordinator should be asked to prepare a preliminary list of records series in advance of the site visit. The list need not be detailed. It should merely provide an overview of the types of records associated with the program unit's business functions. For example:

- A preliminary list for an inventory of records maintained by an academic department in a college or university might include files related to applicants for admission, records of currently enrolled students, records of formerly enrolled students, records pertaining to courses offered by the department, records pertaining to full-time faculty and staff, records pertaining to part-time instructors, and records of departmental committees.

- A preliminary list for an inventory of records maintained by a municipal building department might include building permit files, property history files, drawings and plans, zoning hearing files, code compliance files, and planning board files.

- A preliminary list for an inventory of records maintained by a payroll department might include a payroll database, time and attendance records, direct deposit authorizations submitted by employees, and garnishment records.

- A preliminary list for an inventory of records maintained by the development department of a cultural institution might include records for gifts received, a fundraising database, files for donors and prospective donors, planned giving agreements, corporate sponsorship records, and records for fundraising events.

- A preliminary list for an inventory of records maintained by a labor relations department might include collective bargaining agreements, job action records, a grievance tracking database, employee investigation and disciplinary records, and records related to severance agreements.

A records manager will use a program unit's preliminary list as the starting point for an in-person inventory. Each item on the list will be surveyed and discussed.

If the questionnaire method is utilized, the records coordinator should use the list as the starting point for completing the survey instrument. Presumably, records coordinators can identify and describe the most important records series maintained by their program units. Major records series are notable for both their quantity and importance to program unit operations. Records managers must usually work harder during interviews and site visits to identify minor records series, which are less important and less voluminous. No matter how diligent the inventory procedures, some minor series may be overlooked.

The following sections list and describe the types of information to be collected for each records series maintained by a given program unit. Data collection emphasizes the scope, purpose, and quantity of a records series, as well as the physical and technical characteristics of the records, their storage locations, usage patterns, present and future business value, and retention requirements. Before asking questions about specific records series, the records manager should establish a context for the interview by asking background questions about the mission of the program unit being inventoried, the date the program unit was established, its internal organization and place in the broader organizational structure, the number of employees, and its office locations, if the organization has more than one. The records manager should also identify other program units with which the program unit has working relationships that may impact the use and retention of its records. Some of this information may be available from other sources, such as organization charts, but confirming the availability of those sources at the start of an interview is helpful.

Series Title

The series title is the name by which a records series is known to the program unit where the records are kept. The title will identify the records series in retention schedules, reports, tabulations, analyses, and other documents prepared from inventory data. Consequently, it should be as descriptive as possible. At a minimum, the title must accurately represent the content of the records series and clearly distinguish it from other series maintained by the program unit. Examples of acceptably descriptive series titles include:

- **Employee Benefit Files.** Records maintained by a human resources department related to health insurance, retirement plans, and other benefits elected by individual employees.

- **Human Resources Database.** A computer database that stores information about an organization's employees.

- **Accounts Payable Files.** Include invoices, supporting documentation, and related records maintained by an accounting department.

- **Matter Management Database.** A database of information about legal cases, contracts, insurance claims, and other matters handled by an organization's legal department.

- **Property Records Database.** A database of property descriptions and valuation information maintained by a municipal assessor's office.

- **Facilities CAD Records.** Computer-aided design files of engineering drawings relating to power generation facilities operated by a utility company.
- **Active Student Files.** Records maintained by an academic advisement department for currently enrolled college students.
- **Patient Charts.** Records maintained by a hospital's medical records department.
- **Collection Object Files.** Records about art works maintained by the curatorial department of a museum.
- **Specimen Database.** A database of information about plants maintained by a botanical garden or arboretum.
- **Email Archive.** Email messages and attachments transferred from individual mailboxes to a centralized repository.

Some records series may also be identified by alternative titles, which are sometimes informal. Thus, property records cards may also be known as *assessment cards*, or they may be identified as *yellow cards* or *green cards*, where different colors identify cards for residential and commercial properties, for example. Where a records series consists of standardized forms, the form number often serves as an alternative title. Thus, Employment Eligibility Verification Form, a commonly encountered type of record in human resources departments, is better known as *Form I-9*. Similarly, the Annual Return/Report of Employee Benefit Plan is better known as *Form 5500*.

Summary Description

A brief description, perhaps a paragraph in length, should summarize the business purpose, scope, and content of the records series. With some records series, such as the Active Student Files example previously cited, the title describes the series' content, but additional details can clarify its business purpose and scope. The additional details might indicate the specific types of students—graduate or undergraduate, for example—covered by the series, the types of documents included in student files, and the relationship of the series to other records series maintained in the registrar's office or elsewhere in the organization. Similarly, the description for a seemingly self-evident series title like Patient Charts will indicate the types of patients—in-patient as opposed to ambulatory, for example—to which the records pertain. A brief descriptive paragraph for the Property Records Database series might indicate the specific properties covered and give examples of the type of information included in each database record.

In every case, a statement of purpose should indicate the relationship of the records series to the mission, administrative activities, and business operations of the program unit. The following example provides a summary description for Foundation Files maintained by the Grants and Contracts Office of a cultural institution:

> "These records relate to the organization's involvement with foundations that award grants. Files include grant applications, correspondence, reports, and other documents. Some records originate electronically, but the Grants and Contracts Office prints them in order to create a complete paper/physical file.

Foundation files are consulted regularly and frequently when applying for grant funding or when questions arise about past funding."

Similarly, the following example provides a summary description for Resident Files maintained by an academic medical center:

"A file is maintained for each resident as well as for medical students who do rotations and for post-doctoral fellows. Files include summaries of evaluations from program directors; records of rotations, training experiences and procedures; documentation for disciplinary actions; and recommendations related to board certifications."

Dates Covered

Inclusive (beginning and ending) dates should be determined for each records series. This information is useful when making retention recommendations. In an organization that lacks systematic retention guidance, some records series may span multiple decades, and older records in the series are likely to be obsolete. In the absence of retention guidance, for example, some organizations may be keeping employee time and attendance records indefinitely. On the other hand, newer organizations may have few records eligible for destruction by any parameters that guide retention decisions.

In some organizations, certain records series will date from a singular event such as the incorporation of a company, the establishment of a department, or the introduction of a specific product. If the exact beginning dates for a given records series are not known, an approximation is usually satisfactory. Records series that support ongoing business operations will have open ending dates, which are noted in inventories as "to the present." Many, if not most, business records have open ending dates. Closed records series, to which no new documents are being added, may be associated with discontinued or divested business operations, defunct program units, organizational realignments, or acquired companies that cease to operate independently. Some companies, government agencies, and other organizations may have closed records series inherited from a predecessor entity. With electronic records, closed series may consist of legacy data associated with computer applications that have been replaced. When an organization implements a new human resources database, for example, it may not transfer records for former employees from the predecessor database, which will remain in service as a closed records series until the retention period for records of former employees elapses.

Format

The three principal physical formats for recorded information are paper documents; photographic records, including still-image negatives and plates, slides, motion picture films, x-rays, and microforms; and electronic records, including computer records, audio recordings, and video recordings. As discussed in Chapter 1, certain other objects that are not normally considered records may come within the scope of a records management program and inventorying initiative. Examples include biological specimens, architectural models, soil samples, and product samples that are closely associated with research and development reports, contracts, product specifications, architectural renderings, engineering drawings, medical test reports, environmental test reports, or other records.

For descriptive purposes, paper records are often categorized by page size. North American paper sizes—used in the United States, Canada, and, to a limited extent, in some Latin American countries and the Philippines—are measured in inches. International standard paper sizes, which have metric measurements, are specified in ISO 216, *Writing Paper and Certain Classes of Printed Matter—Trimmed Sizes—A and B Series, and Indication of Machine Direction*. ISO standard sizes are identified by alphanumeric designations. Most North American paper sizes have an international counterpart that is slightly larger or smaller but is intended for the same business purpose:

1. In the United States, 8.5 inches by 11 inches (U.S. letter-size) is the most commonly encountered page size for correspondence, reports, and other office records. Its international counterpart is the A4 size, which is slightly narrower and longer (approximately 8.27 inches by 11.7 inches). In the 1920s, the U.S. government, the world's largest purchaser of office papers, adopted an 8-inch by 10.5-inch page size for government forms. It was subsequently used for correspondence and other office documents generated by federal agencies, but that practice was discontinued in the 1980s.

2. Since the 1980s, the records management profession, led by ARMA International, has strongly opposed the use of U.S. legal-size (8.5-inch by 14-inch) papers, which were once commonplace for contracts, legal briefs, depositions, and other documents. When compared to letter-size papers, legal-size pages require larger, more expensive filing cabinets that occupy more floor space. Legal-size documents also require larger, more expensive file folders, and they must be microfilmed at higher reduction ratios than their letter-size counterparts. Legal-size pages, when scanned, are typically reduced to letter-size for display or printing.

3. U.S. computer printout pages, which measure 11 inches by 14 inches, are the largest office records that can be packed into cubic-foot containers without folding. The closest international paper size is B4, which measures approximately 9.8 inches by 14 inches. Since the 1990s, most computer reports have been printed in a reduced format on 11-inch by 8.5-inch paper, but—paper sizes aside—the proliferation of online systems has greatly reduced the quantity of printed reports.

4. U.S. ledger-size pages, which measure 11 inches by 17 inches, are the largest office records that can be digitized by a desktop scanner or recorded on 16mm microfilm at a reasonable reduction in a single exposure. The international counterpart is the A3 page size, which measures approximately 11.7 inches by 16.5 inches.

Multinational companies, universities, cultural institutions, government agencies, and other organizations with international activities or operations will likely have records in both North American and international paper sizes. Although comingled North American and international papers cannot be precisely stacked, minor size variations pose no significant problems for filing, scanning, microfilming, or other records management work. Table 2-1 lists commonly encountered

Table 2-1

Commonly Encountered North American Paper Sizes

Commonly Encountered North American Paper Sizes		
	Dimensions	
Page Type	Inches	Millimeters
Letter	8.5 x 11	216 x 279
Legal	8.5 x 14	216 x 356
Printout	11 x 14	279 x 356
Ledger	11 x 17	279 x 432
Index Card	3 x 5	76 x 127
Index Card	4 x 6	102 x 152
Index Card / Invoice	5 x 8	127 x 203
Engineering Drawing A	11 x 8.5	279 x 216
Engineering Drawing B	11 x 17	279 x 432
Engineering Drawing C	17 x 22	432 x 559
Engineering Drawing D	22 x 34	559 x 864
Engineering Drawing E (new)	34 x 44	864 x 1118
Engineering Drawing E (old)	36 x 48	914 x 1219

Table 2-2

Commonly Encountered International Paper Sizes

Commonly Encountered International Paper Sizes			
	Dimensions		
ISO Designation	Millimeters	Inches	Typical Uses
A4	210 x 297	8.25 x 11.7	Office documents
B4	250 x 353	9.8 x 13.9	Computer printouts
A3	297 x 420	11.7 x 16.5	Ledgers
A5	148 x 210	5.8 x 8.3	Index cards
A6	105 x 148	4.1 x 5.8	Index cards, microfiche
A2	420 x 594	16.5 x 23.4	Engineering drawings
A1	594 x 841	23.4 x 33.1	Engineering drawings
A0	841 x 1189	33.1 x 46.8	Engineering drawings

paper sizes for office records in North American. Table 2-2 lists commonly encountered international paper sizes.

Apart from size, a records inventory should collect information about the physical attributes of paper documents, including thickness, color of pages and ink, legibility, fragility, and two-sided pages. These attributes are particularly important if retention recommendations will include document scanning or microfilming.

Original engineering drawings may be created on polyester, vellum, or other nonpaper materials, but they are treated as paper records for inventorying purposes.

U.S. and international page sizes for engineering drawings, architectural plans, and other large-format documents are specified in ANSI/ASME Y-14.1, *Decimal Inch Drawing Sheet Size and Format*, and ASME Y-14.1M, *Metric Drawing Sheet Size and Format*. Both standards are published by the American Society of Mechanical Engineers (ASME International).

U.S. drawing sizes are identified by alphabetic designations, while international drawing sizes use alphanumeric identifiers in the ISO A Series. The most common drawing sizes are U.S. D and E and their international counterparts, A1 and A0. The E and A0 sizes are the largest drawings that can be readily scanned or recorded on 35mm microfilm in a single exposure. E and A0 drawings are also the largest sizes that can be filed flat in a drawer or hanging cabinet. While U.S. letter designations are available for drawings larger than E size, they are sometimes collectively categorized as O (oversize). Such large drawings are typically rolled for storage, and they must be digitized or microfilmed in segments.

Photographic records include, but are not necessarily limited to, still-image negatives, photographic plates, slides, x-rays, and motion picture films. These records are usually described by type, size, format, color status, and special attributes. Examples include 4-inch by 5-inch black-and-white negatives, 2-inch by 2-inch color slides in paper mounts, and 35mm color motion picture film on reels. Note that photographic prints are considered paper records for inventorying purposes. They may be filed separately or comingled with other paper documents in folders. As previously noted, microforms are considered photographic records. They include 16mm and 35mm reels, 16mm cartridges, microfiche, microfilm jackets, and aperture cards. When inventorying microforms, the reduction ratio, image placement, and film type are typically noted. These attributes are discussed in Chapter 5.

Electronic records media include tapes, disks, and solid-state media. As with photographic records, these media are described by type, size, format, and special attributes. Examples of computer tapes include 9-track reels, half-inch data cartridges, DLT and Super DLT cartridges, LTO Ultrium cartridges, 8mm data cartridges, and DAT cartridges. Although hard drives dominate computer storage, magnetic tapes continue to be used for backup and data archiving. Examples of removable computer disks include compact discs, DVDs, and Blu-ray media in read-only and recordable formats; hard disk cartridges, floppy disks, and magneto-optical (MO) disk cartridges, all of which have been discontinued; and ultra density optical (UDO) disks cartridges, which remain in use but have a limited market. Examples of video recording media include DVDs, Blu-ray discs, VHS and beta tapes, 8mm videotapes, and digital video cartridges. Examples of audio recording media include compact discs and audiotapes on reels and in cassettes. Some of the media types listed in this paragraph are obsolete, but records managers may encounter them during the inventory process.

Arrangement

Arrangement refers to the physical sequence of records or groups of records within a series. In paper filing systems, documents pertaining to a given person, case, subject, or other matter are typically grouped into folders that are arranged by their principal retrieval parameter. In a hospital, for example, folders that contain patient records may be arranged alphabetically by the patient's name. In a law office, case folders may be arranged sequentially by case number. In a municipal building department, folders that contain building permit applications and related documents may be arranged by a geographic designator such as property address or tax map identifier. In a sales department, folders that contain order documents may be arranged by customer name or order number. Many program units maintain general subject files with folders arranged alphabetically by topical headings. These and other filing arrangements are discussed more fully in Chapter 7.

Microforms are often arranged in the same sequence as the paper records from which they were made. Thus, microfiche copies of student records may be arranged by student name, while aperture cards produced from engineering drawings may be arranged by drawing number.

Arrangement concepts are also applicable to magnetic tapes, optical disks, and other removable media that contain electronic records. In computer installations, for example, backup tapes may be shelved chronologically or by a serially assigned number. Similarly, videotape recordings of building inspections may be arranged by building number or project number, while dictated correspondence and other office documents may be arranged chronologically within a series of audio tapes, which may themselves be arranged chronologically in cabinets or on shelves.

In computer installations, electronic records are often grouped in folders that relate to specific matters. These folders, which can be browsed in hard drive directories, are the electronic counterparts of paper files, but—unlike paper filing systems—logical arrangements do not coincide with physical arrangements. A computer's operating system determines where electronic records are physically located, often on a space available basis. In many cases, unrelated documents and files are intermingled within a hard drive, and a given file may be fragmented among several hard drive locations.

Quantity

For each records series, an inventory must collect information about the quantity of records as well as the locations and conditions in which the records are stored. Quantity estimates provide useful information about the amount of physical storage space required by a given records series. In particular, such measurements alert the records manager to potential space problems posed by voluminous records series.

For office documents and other paper records, quantity is customarily measured in cubic feet, a practice that facilitates the tabulation and comparison of records regardless of paper size or the cabinets in which they are stored. In records management, a cubic foot is defined as the contents of a container with interior dimensions of 10 inches high by 12 inches wide by 15 inches deep, which is slightly greater than one cubic foot. That container can conveniently store the three most commonly encountered sizes of office records: letter-size pages, legal-size pages, and computer printouts. It can also store index cards and other small records packed or stacked in multiple rows and layers.

Active records are rarely packed into cubic-foot containers; they are typically stored in drawer or shelf-type filing cabinets. Estimate the number of cubic feet in such cases by measuring the number of linear inches of drawer or shelf space that the records occupy and applying the following simple conversion rules:

1. For letter-size pages, 15 linear inches of records equals 1 cubic foot.

2. For legal-size pages, 12 linear inches of records equals 1 cubic foot.

3. For 11-inch by 14-inch computer printouts, 10 linear inches of records equals 1 cubic foot.

Therefore, a file cabinet drawer with 26 linear inches of filing space contains slightly less than 2 cubic feet of letter-size pages or 2.5 cubic feet of legal-size pages when filled. Because many file drawers are partially filled to facilitate the insertion and removal of folders, a reasonable volume estimate is 1.5 cubic feet of letter-size pages or 2 cubic feet of legal-size pages per drawer, which works out to 6 cubic feet of letter-size files or 8 cubic feet of legal-size files per four-drawer cabinet.

For small records, which may be packed into cubic-foot containers in the most practical manner, reasonable volume estimates are as follows:

1. 12,000 3-inch by 5-inch cards per cubic foot

2. 6,000 4-inch by 6-inch cards per cubic foot

3. 4,500 5-inch by 8-inch cards per cubic foot

4. 10,000 tabulating-size cards per cubic foot

When inventorying records, emphasizing the most voluminous series and surveying them first is often advisable. When retention recommendations are developed and implemented, large records series usually offer the greatest potential for floor space reduction, elimination of new filing equipment purchases, and other savings.

Quantity estimates for engineering drawings and other large format documents are usually based on the number of individual items. The same method applies to photographic and electronic storage media. An inventory typically estimates the number of film negatives, slides, motion picture reels, microforms, disks, tapes, or other media. With high-capacity computer disks and tapes, several records series may be comingled within a given medium, in which case the percentage occupied by each series should be indicated.

Estimated Growth

Information about the annual growth of records is essential for planning future storage requirements. As discussed in Chapter 1, record-keeping is an ordinary and necessary aspect of all business operations. Unless the activities they support are discontinued or severely curtailed, the quantity of records created and maintained by a company, government agency, or other organization will increase over time. In presentations to management, growth estimates can promote a sense of urgency about records management initiatives, particularly for records series that are growing at a rapid rate.

Anticipated annual growth rates for a given records series are most easily and conveniently determined when the series is subdivided by year or other chronological periods, a practice known as **breaking files**. Financial records and other transaction-oriented documents are often subdivided. The sizes of annual segments can be measured and compared to calculate growth. Thus, if a series of vouchers in an accounting department occupied 15 file drawers in the 2013 fiscal year and 18 file drawers in the 2014 fiscal year, the growth rate from one year to the next is 20 percent.

Where a given records series is not subdivided by year, the annual growth rate must be estimated in other ways such as relating the growth of records to some measurable factor. The creation of records never occurs in a vacuum. Records are typically linked to events or transactions such as the receipt of orders in a sales department, the issuance of policies or receipt of claims in an insurance company, the acceptance of new clients in a social services agency, the enrollment of students in an academic institution, the admission of patients to a hospital, the hiring of new employees in a human resources department, or the initiation of projects in an engineering firm. If such events or transactions are increasing at a specific annual rate, records associated with such transactions will likely grow at a corresponding rate. Thus, if a file is created each time a school district enrolls a new student and if enrollment is increasing by 10 percent per year, the number of files for newly enrolled students should also increase by 10 percent, all other things being equal. If 5,000 new student files were created this year, 5,500 files will be created next year.

Where the foregoing methods are inapplicable, paper files, database records, or other records can be examined, their creation dates determined, and a tabulation of annual quantities prepared, but that procedure is labor-intensive, time-consuming, and difficult to apply. Methods aside, unusual circumstances often defy estimation. None of the above methods could have predicted the explosive growth of email, for example. A new business function can create a fast growing record group where none existed previously. As an example, New York State's School Tax Relief (STAR) program created a homestead exemption with very broad eligibility. When it was introduced in the late 1990s, municipalities previously accustomed to tax exemptions that affected a limited subset of homeowners were inundated with STAR applications for owner-occupied residences.

Storage Location and Equipment

Records may be stored in departmental offices, in file rooms or other centralized repositories, in offsite warehouses, or in other facilities. Records from a given series are often housed in multiple locations; newer records may be kept in departmental offices, while older records are transferred to offsite storage. An inventory should indicate all storage locations for each records series and for all copies of a given series. If storage facilities have special security or environmental characteristics, whether suitable or unsuitable, they should be noted.

An inventory should also indicate the types, quantities, and physical conditions of filing cabinets or other containers that house a given records series. This information is important because records retention initiatives typically result in the destruction of older records or their transfer from office areas to offsite storage. As part of that process, filing cabinets may be emptied. Using information collected during an inventory, a records manager can estimate the number of file cabinets that will be made available and are suitable for reuse, thereby eliminating the need to purchase an equivalent quantity of new cabinets. Certain types of file folders may also be reusable.

Reference Activity

Reference activity means the frequency with which a given records series is consulted for business or other purposes. An analysis of reference activity should consider the business processes or operations that a given records series supports, the departments or other organizational units that use the records, and access privileges or restrictions associated with specific users and/or business operations.

This information is best obtained by interviewing knowledgeable users of a records series. Ideally, a knowledgeable user will be able to make a reasonable estimate of the number of times that all or part of a given records series is consulted per month, year, or other time period. With most recorded information, as explained in Chapter 1, frequency of reference diminishes over time. Within a series, the newest records—the current year's accumulation, for example—are consulted most frequently. As records age, they typically become less valuable, and they are consulted less often. The oldest records in a series may be consulted occasionally, if at all.

During interviews with program unit personnel, a records manager should identify events—such as the payment of an invoice, expiration of a contract, completion of a project, graduation of a student, or discharge of a hospital patient—that may cause records within a given series to become less active and, ultimately, inactive. The records manager should also determine the users' speed expectations when retrieving information from a given records series, because such requirements will dictate locations and/or media for records storage. Information that must be immediately and continuously available for unpredictable but urgent consultation will be handled differently than information for which retrieval delays, measured in hours or days, are acceptable. Thus, records for patients who have regularly scheduled appointments for chronic conditions must be conveniently available in physicians' offices or medical clinics. Records for former patients may be retained for regulatory or research purposes, but they can be stored offsite.

Retention Requirements

As previously discussed, a records inventory is a means to an end, rather than an end in itself. Its principal purpose is to provide the information necessary to prepare retention schedules for records covered by the inventory. As explained in the next chapter, many retention recommendations rely on the perceived requirements of employees who create, maintain, and use records. Such requirements are typically based on operational experience with records and their relationship to specific business processes or operations. Knowledgeable persons in a program unit contend that they must retain a given records series for seven years, for example, because they have consulted records from the series that were seven years old. During the inventory, the records manager must ask about the program unit's operational retention requirements.

The records manager must also ask about the program unit's existing retention practices. In the absence of systematically developed retention schedules, some program units formulate their own retention guidelines, and the time period and appropriateness of existing retention practice must be determined. In particular, the records manager must ask about the program unit's reason for adopting the existing practice, which may be based on the program unit's understanding of specific laws or regulations. In some cases, however, these legal and regulatory retention requirements are misinterpreted. Whenever a law or regulation is cited during an interview, the records manager must verify the retention requirement by consulting the full text of the cited item as discussed in Chapter 3.

Confidentiality

Records that contain confidential or otherwise sensitive information must be identified and access restrictions fully understood, including any restrictions imposed by privacy and data protection legislation. Examples of such information include:

- Personally identifiable information (PII) of any type about an organization's employees, clientele, or suppliers

- Protected health information (PHI) about an organization's employees, job applicants, or others, including physicians' notes to explain absences or other medical information contained in employees' files and students' files as well as patient information held by healthcare providers, insurance companies, or others

- Business plans and proposals

- Proprietary information about an organization's products, services, and facilities, including plans or drawings of an organization's buildings

- Trade secrets and other intellectual property

- Marketing and pricing strategies

- Competitive intelligence

- Government records that are exempt from public inspection as specified in statutes or regulation.

- Records covered by attorney/client privilege.

- Information given to an organization in confidence.

Duplication

An inventory must determine whether other program units keep copies of all or portions of a given records series, and the business purpose and relationship of such copies must be identified. During inventories, some records managers differentiate originals from copies for purposes of determining the **official copy**—the copy that will satisfy an organization's retention requirements for information that exists in multiple copies. Official copy concepts are explained more fully in the next chapter.

As part of an organization's computer security and disaster recovery precautions, backup copies are routinely produced for electronic records that are stored on centralized computers or network servers. As discussed in subsequent chapters, such backup copies are typically stored offsite, but their existence should be noted during inventories. Backup copies are much less common for electronic records stored on desktop or mobile computers.

A given record may exist in multiple formats. Many electronic records are related to, and often duplicate, human-readable information recorded on paper or microfilm. Many word processing documents and email messages, for example, are printed for filing or distribution. Databases are used to print paper reports that provide a snapshot of information at a particular point in time or for a particular set of variables. Whenever paper or microfilm records are encountered during an inventory, a records manager should inquire about electronic records with identical or similar contents. Whenever electronic records are encountered, the records manager should inquire about corresponding paper or microfilm records.

Hardware and Software Requirements

Electronic records and microforms require specific hardware and/or software components for reference or other uses. An inventory must include descriptions of all equipment and software required to retrieve or process a given records series. In some cases, a generic description will suffice. Examples include "a 16mm microfilm cartridge reader/printer with 24x magnification," "a Windows-compatible computer system," "a video cassette recorder with Super-VHS playback capabilities," or "an audio cassette deck with Type IV tape compatibility." Some electronic records, however, require specific brands and/or models of computers, storage peripherals, and software. Further, inventories may encounter older electronic records that can only be read by discontinued hardware or software components.

Supporting Files

An inventory should identify and briefly describe any related records that support the creation, maintenance, or use of a given records series. As an example, a litigation file arranged by case number may be supported by an alphabetic index that permits retrieval by the litigant's name where the number is not known. Such indexes are essential, and their retention periods should be coordinated with retention recommendations for the records series they support.

Vital Record Status

Vital records contain information that is essential to an organization's mission-critical operations. To eliminate the need for a separate survey of vital records, identify such records during a records inventory conducted for retention purposes. The identification of vital records is discussed in Chapter 6.

Execution and Followup

Information collected during an inventory will be used to prepare retention recommendations for specific records series.

Responses to questions contained in the survey instrument need to be both accurate in content and correctly interpreted by the records manager. If the questionnaire method is used, the records manager should review the responses with departmental coordinators or others responsible for completing the questionnaire in each program unit. To avoid misunderstandings that can lead to inappropriate retention recommendations, the records manager's interpretation of major points should be confirmed by knowledgeable persons in the program units where records are kept and used. Clarification should always be requested for vague or incomplete responses.

If the consultation method is used, the interview technique will have a significant impact on the success of an inventory. Above all, the records manager must elicit useful responses to questions about recorded information.

Although a comprehensive discussion of interviewing techniques is beyond the scope of this book, the following points summarize widely cited interviewing suggestions for records inventories:

1. *Obtain the information necessary to draft retention recommendations for records created and maintained by a given program unit.* In order to fulfill this purpose for conducting the records inventory, the interviewee must be talking, and the interviewer must be listening. The records manager should ask brief questions and, when necessary, clarify them with succinct explanations.

2. *Begin the interview by briefly describing its purpose, methods, and intended outcome.* Emphasize the need to obtain information from knowledgeable persons in order to prepare retention recommendations that meet the program unit's requirements.

3. *Emphasize that the inventory is exclusively a data-gathering exercise limited to recorded information and that job duties and job performance are not being evaluated.* Specifically disavow any interest in evaluating the job descriptions or work performance of program unit employees. When describing the interview's purpose, avoid words such as "investigate" and "inspect" that have evaluative connotations.

4. *Work with a pre-formulated interview script based on the survey instrument described in preceding sections.* After a few interviews have been completed, re-evaluate the interview script for effectiveness and make any necessary modifications.

5. *Explain that a list of questions will be asked about each records series.* Anything that the interviewee says about the creation and use of recorded information in their program units will contribute to the inventory. Let the interviewee talk, but the records manager is responsible for keeping the interviews on track and the responses on point.

6. *Take notes during the interview.* Tape recording inhibits open discussion. Note-taking forces the interviewer to be involved and attentive. It also confirms for interviewees that the interviewer is listening to and interested in their responses.

7. *Be honest about a lack of knowledge of a specific records series.* Obtaining this knowledge is the reason that a records inventory is necessary. Ask the interviewee to define specialized terms and describe unfamiliar business processes or operations.

8. *Obtain information during the interview instead of giving it.* Until the inventory is completed and its findings are evaluated, a records manager cannot knowledgeably advise program units about their recordkeeping practices. Such advice should be deferred until draft retention recommendations are prepared.

9. *Avoid criticizing the program unit's recordkeeping practices during an interview.* Unacceptable practices should be noted and corrective actions incorporated into retention recommendations.

10. *Visit the file rooms, storage areas, or other locations where records are kept and used.* These visits may be done at the beginning of the interview to provide an overview of the program unit's records or at the end of the interview after the records have been described in detail. In particular, ask to see any unfamiliar records series or unusual storage conditions.

11. *Ask for copies of program unit written policies and procedures for recordkeeping if they are available.*

12. *Strive to complete the site visit in 90 minutes or less and inform the interviewee when scheduling the meeting.* Longer sessions are often difficult to arrange and will likely disrupt the interviewee's work schedule. If additional time is required for large or complicated collections of records, schedule a follow-up meeting.

13. *Prepare a written summary of information obtained and the points discussed when the interview is completed.* The summary can be written as if it were the minutes of a meeting. The written summary should be submitted to the interviewee for review and, where necessary, correction or clarification. Such follow-up work steps will increase the time required to inventory records, but they are highly advisable. The time and effort required to conduct thorough inventories and prepare accurate interview summaries will be repaid in appropriate retention recommendations that are less likely to require time-consuming negotiation and revision.

Most of these suggestions are applicable to interviews associated with other records management activities, such as the development of filing systems or computer-based document storage and retrieval systems, that depend upon interviews to obtain information about business processes, operations, and requirements associated with recorded information.

Summary of Major Points

☑ An inventory is a fact-finding survey that identifies and describes records maintained by all or part of an organization. The purpose of the inventory is to gather information about the quantity, physical characteristics, storage conditions, use, and perceived value of records that the organization maintains.

☑ A thorough inventory is the initial step in a scientific approach to systematic control of recorded information. It is an essential component of an effective records management program.

☑ A records inventory is a means to an end rather than an end in itself. Information collected during the inventory is used to prepare retention schedules.

☑ Records are inventoried in the program units where they are kept. A program unit is a division, department, section, or other organizational unit that maintains recorded information. Some program units may be large departments with hundreds of employees and huge quantities of records in multiple formats; others may be small offices staffed by one or two persons who maintain a few paper files or electronic records.

☑ Inventorying, retention scheduling, and related operations are applied to records at the series level, as opposed to the document, folder, or item level. A records series is a group of logically related records that support a specific business or administrative operation performed by a given program unit. A records series typically consists of multiple documents, folders, or items that are stored and/or used together.

☑ Departmental coordinators play an important role in records inventories and other records management initiatives. They are the principal contact persons for all records management activities within their program units. They assist the records manager in conducting inventories and in formulating retention recommendations. Once retention schedules are finalized, departmental coordinators are responsible for implementing them.

☑ Records inventories are based on a formalized survey instrument, which may be distributed as a questionnaire to departmental coordinators. Even better, records managers can personally collect the information required by the survey instrument, which is treated as a script and checklist to be followed when conducting site visits and interviewing program unit personnel.

☑ Responses to questions contained in the survey instrument must be accurate in content and correctly interpreted by the records manager. If the questionnaire method is used, the records manager should review the responses with departmental coordinators or others responsible for completing the questionnaire in each program unit. Clarification should always be requested for vague or incomplete responses.

[This page intentionally left blank]

Chapter 3

Preparing Retention Schedules II: Making Retention Decisions

As described in the preceding chapter, a records inventory is a means to an end. Its principal purpose is to collect the information needed to prepare retention schedules for records covered by the inventory. Broadly defined, a **retention schedule**—variously described as a *retention and disposal schedule* or a *retention and disposition schedule*—is a list of records series maintained by all or part of an organization together with the period of time that each records series is to be kept. Some retention schedules also include information about the reasons that records are to be kept for specified time periods, as well as instructions regarding the locations and formats in which records are to be retained. Retention schedules are themselves records. They may be maintained in paper or electronic form. In the latter case, they may be printed for distribution and reference, although companies, government agencies, and other organizations are increasingly posting web-based versions of retention schedules on intranets or otherwise making them accessible online as alternatives to printed copies.

Retention schedules may be organized by program units or by functional categories:

1. A **program-specific retention schedule** *is limited to records series held by a given department, division, office, or other program unit.* In program-specific schedules, each records series has a unique identifier, the so-called record code. It might be a serially assigned number or an alphabetic abbreviation for the program unit with a serial number for the records series. As an example, the record code for the first records series listed in a program-specific retention schedule for a human resources department might be "HR001." Sometimes described as *activity-oriented* or **departmental retention schedules**, program-specific retention schedules are custom-prepared for each program unit within an organization. A given organization will have multiple program-specific schedules. (See a sample format for a typical departmental or program-specific retention schedule in Figure 3-1.)

2. A **functional retention schedule**, *by contrast, categorizes records series by the business functions to which they pertain rather than by the program units where*

Figure 3-1

Sample Departmental or Program-specific Retention Schedule Format

Records Retention Schedule						
Division	Department	Records Coordinator	Issue/Revision Date	Page 1 of ___	Schedule No.	

Records Title	Records Description	Retention Period Office / Storage / Total	Office of Record	Remarks

Key for Retention Codes:

01 – Annual Review	02 – Until Superseded	03 – While Active	04 – Retain for Audit	05 – Tax Audit Requirements	06 – User Override
07 – Litigation	08 – Until Terminate	09 – Permanent	10 – Life of Corporation	11 – Life of Equipment/Facility	12 – Life of System
13 – Life of Project	14 – Until Expiration	Number of Years (Excluding the Current Year)		

Records Administration Approval (Print)	Date	Department Manager Approval (Print)	Date	Tax Representative Approval (Print)	Date	Law Representative Approval (Print)	Date
Signature		Signature		Signature		Signature	

(Source: Sample Forms for Archival & Records Management Programs, *published by ARMA International and the Society of American Archivists*)

the records are maintained. Examples of functional categories include administrative records, accounting records, procurement records, personnel records, legal records, project records, research and development records, manufacturing records, sales and marketing records, and customer service records. As with program-specific schedules, functional schedules assign record codes to individual records series. Typically, the record code identifies the functional category and the series number within that category. Thus, the record code "CS001" would identify the first records series listed in the customer service category. An organization may prepare separate schedules for each functional category or issue a single retention schedule for the entire organization with records grouped by functional categories. Such enterprise-wide functional schedules are sometimes described as *master retention schedules.*

As their principal advantage, program-specific retention schedules are typically short and highly prescriptive. They list only those records series that a given program unit has in its custody or under its control. Each records series is identified by the name that the program unit uses. Series descriptions relate the records to the specific business operations that they support, and retention periods are tailored to the program unit's requirements. Consequently, program-specific retention schedules are easy to understand and can include detailed implementation instructions for individual records series.

Functional schedules are comparably easy to use if a program unit's records are principally or entirely covered by one functional category. In an elementary or secondary school, for example, records held by a special education department will be covered by the functional category for special education. In a company, records held by an employee benefits department will be covered by the functional category for human resources. In a hospital, records held by the medical records department will be covered by the functional category for patient records. Problems can arise, however, when a program unit's records are covered by multiple functional categories. Comprehensive functional schedules for large organizations can encompass dozens of functional categories, some of which may be divided into multiple subcategories, and hundreds or even thousands of records series. Any given program unit will have a limited subset of the listed records—10 to 15 records series in most cases. Those records series may be scattered throughout a functional schedule. Interpretation is required to match a program unit's records to the functional categories and records series that are most closely related to the business operations that the records serve. As an added complication, program units may identify their records by different titles than those listed in the functional schedule, and there may be slight variations in the scope and content of records series maintained by different program units.

To address these concerns, a "big bucket" retention schedule emphasizes functional groups rather than records series. In a conventional functional schedule, accounting ledgers, invoices, payment vouchers, accounts receivable files, and other financial transaction records might be individually listed as records series in an accounting category. Each records series would have its own retention period. A big bucket schedule, by contrast, specifies a uniform retention period—10 years from the end of the fiscal year to which the records pertain, for example—for all accounting records. Ledgers, invoices, vouchers, and other records might be listed as examples of records included in that functional category, but a big bucket schedule does provide a comprehensive listing of records series.

Whether the conventional or big bucket approach is utilized, proponents of functional retention schedules claim that they are easier and faster to create than program-specific schedules and that they promote consistent retention practices for specific types of records and across program units. They also note that program-specific schedules can be difficult to update when reorganizations, mergers, divestitures, and other changes realign or eliminate program units. Functional schedules are particularly well suited to multinational organizations where specific business functions, such as research and development or sales and marketing, are encountered in multiple locations. Compared to program-specific schedules, a functional schedule prepared for a company's primary location can be more easily adapted for use in other countries.

By definition, functional retention schedules present retention guidelines for multiple program units. The retention designations are based on input from some, but not necessarily all, program units that maintain a given records series. Presumably, the retention designations reflect the longest retention requirements for a listed series. For records that exist in multiple copies, however, a program unit may want to discard its copies of a given records series before the specified retention period has elapsed. To address this requirement, a functional schedule may designate an office of record that is responsible for retaining the official copies of a specific records series for the complete designated time period. Copies held by other program units are considered duplicate records. They can be discarded when no longer needed, but they must not be retained longer than the designated retention period. Program-specific schedules designate official copies in a different way: A given program unit is, by definition, the **office of record** for those series that are listed in its retention schedule. Any records not listed are considered duplicate copies. The official copy concept is discussed more fully elsewhere in this chapter.

Functional and program-specific schedules are not mutually exclusive options. They can, and often do, coexist in a given organization. Functional schedules are particularly useful for commonly encountered records held by many program units. Examples include accounting and procurement records, correspondence and electronic mail, budget preparation records, committee minutes, departmental publications, and records relating to personnel matters. An organization may issue enterprise-wide retention guidelines for these commonly held records series and prepare customized program-specific schedules for records that are unique to particular departments, divisions, offices, or other program units. In the U.S. government, for example, so-called general schedules prepared by the U.S. National Archives and Records Administration (NARA) cover records in over two-dozen major categories. Federal government agencies must prepare retention schedules for records that are not covered by the general schedules and submit those schedules to the U.S. National Archives and Records Administration for approval. The Library and Archives of Canada has issued retention guidelines for federal government records in five functional categories: general administration, real property management, materiel management, comptrollership, and human resources. In the United Kingdom, the National Archives has issued general retention guidelines for commonly held government records. The Administrative Functions Disposal Authority, issued by the National Archives of Australia, specifies minimum retention periods for Commonwealth records associated with eighteen common administrative functions. A sample general retention schedule is shown in Figure 3-2.

Whether functional or program-specific in scope, a retention schedule must, at a minimum, list records series and indicate the period of time, usually in years, that each series is to be kept. Most retention schedules specify the number of years for a given records series followed by the trigger event on which the retention period is based. The most common trigger event is the end of the calendar year, fiscal year, or other chronological period to which the records relate, but some retention periods are based on specific circumstances such as the completion of an audit, termination of a project, resignation or retirement of an employee, settlement of legal proceedings, closing of a customer account, payment of an insurance claim, graduation of a student, or discharge of a hospital patient. Some schedules utilize flexible rather than precise retention periods. Flexible retention periods specify the minimum amount of time that a given records series must be kept. Longer retention is permitted if the records remain useful for some business purpose. Some retention schedules specify that a given records series is to be discarded when no longer needed. This instruction may be accompanied by a maximum period of time that the records series is to be kept.

In addition to retention periods, a retention schedule may provide additional instructions for specific records series. Examples include the physical storage media to be used, the location(s) where the records are to be stored, the date and method of records destruction where applicable, and storage or records transfer instructions if destruction is not authorized. If this information is not contained in the retention schedule, an accompanying procedure or other supporting documentation must provide it. Some retention schedules also include citations to legal statutes or government regulations on which specific retention periods are based. Alternatively, such citations may be included in working papers associated with legal research relating to records retention.

A retention schedule may specify more than one physical storage medium and/or location for a records series. As an example, a municipal building department may store applications for building permits and zoning variances in paper form in the departmental office while the applications are under active review and for a short time thereafter. Periodically, records relating to building permit applications may be microfilmed or scanned for long-term retention and the paper copies discarded. A security copy of the microfilm or digital images may be stored offsite. Similarly, a retention schedule may stipulate that records relating to withdrawn

Figure 3-2

Sample Use
General
Retention
Schedule

Transmittal No. 24
August 2015

General Records Schedule 3.2

GENERAL RECORDS SCHEDULE 3.2: Information Systems Security Records

This schedule covers records created and maintained by Federal agencies related to protecting the security of information technology systems and data, and responding to computer security incidents. This schedule does not apply to system data or content.

Item	Records Title/Description	Disposition Instruction	Disposition Authority
010	**Systems and data security records.** These are records related to maintaining the security of information technology (IT) systems and data. Records outline official procedures for securing and maintaining IT infrastructure and relate to the specific systems for which they were written. This series also includes analysis of security policies, processes, and guidelines, as well as system risk management and vulnerability analyses. Includes records such as: • System Security Plans • Disaster Recovery Plans • Continuity of Operations Plans • published computer technical manuals and guides • examples and references used to produce guidelines covering security issues related to specific systems and equipment • records on disaster exercises and resulting evaluations • network vulnerability assessments • risk surveys • service test plans • test files and data	**Temporary.** Destroy 1 year(s) after system is superseded by a new iteration or when no longer needed for agency/IT administrative purposes to ensure a continuity of security controls throughout the life of the system.	DAA-GRS-2013-0006-0001
020	**Computer security incident handling, reporting and follow-up records.** A computer incident within the Federal Government as defined by NIST Special Publication 800-61, Computer Security Incident Handling Guide, Revision 2, (August 2012) is a violation or imminent threat of violation of computer security policies, acceptable use policies, or standard computer security practices. This item covers records relating to attempted or actual system security breaches, including break-ins ("hacks," including virus attacks), improper staff usage, failure of security provisions or procedures, and potentially compromised information assets. It also includes agency reporting of such incidents both internally and externally. Includes records such as: • reporting forms • reporting tools • narrative reports	**Temporary.** Destroy 3 year(s) after all necessary follow-up actions have been completed, but longer retention is authorized if required for business use.	DAA-GRS-2013-0006-0002

(Source: The U.S. National Archives and Records Administration)

building and zoning applications are to be kept in the departmental office for two years then transferred to offsite storage for five additional years, at the end of which time they will be discarded.

Retention Concepts

Retention schedules are the core component of a systematic records management program.

Retention schedules provide a foundation upon which other records management activities discussed in this book are based. The formulation of retention guidance is a defining characteristic of records management work. No other information management discipline can properly claim responsibility for retention-related activities. Retention and its counterpart, **disposition**, are two of the eight Principles discussed in Chapter 1.

As explained in Chapter 1, recorded information is the property of the company, government agency, not-for-profit organization, or other entity that creates and maintains it. By preparing retention schedules, an organization acknowledges that systematic disposition of its records is a critical information management activity to be governed by formalized operating procedures rather than the discretion of individual employees.

For government records, this concept often has the force of law. In the United States, 44 U.S. Code, Chapter 33 prohibits the destruction of federal government records without authorization from the Archivist of the United States. The Library and Archives of Canada Act prohibits the destruction of government and ministerial records without the consent of the Archivist of Canada. In the United Kingdom, the Public Records Act authorizes the Public Records Office to work with government departments to determine retention requirements and identify records for permanent preservation. Under the Archives Act 1983, the National Archives of Australia regulates the destruction of public records. Similar provisions limit the destruction of government records in other countries. In the United States, Canada, and elsewhere, state and provincial archives have retention authority over records created by government agencies within their jurisdictions.

A retention period places a value on a records series. The value is an estimate of the series' future usefulness or lack thereof. Because retention periods are estimates, uncertainty and risk are unavoidable, but a careful analysis of retention requirements, based on an understanding of the purpose and characteristics of a given records series, will increase the likelihood of a satisfactory determination.

A comprehensive inventory, as described in Chapter 2, will identify the records series to be included in retention schedules. The inventory collects information about the business purpose, characteristics, and quantity of records in each series, the ways in which the records are organized and used, and the relationship between a given records series and other records maintained by an organization. The records manager, in consultation with program unit personnel and others, will use the inventory information, supplemented in some cases by additional research, to determine appropriate retention periods for specific records series.

Retention Criteria

Retention decisions are based on the content and purpose of records. Retention periods are determined by legal, operational, and scholarly (research) criteria:

1. **Legal retention criteria.** Legal criteria may be defined by laws, regulations, or other legal instruments that mandate the retention of certain records for specific periods of time. A broader group of legal considerations is concerned with the retention of records for use as evidence in litigation and other legal proceedings. Some records managers consider fiscal and tax-oriented retention criteria, which are concerned with the management and expenditure of public or private funds, to be distinct from legal parameters. Some fiscal and tax retention criteria, however, are embodied in laws and regulations. For purposes of this discussion, they are considered a subset of legal criteria.

2. **Operational retention criteria.** Operational criteria are based on the continued need for specific records series to support an organization's mission, the public interest (in the case of government records), owners or stockholders' interest (for records of private or publicly held companies, including sole proprietorships and partnerships), or the interests of founders, trustees, donors, clients, members, or other parties (for records of social services agencies, healthcare facilities, educational institutions, cultural institutions, philanthropic foundations, charities, and other not-for-profit organizations). Such criteria are concerned with the availability of records for long-term administrative consistency and continuity, as well as for the day-to-day operations of individual program units. Operational criteria are the most important considerations when determining retention periods for many, if not most, records. This statement does not denigrate the importance of legal criteria; it merely recognizes that many records are not subject to legally mandated recordkeeping requirements and have no value as evidence in legal proceedings.

3. **Scholarly retention criteria.** Records maintained by companies, government agencies, not-for-profit organizations, and other entities may contain information of interest to historians, political scientists, sociologists, economists, demographers, or other scholars. Some records are also of interest to genealogists, private investigators, market trends analysts, and others who are not necessarily scholars but are nonetheless involved in research. Scholarly retention criteria are sometimes characterized as secondary value to distinguish them from the primary business purposes for which records are created and maintained.

This chapter discusses legal and operational criteria for records retention. (As noted previously, legal criteria include fiscal and tax considerations.) Scholarly retention criteria are beyond the scope of this book and of records management generally, although portions of the discussion of operational criteria may be relevant for scholarly applications. As noted in Chapter 1, determination of scholarly value is principally the concern of archival administration. Such determination, sometimes described as *archival appraisal*, requires specialized knowledge about the scholarly disciplines and research activities for which particular records may be relevant. Many archivists have advanced academic degrees in a subject discipline, such as history or public administration, as well as training in archival management or library science. Archivists work closely with records managers to identify records of scholarly value and ensure that they are preserved. This work is often done at the time that retention schedules are prepared. In government agencies, academic institutions, and other organizations where preservation of records of scholarly value is required by law or institutional policy, the archivist typically has review and approval authority over retention schedules.

Official Copies vs. Duplicate Records

Much information maintained by corporations, government agencies, and other organizations exists in multiple copies and multiple formats. Accounting, purchasing, and other business transactions rely on multipart forms. Correspondence, reports, and other office documents are widely photocopied for distribution. Prints of engineering drawings, architectural renderings, and other large-format documents are routinely included in project files. Many office records and engineering drawings are microfilmed and/or scanned, and the resulting microforms or digital images may themselves be duplicated for distribution or offsite storage. Increasingly, electronic records are the originating sources for paper documents—with word processing files and computer-aided design files, for example. Conversely, information from paper documents, such as invoices or employee time sheets, may be entered into databases or other electronic records.

Where a given record exists in multiple copies, the copy that will satisfy an organization's legal and operational retention requirements is termed the *official copy* or the *record copy*, a confusing designation that implies that other copies are outside the scope of records management authority. The program unit that has custody of the official copy is designated the *office of record* for retention purposes. Copies maintained by other program units are considered duplicate records. Where information is unique to a given record, that record is necessarily an official copy.

The official copy concept has a straightforward rationale: Not all copies of a given record need to be kept for the same amount of time. This principle is subject, however, to significant variations in application. Possibilities include, but are not necessarily limited to, the following:

* *A retention schedule separately enumerates and specifies retention periods for all copies of a given records series in*

A duplicate record may be in the same format or medium as the official copy or in a different format or medium. For example:

* The official copy may be a paper document and the duplicate record a photocopy of it.

* The official copy may be a database, word processing document, spreadsheet, email message, or other electronic record, in which case any printed copies are considered duplicate records.

* The official copy may be a paper document and the duplicate record a digital image or microfilm image made from it.

* A microfilm image or digital image produced from a paper document may be designated as an official copy for retention purposes, in which case the original paper document is considered a duplicate record.

all formats. Retention periods may differ among the copies. Where legal or regulatory retention requirements exist, one copy is designated as the official copy to satisfy those requirements. This approach requires the time-consuming identification of individual copies. It can be applied to multipart business forms and periodic reports with predefined distribution lists. With many business forms, distribution instructions are printed on the forms. Separate identification of all copies is impractical, however, for records with unpredictable copying and distribution patterns.

- *One copy of a record is designated as the official copy to be kept for the time period specified in an organization's retention schedule.* Other copies, which are not identified in the retention schedule, can be discarded when no longer needed, but they must not be kept longer than a specified period of time—perhaps one to three years.

- *One copy of a record is designated as the official copy to be kept for the time period specified in an organization's retention schedule.* Other copies, which are not identified in the retention schedule, can be kept as long as the official copy or discarded sooner if no longer needed. As its principal shortcoming, this discretionary approach permits the permanent retention of duplicate records where the official copy is a permanent record.

Note that the foregoing discussion is limited to duplicate records that are created for information purposes. It does not apply to backup copies that are produced for disaster recovery purposes. Retention periods for backup copies are determined by an organization's disaster recovery requirements and procedures. In some retention schedules, backup copies are listed as a records series, usually in the functional category for information technology.

Official copy determinations are based on the assumption that all copies of a record are equivalent in content and functionality, but they are not equivalent in all cases. One copy may contain more information or be more useful than another. Contracts, correspondence, and other documents generated from word processing files may be signed or amended after printing. A photocopy of a document may contain significant handwritten annotations that are absent from the original. Individual copies in multipart form sets may differ in color and legibility. Microfilm copies of engineering drawings may not satisfy all reproduction requirements for scaled documents. Digital images of certain documents may be easier to retrieve than their paper counterparts, but, in some localities, government regulations may prohibit their retention in lieu of paper records.

By definition, duplicate records contain the same information as official copies or a subset of that information, as is the case where official copies contain information that is omitted or redacted from duplicate records. Duplicate records never contain information that is absent from official copies. Thus, photocopies that contain annotations are not considered duplicate records. Drafts that contain information omitted from final versions are not considered duplicate records.

Legally Mandated Recordkeeping Requirements

Recorded information documents an organization's business operations, including hiring employees, paying taxes, and other activities that are subject to government regulation.

Auditors, investigators, and other government officials examine an organization's records practices to determine compliance with laws and regulations to which the records relate. To ensure the availability of adequate information for that purpose, various laws, regulations, ordinances, directives, and other legal instruments specify retention periods for certain types of records. Such retention periods are collectively described as *legally mandated recordkeeping requirements*. Avoidance of costly fines or other penalties for noncompliance with such **recordkeeping requirements** is an important benefit of a systematically developed records retention program. Where such requirements exist, they typically establish minimum retention periods for the recorded information to which they pertain. Retention periods determined by other criteria discussed in this chapter may be longer than those defined by legally mandated recordkeeping requirements, but they can never be shorter.

Given concerns about fines, penalties, and other risks associated with noncompliance, legally mandated recordkeeping requirements are often the first criteria to be considered when determining how long records must be kept. As a more efficient approach, however, an organization should first determine whether a given records series merits permanent retention for its scholarly or operational value. If it does, legal retention periods are irrelevant. Permanent is the longest possible retention period. In theory, this retention period should eliminate the need to do legal research to determine retention requirements for such records, but some recordkeeping regulations impose restrictions on storage locations and formats. As an example, the Securities and Exchange Commission's Rule 17a-4 specifies that broker-dealers must retain certain records for a minimum of six years, "the first 2 years in an easily accessible place." According to New York State Codes, Rules, and Regulations (NYCRR), Title 10, Section 58-1.11, hospitals must keep laboratory copies of pathology records onsite for two years, after which they can be transferred to offsite storage. These records must be retained in their original formats for a minimum of three months, after which they can be microfilmed or scanned. In some countries, laws and regulations specify that accounting or tax records must be retained in the country and that certain records related to employee safety and health must be kept in the workplace.

Recordkeeping laws and regulations apply to all organizations that operate within a specific governmental jurisdiction. An organization's headquarters location or the governmental jurisdiction in which it is incorporated or chartered is not the determining factor. A company, government agency, not-for-profit organization, or other entity is considered to operate in a given location if it maintains an office, employees, or property there. Thus, a multinational consumer products company headquartered in the United States must comply with applicable record-keeping requirements in all countries where its products are sold. A multinational bank headquartered in Australia must comply with all applicable recordkeeping requirements in all countries where it offers financial services. A multinational philanthropic organization or religious group headquartered in the United Kingdom must comply with all applicable recordkeeping requirements in every country where it maintains offices, has employees, or offers programs.

Identification of applicable laws and regulations is the essential first step toward compliance with legally mandated recordkeeping requirements. For organizations that operate in the United States, recordkeeping requirements for business operations regulated by the federal government can be found in the U.S. Code, which is the codification by subject matter of the general and permanent laws of the United States, and, more commonly, in the Code of Federal Regulations (CFR), which is the codification of regulations issued by executive branch agencies of the U.S. government. The CFR is updated daily by the Federal Register. Recordkeeping requirements for business operations regulated by U.S. states and local governments can be found in compilations of statutes, codes, rules, and regulations issued by those jurisdictions. Where federal, state, and local recordkeeping requirements differ, the longest retention period applies. As an example, federal regulations require hospitals to keep patient records for five years following discharge or death as a condition for participation in Medicare and Medicaid programs. Many states, however, mandate longer retention periods. In New York State, hospitals records for adult patients must be kept for six years following discharge or death, while records for minors must be retained for six years following discharge or death or until the patient attains age 21, whichever is longer. In Massachusetts, hospitals must retain patient records for a minimum of 20 years following discharge or final treatment.

In other countries, recordkeeping requirements are contained in similar codifications. A country's governmental structure has a significant impact on records retention requirements and on the amount of research that must be done to identify applicable laws and regulations:

- *Most countries are unitary states in which a central government issues laws and regulations that apply to the entire nation.* In such countries, subnational jurisdictions have administrative responsibilities that do not impact records retention.

- *In federated countries, like the United States, a national government shares legislative authority with subnational jurisdictions.* Examples of federated countries include Argentina, Australia, Belgium, Brazil, Canada, Germany, India, Mexico, Pakistan, the Russian Federation, South Africa, Spain, and the United Kingdom. In federated countries, both federal and subnational jurisdictions must be researched individually to identify legal requirements for records retention. Organizations with business operations in Canada, for example, must comply with recordkeeping requirements in Canadian Consolidated Acts and Consolidated Regulations and with provincial and local laws and regulations that specify retention periods for certain records. Similarly, organizations that operate in Australia must comply with recordkeeping provisions in Commonwealth Consolidated Acts and Commonwealth Consolidated Regulations as well as records retention requirements in various state laws and regulations. Significant time and effort will be required to thoroughly research subnational jurisdictions. Mexico, for example, has 31 states. India has 29 states and seven union territories. Brazil has 29 states.

• *Some countries are member states of supranational entities to which they delegate some legislative powers.* The European Union is the best-known supranational entity. Other examples include the Commonwealth of Independent States and the Organization for Harmonization of Business Laws in Africa. The legal harmonization provided by a supranational entity can simplify legal research and formulation of retention guidance for organizations with business operations in multiple countries, but member states must transpose the supranational entity's legislation and directives into their own national laws.

Various online and printed reference sources identify, excerpt, categorize, and index legally mandated recordkeeping requirements. Many countries have government-operated databases of laws, regulations, ordinances, directives, and other legal instruments. These databases, which are publicly accessible through governmental websites, contain full texts of legal instruments. In unitary states, the databases are comprehensive. In federated states, however, they principally cover national requirements. Coverage of subnational jurisdictions is often less extensive or nonexistent. Even when all information is available online, the identification of applicable laws and regulations is a formidable task requiring careful study. To identify 10 relevant laws or regulations, 100 or more must be located, read, and analyzed.

As a significant complication, recordkeeping requirements can be difficult to interpret. Some government regulations merely state that certain records must be kept without specifying a retention period for them. In such situations, an organization may adopt long retention periods for the indicated records as a seemingly prudent precaution; but unless a demonstrable business need for the records exists, that approach may not be necessary or advisable. Relatively short retention periods are legally acceptable for many records. In the U.S., for example, Georgia, Illinois, Maryland, New Hampshire, North Dakota, Oklahoma, and Texas have adopted laws that permit the destruction of business records after three years unless "express provision is made by law" for a longer retention period.[2] Exceptions

---

[2]   These laws are based on the Uniform Preservation of Private Business Records Act (UPPBRA), which was issued in 1954 by the National Conference of Commissioners on Uniform State Laws, also known as the *Uniform Law Commission.* Uniform laws are proposed state laws developed by judges, attorneys, and other legal experts to promote uniformity in legal practice relating to commonly encountered matters. States may adopt, modify, or reject a given uniform law. In the latter case, a uniform law's provisions may be adequately covered by an existing state statute. Although it was subsequently withdrawn by the Uniform Law Commission, the UPPBRA continues to play a role in records management. Other uniform laws are cited elsewhere in this book.

include minute books of corporations and sales records relating to weapons, explosives, or other dangerous substances. These laws interpret business records broadly to include records maintained by nongovernmental institutions, including private schools and universities, philanthropic foundations, professional associations, cultural institutions, and other not-for-profit organizations. U.S. federal regulations associated with the Paperwork Reduction Act (44 U.S. Code 3501 et seq.) recognize three years as a reasonable records retention period. As specified in 44 CFR 1320.5, the Office of Management and Budget provides a default retention period of three years, subject to exceptions, for U.S. government records that do not have a retention period mandated by other laws or regulations.

Legally mandated recordkeeping requirements apply to a subset of an organization's records, but, in some cases, the subset can be large. An important and widely publicized group of recordkeeping requirements applies to specific industries or business activities that are regulated by one or more government agencies. Examples include banking, food processing, insurance, securities, public accounting, pharmaceuticals, communications, transportation, energy, healthcare, foreign trade, and waste management. In those industries, government regulations mandate minimum retention requirements for many records, including those that are unique to specific work environments.

Although most often associated with private businesses, some legally mandated recordkeeping requirements apply to government agencies and not-for-profit organizations. In many countries, government agencies are subject to laws that specify the retention authority of archival agencies over public records. The U.S. National Archives and Records Administration (NARA), as previously noted, has retention authority over records maintained by U.S. government agencies. State archival agencies have similar retention authority over state government records and, in many cases, records maintained by county governments, municipalities, school districts, quasi-governmental authorities, public benefit corporations, and other entities. Many state archives have issued functional schedules that specify minimum retention requirements to which agencies within their jurisdiction must conform.

To illustrate the scope and characteristics of legally mandated recordkeeping requirements, the following sections cite examples of laws and government regulations that specify minimum retention periods for selected records related to three commonly encountered business operations: tax, accounting, and human resources. As previously noted, tax auditors, compliance officers, and other government officials require these records to determine compliance with laws or regulations to which the records pertain. The cited laws and regulations emphasize U.S. requirements, but representative examples from other countries are also cited. The discussion is illustrative rather than comprehensive and prescriptive. It does not cite all applicable laws and regulations, nor does it provide authoritative retention recommendations. It merely provides examples of records that are subject to statutory or regulatory retention requirements. Retention periods for an organization's records are determined by legal requirements in combination with other factors discussed in this chapter. Readers are further cautioned that retention guidelines discussed here are subject to change.

Tax Records

All countries have laws and regulations that specify minimum retention requirements for financial records pertaining to tax assessments. Such retention requirements ensure that revenue officials will have sufficient information to determine taxes owed and paid. Section 6001 of the U.S. Internal Revenue Code requires that taxpayers keep sufficient records to determine their income tax liability. Section 7062 authorizes the Internal Revenue Service to examine these records to determine the accuracy of federal income tax returns. Similar provisions apply to state and local income tax records.

At a minimum, federal and state tax records—including tax returns and supporting documentation, such as income statements, canceled checks, and receipts—must be retained as long as the tax returns to which they pertain are subject to audit. In most cases, that time period is three years after the original due date of the return or the date the return is filed, whichever is later. The audit period increases to six years, however, for tax returns that understate income by more than 25 percent. Other factors warrant longer retention periods for certain tax returns and supporting documentation. For example, records relating to properties purchased and capital improvements made to those properties will be needed for tax basis adjustments if the properties are sold in the future. Similarly, certain depreciation deductions are subject to recapture if qualified business use falls below a certain percentage in future years. Records older than three years may be needed to substantiate business use in years subject to recapture. To address these issues, some authorities recommend that copies of tax returns and supporting documentation be retained for several decades or longer. As a further complication, tax audits and any ensuing litigation may take years to resolve, forcing the retention of tax records while those matters are pending.

In other countries, laws and regulations typically mandate the retention of tax-related records for 3 to 10 years following the end of the tax year to which the records pertain. According to Section 230 of the Canadian Income Tax Act, for example, tax-related books and records must be retained for six years from the end of the tax year to which they relate. In the United Kingdom, the Taxes Management Act 1970 specifies that tax-related records must be kept for five years after January 31 of the year following the year of assessment. In France, the Book of Tax Procedures specifies a six-year retention requirement for records that are subject to audit and that support deductions claimed by the taxpayer. According to the Fiscal Code of Germany, tax-related records must be retained for 10 years from the end of the calendar year to which they relate. Depending on the country, a longer retention period may apply where a taxpayer files a late return or fraud or negligence is suspected.

Value-added tax laws and regulations specify retention periods ranging from 5 to 10 years for invoices, vouchers, credit notes, debit notes, receipts, customs clearance documents, and other relevant records. Longer retention periods may be specified for records related to the purchase or renovation of immovable property.

Tax laws assume or explicitly state that tax-related records will be stored at the taxpayer's domestic location where they will be available for tax audits or other government inquiries. Some countries allow electronic records to be retained abroad if tax officials can access them online.

Accounting Records

Apart from tax laws, many countries have laws and regulations that specify minimum retention requirements for accounting records that document an organization's business transactions and disclose its financial position. Examples include accounting books and ledgers, charts of accounts, balance sheets, financial reports, auditors' reports, records of goods purchased and sold, inventories, and supporting documentation such as contracts, invoices, payment vouchers, receipts, and reconciliation documents. Retention periods—which may be specified in a commercial code, a companies law, a civil code, an accounting act, bookkeeping regulations, and/or tax laws—range from 3 years to more than 10 years, depending on the country and the types of records involved. The retention requirements typically apply to for-profit companies. Examples include the following:

1. In the Czech Republic, Denmark, and Slovakia, companies must retain ledgers, journals, transaction documents, and other accounting records for five years.

2. In Canada, Ireland, and Spain, companies must retain accounting records for six years from the date to which they relate.

3. In Australia, Belgium, Hong Kong, the Netherlands, and Sweden, companies must retain accounting books and supporting documentation for seven years.

4. In India, accounting books and records must be retained for eight financial years immediately preceding the current year.

5. In France, Germany, Indonesia, Italy, Japan, Norway, Pakistan, Portugal, South Korea, and Switzerland, companies must keep accounting books and records for 10 years.

The retention period for accounting records may begin on the date that the records were created or, more commonly, at the end of the calendar year, the end of the fiscal year, or the conclusion of the accounting transaction to which the records relate.

Hiring Records

In the United States, federal and state laws prohibit hiring practices that discriminate against qualified job applicants on the basis of race, skin color, national origin, citizenship, gender, age, religion, union membership, or disability. Employment application records include application forms, correspondence, resumes, and other documents submitted by or pertaining to job applicants. U.S. law requires the retention of these records to confirm that an organization's hiring practices are not discriminatory, but the mandated retention periods are short. Under Title VII of the Civil Rights Act of 1964 (42 US Code 2000(e)(8)(c) and 29 CFR 1602.14) and the Americans with Disabilities Act of 1990 (42 US Code 12101 and 29 CFR 32.15d), employers must retain all hiring records, including application files, for one year from the date the records were made or the personnel action was taken, whichever is later. The Age Discrimination in Employment Act (29 US Code 62 and 29 CFR 1627.3) requires retention of hiring records, including job applications, inquiries, and resumes, for one year from the date of the personnel action. The time period for filing a complaint with the Equal Employment Opportunity Commission is 360 days. Some U.S. states, however, allow up to three years for filing discrimination lawsuits.

In some other countries, laws and regulations specify retention and disposition requirements for records related to prospective employees. According to Article 32 of the Portuguese Labor Code, for example, job advertisements, summary data about applicants, the results of testing and selection, information about the gender of applicants, and other records that document the hiring of new employees must be retained for five years after the recruitment process is completed. In Switzerland, guidelines issued by the Federal Data Protection and Information Commission require that records related to rejected job applications must be returned to the applicant after the selection procedure is completed, and any copies must be destroyed. Letters of reference, test results, and certain other documents may be retained only if they will be reused in the short term and the applicant agrees to their retention. In the Netherlands, information about rejected job applicants must be deleted upon request by the person concerned within four weeks after completion of the hiring process unless the rejected applicant consents to a retention period of one year after completion of the hiring process. In France, information collected during the recruitment process about a successful or rejected job applicant must be discarded within two years after last contact with the applicant.

Personnel Records

Companies, government agencies, and other organizations maintain database records and/or paper files that contain performance appraisals, commendation letters, training records, warnings about possible disciplinary actions, and other information about their employees. Most organizations retain these records for a reasonable period of time following termination of employment to be able to confirm the dates of employment, to allow for the possibility that a former employee may return, or for other reasons. Certain employee records are subject to legally mandated recordkeeping requirements, but the retention periods specified in laws and government regulations are typically shorter than the business need to retain such records. U.S. examples include:

- The Equal Pay Act of 1963 (29 US Code 206 and 29 CFR 1620.32) requires employers to retain job descriptions, job evaluations, and other records related to payment of wages for two years. The same retention applies to records that explain the basis for gender-based wage differentials.

- Under the previously cited Civil Rights Act of 1964, the Americans with Disabilities Act of 1990, and the Age Discrimination in Employment Act, records relating to employee promotion, demotion, layoffs, recalls, discharges, or selection for training must be retained for one year from the date of the personnel action.

- Records relating to leaves of absence under the Family and Medical Leave Act (29 U.S. Code 2616 and 29 CFR 825.500) must be retained for three years.

- Under the Employee Polygraph Protection Act (29 U.S. Code 2001 and 29 CFR 801.30), employers must retain polygraph test results and the reasons for administering the test for three years.

- Federal government contractors and subcontractors are subject to the Rehabilitation Act of 1973 (29 U.S. Code 793 and 34 CFR 104) and the Vietnam Era Veterans Readjustment Assistance Act (38 U.S. Code 4212 and 41 CFR 60-250), which require that employment records be retained for one or two years from the date the record was created or the personnel action involved, depending on the number of employees hired and the value of the government contract. The same retention requirements are specified in 41 CFR 601-12 for compliance with Executive Order 11246, which deals with equal opportunity in employment by federal government agencies and contractors.

- Under the Immigration and Nationality Act of 1952 (8 U.S. Code 1324 and 8 CFR 274), Employment Eligibility Verification Form I-9 must be retained for three years following the date of hiring or one year following termination of employment, whichever is later. This retention period also applies to supporting documentation that confirms identity and eligibility. All U.S. employers must complete and maintain Form I-9 for each employee hired to work in the United States after November 6, 1986, whether the employee is a citizen or not.

Other countries have laws and regulations that require employers to create and keep certain information about their employees, such as names and addresses, job titles, the dates that employment began and termination, regular and overtime hours worked, and annual leave taken. Among the many examples that might be cited:

1. *In Canada,* according to Canada Labour Standards Regulations, records indicating the dates that employment began and terminated for each employee must be retained for 36 months after termination of employment. Information about wage rates, hours worked, earnings, paid holidays granted, medical leave, and certain other matters must be retained for three years after the work to which the records relate is performed. Provincial laws and regulations specify similar requirements.

2. *In France,* according to the French Labor Code, every employer must keep a single register of staff that contains the name, nationality, date of birth, gender, dates of employment, and other information for each employee in chronological order by the date of hiring. This register must be kept for five years after an employee leaves the organization.

3. *In Italy,* employers must keep a single personnel ledger that contains personal information, job titles, payroll information, and attendance information for each employee. The ledger must be retained for five years from the date of last entry.

4. *In Belgium,* an employer must keep a personnel register for five years from the date of last entry and records for individual employees for five years after termination of employment.

5. *In Malaysia,* the Employment Act specifies a six-year retention period for registers that contain information about employees.

6. *In Singapore,* employment records must be kept for a minimum of three years from the date of last entry in the records.

7. *In Japan,* employment records, including records related to hiring and retirement of employees, must be retained for three years after termination of employment.

8. *In South Korea,* records related to employment, dismissal, retirement, leaves of absence, promotion, demotion, and other matters must be kept for three years after termination of employment.

9. *In Finland,* an employer must provide an employee with a written certificate of employment for up to 10 years following termination of the employment relationship.

10. *In some countries,* records retention requirements are specified for special situations such as foreign workers, child labor, maternity, or workers in specific occupations. Various countries mandate retention of records that verify the eligibility of foreign workers.

    - *In Finland,* for example, an employer must keep records related to foreign workers for four years after termination of employment.

    - *In the Netherlands,* employers must keep copies of foreign workers' identification papers and work permits for five years following the end of the year in which work was performed.

    - *In India,* employers must maintain a register of children employed, including ages, the nature of the work, hours work, and rest intervals, for three years following the date of last entry.

    - *In Pakistan,* a register of child workers must be retained for three years from the date that work began.

    - *In Germany,* employers must keep records of the names, job duties, work hours, and wages of expectant and nursing mothers for two years after the last entry.

    - *In the United Kingdom,* employers must keep records related to maternity pay for three years after the end of the tax year in which the maternity pay period ends.

    - *In European Union (EU) member states,* Directive 2002/15/EC specifies a two-year retention period for records of hours worked by truck drivers or other employees involved in the transport of passengers or goods by road.

Employment Contracts

According to the Fair Labor Standards Act of 1938 (20 US Code 206 and 29 CFR 516.5), employment contracts, including collective bargaining agreements, must be retained for three years from their last effective date. Some other countries have similar requirements. In the Czech Republic and the Slovak Republic, for example, the Collective Bargaining Act specifies that collective bargaining agreements and arbitration decisions must be kept for five years after they are no longer in effect. In Ireland, the Industrial Relations Act 1990 specifies a three-year retention period for registered employment agreements.

Occupational Health and Employee Medical Records

An employee medical record is defined in 29 CFR 1910.1020 as any "record concerning the health status of an employee which is made or maintained by a physician, nurse, or other health care personnel or technician." This definition specifically encompasses medical and employment questionnaires or histories; results of medical examinations; medical opinions, diagnoses, progress notes, and recommendations made by medical practitioners; descriptions of treatments and prescriptions; and employee medical complaints. Employers can maintain medical information about employees, but under the Americans with Disabilities Act, such records must be filed separately from other employee records.

Regulatory retention requirements for employee medical records depend on the circumstances in which the records were created and the duration of employment:

- **Hazardous or toxic substances.** Medical records related to an employee's exposure to hazardous or toxic substances must be retained for 30 years following termination of employment as specified in 29 CFR 1910.1020 for employees who have worked for an organization for one year or longer and three years following termination of employment for employees who worked for an organization for less than one year, provided that copies of the records are given to the employee upon termination of employment. If copies are not provided, the records must be retained for 30 years following termination of employment. Some other countries have longer retention requirements for records related to workers' exposure to hazardous substances. In EU member states, such records must be kept for 40 years after exposure to carcinogenic substances, mutagenic substances, or asbestos ceases. Records of workers exposed to hazardous biological agents must be retained for 10 years following the last known exposure. Where exposure may result in infections in the future, the records must be retained for 40 years following the last known exposure.

- **Minor illnesses and injuries.** For records relating to first-aid treatment by a nonphysician of minor illnesses and injuries, including cuts and scratches, as defined in 29 CFR 1910.1020 (d1)(iB), the retention requirement is three years following treatment.

- **Medical records unrelated to hazardous substances or toxins.** In the United States, there are no legally mandated retention requirements for medical records unrelated to an employee's exposure to hazardous or toxic substances, although organizations that operate clinics that provide medical treatment to employees may be subject to retention requirements for patient records maintained by healthcare facilities. Such retention requirements, which vary from state to state, typically specify that such records must be retained for 5 to 10 years from the date of last treatment. In other countries, where employers are responsible for health surveillance of workers through periodic medical examinations, employee medical records must be retained for specific periods of time. In Belgium, for example, employee medical records must be kept for 15 years after termination of employment. In Italy, Latvia, and Luxembourg, employee medical records must be kept for a minimum of 10 years.

- **Work-related injuries and illnesses.** Under the Occupational Safety and Health Act (29 U.S. Code 651 and 29 CFR 1904.33), employers must keep a log and incident reports of work-related injuries and illnesses. The Occupational Safety and Health Administration (OSHA) provides forms for that purpose, although an equivalent insurance form or computer records can be substituted. The log and incident reports must be available within four hours when requested by an authorized government official. These records must be retained for five years following the year to which they relate. The same recordkeeping requirements apply to states that operate their own OSHA programs as approved by the Occupational Safety and Health Administration. In Canada, Section 15.11 of the Occupational Safety and Health Regulations (SOR/86-304) specifies a 10-year retention period for records related to hazardous occurrences. The same retention period applies in Poland. In Estonia, employers must keep records related to occupational accidents and illnesses for 55 years. In the Russian Federation, lists of employees exposed to hazardous working conditions and records related to occupational illnesses and injuries must be retained for 75 years.

As specified in 29 CFR 1910.1020, employers must retain material safety data sheets or other records that identify hazardous substances used in a specific workplace for 30 years. In EU member states, organizations must keep material safety data sheets for 10 years after a hazardous substance is no longer in use.

Workers' Compensation Records
As an alternative to litigation, workers compensation laws provide monetary and medical benefits related to workplace injuries and illnesses. In the United States, workers' compensation laws and their associated recordkeeping requirements vary from state to state. In New York State, for example, case files and other records for workers' compensation awards must be kept for eighteen years after the injury or illness or eight years after final payment of the award, whichever is longer. Records for claims that are disallowed or otherwise disposed of without an award must be kept for eighteen years after the injury or illness for the basic record of injuries or illnesses and seven years after the injury or illness for case files, excluding the basic record of injuries and illnesses. Records relating to injuries or illnesses that do not

result in workers' compensation claims must be kept for eighteen years after the injury or illness. Case records are subject to audit by state workers' compensation boards throughout their retention periods.

As specified in the Canada Labour Standards Regulations, an employer must keep records for an injured employee for three years after the employee returns to work. In Japan, records related to compensation for workplace injuries must be retained for three years after the last payment.

Payroll Records

In the United States, government regulations require the retention of certain payroll records to confirm that an organization's wage rates are not discriminatory. Under the Equal Pay Act of 1963, Fair Labor Standards Act, and Age Discrimination in Employment Act, payroll records that indicate employees' dates of birth, occupations, and rates of pay must be retained for three years. Such records may contain information about wage rates, hours worked per pay period, total wages per pay period, and additions to or deductions from wages paid.

Federal government contractors and subcontractors are subject to the Davis-Bacon Act (40 U.S. Code 3141 and 29 CFR 5.5), which specifies wage rates for public works projects; the McNamara-O'Hara Service Contract Act (41 U.S. Code 351 and 29 CFR 4.6), which specifies wage and benefit levels for work performed for the U.S. Government or the District of Columbia; and the Walsh-Healy Public Contracts Act (41 U.S. Code 35 and 41 CFR 50-201.501), which defines minimum wage and overtime requirements. These laws specify a three-year retention period for wage and hour records for employees working on U.S. government contracts.

Under the Federal Insurance Contribution Act (26 U.S. Code 21 and 26 CFR 31.6001-2) and the Federal Unemployment Tax Act (26 U.S. Code 23 and 26 CFR 31.6001-4), records relating to income taxes withheld from employees' wages, including W-4 withholding forms, must be retained for four years from the date the taxes are due or paid, whichever is later. As with personnel records, legally mandated retention requirements for payroll records may be shorter than the administrative value of such records. In government agencies and other organizations where pension eligibility is determined by employees' length of service, for example, payroll records may need to be retained for decades.

The Ledbetter Fair Pay Act of 2009 (Public Law 111-2) amends Section 706e of the Civil Rights Act of 1964. Every time a violating paycheck is issued, the Ledbetter Fair Pay Act resets the three-year time period for legal action under the Equal Pay Act. In effect, the time period is now three years after the last violating paycheck for a given employee was issued. The Act does not specify retention periods for payroll or compensation records, but the implication is that payroll records for individual employees should be kept for three years after termination of employment.

Most other countries have laws and regulations that specify retention periods for payroll records. In Germany, for example, employers must keep payroll records for each worker for six years following the last payment of wages. In the United Kingdom and Ireland, employers must retain payroll records for three years as evidence that employees are not being paid less than the minimum wage to which they are entitled. In Spain, employers are required to store information about payment of employees' wages and benefits for four years. In India, employers must keep records of wages paid for three years following the date of the last entry. In Taiwan, payroll rosters must be retained for five years. In Austria, employers must keep a record of each worker's wages until termination of employment.

Employee Benefit Records

In the United States, the Employee Retirement Income Security Act of 1974 ((29 USC 1027) and (29 CFR 209)) defines responsibilities and recordkeeping requirements for organizations that offer pension plans, disability plans, health insurance, or other benefits to employees. Such organizations must maintain sufficient records to determine the benefits due to those employees, but the Act does not specify how long individual employee benefit files must be kept. Most organizations must file Form 5500 Annual Report/Return for Employee Benefit Plan for each pension or benefit plan offered to employees. Under the Employee Retirement Income Security Act, Form 5500 and supporting documentation must be kept for six years after the filing date.

In other countries, laws and regulations specify retention periods for records related to an employer's contributions to social security or pension plans. For example:

- *In Germany,* employers must keep records for contributions to occupational pension accounts for 10 years following the end of the contribution year.

- *In the United Kingdom,* employers must retain records related to payment of benefits, refund of contributions, purchase of annuities, and other retirement matters for five years from the end of the year to which they pertain.

- *In Spain,* employers are required to keep social security records, including registration documents and coverage for temporary disability benefits, for five years.

- *In Taiwan,* employers must maintain information about pension contributions for each employee for five years following termination of employment.

- *In the Czech Republic,* employers must retain records related to pensions and disability benefits for 10 years following the year to which they relate. Records related to pension insurance for occupational illnesses and injuries must be retained for 30 years following the year to which they relate.

- *In Poland,* records related to employee pensions must be retained for 50 years following termination of employment.

- *In Switzerland,* occupational pension plan benefits lapse at age 100, which establishes the retention period for records related to such benefits.

Records Retention and Data Protection Laws

Most recordkeeping laws and regulations specify minimum retention periods for specific types of records. Records can be retained longer than the specified time period if warranted by operational or historical considerations. In the United States, exceptions are few in number and limited to specific situations. As an example, 34 CFR 300.573 requires public school districts to destroy personally identifiable information about special education students at a parent's request when the information is no longer needed to provide educational services to the child, although the school district is allowed to retain a permanent record of the student's name, address, telephone number, grades, attendance record, classes attended, grade level completed, and year completed. Some laws specify maximum retention periods for specific records. As an example, Title 5, Section 72.051 of the Texas Business Commerce Code requires a business to delete any record related to dishonored checks within 30 days if the business and the customer agree that the record is incorrect or if the customer affirms that the dishonored check was unauthorized. According to Section 19589 of the California Government Code, a letter of reprimand must be removed from a state employee's personnel file and destroyed within three years after the letter was issued. Even more unusual, some laws specify absolute retention periods for specific records. According to the New York State Social Services Law, for example, social services agencies must destroy an unsubstantiated report of a child abuse investigation 10 years after the report is submitted to the State Central Register unless an earlier destruction date is ordered by the New York State Office of Children and Family Services. Substantiated reports must be destroyed 10 years after the youngest child mentioned in the report attains 18 years of age.

Some countries have data protection laws that mandate the prompt destruction of records containing personally identifiable information when the information is no longer needed for the purpose for which it was originally created or collected. Many of these laws are modeled after Directive 95/46/EC of the European Parliament and of the Council of 24 October 1995 on the Protection of Individuals with Regard to the Processing of Personal Data and on the Free Movement of Such Data. That directive defines personal data as "any information relating to an identified or identifiable natural person." The personal data may be an identification number or information about the subject's "physical physiological, mental, economic, cultural, or social identity."

This data protection requirement can affect retention periods for employment records, payroll records, workplace health and safety records, shareholder records, tax records, email, customer records, patient records, student records, and other records, all of which may contain personally identifiable information. In the Netherlands, for example, personal information about an employee—including name, address, date and place of birth, positions held, performance assessment, training information, and the reason for termination—cannot be retained longer than two years after termination of employment. In France, information of this type is not to be retained beyond the period of employment unless a longer retention period is specified in laws or regulations.

In some contexts, data protection laws require interpretation to determine the point when the original purpose for which personally identifiable information was collected has been fulfilled. In the case of student records, for example, information about classes taken and grades received remains useful after a student graduates because a student may request an academic transcript to support graduate school or employment applications, but it is not clear when the information is no longer needed for that purpose. Similarly, the personnel records of a former employee may be useful if the employee wants to return to the organization, but that consideration does not warrant indefinite retention. As a complicating factor, data protection requirements do not take precedence over other laws and regulations that specify minimum retention periods for specific records.

Some countries have laws or regulations that mandate short retention periods for surveillance images produced by closed circuit television cameras or other video devices installed in public spaces. In the absence of legislation that deals expressly with video surveillance, some countries invoke data protection laws to limit retention of video recordings that contain personally identifiable information.

Formats for Official Copies

As a group, recordkeeping laws and regulations require the creation of information and its retention for designated time periods. In some cases, acceptable records storage formats and media—paper, microfilm, or electronic—are specified. With many recordkeeping laws and regulations, however, requirements for storage formats and media are omitted or implied rather than clearly stated. This situation is typically the case with recordkeeping laws and regulations that predate widespread computerization of business operations. Those laws and regulations are based on the assumption that required information is contained exclusively in paper documents; the acceptability of electronic media is not mentioned.

Increasingly, however, recordkeeping laws and regulations are being revised to explicitly accept computer databases, word processing files, and other electronic records for retention of specified information. According to 15 US Code 7001(d)(3), for example, electronic records can satisfy statutes and regulations that require the retention of a contract or other record "in its original form." Section 12 of the Uniform Electronic Transaction Act (UETA)—which has been adopted by 47 states, the District of Columbia, Puerto Rico, and the U.S. Virgin Islands—contains virtually identical provisions. (The nonadopting states have their own statutes pertaining to electronic transactions.) Section 13 of the UETA provides that "evidence of a record or signature may not be excluded solely because it is in electronic form." In Canada, all provinces and territories, with the exception of the Northwest Territories, have

Many other countries have electronic transaction laws or electronic signature laws that affirm the legal status of electronic records, which are variously described as electronic documents or data messages. For the most part, these national laws draw upon model laws developed by the United Nations Commission on International Trade Law (UNCITRAL). They accept electronic records as official copies to satisfy retention requirements subject to certain conditions, the most common being that the electronic records accurately preserve all content, that the records remain readable throughout their retention periods, and that printed copies can be created when requested by government officials. Computer equipment and software to support retrieval, display, and printing of electronic records must be available through their retention periods.

adopted the Uniform Electronic Commerce Act, which establishes functional equivalency rules that allow electronic records to satisfy legal requirements for written communications and recordkeeping. The Canadian Personal Information Protection and Electronic Documents Act (2000, c. 5) specifies that electronic documents can satisfy regulatory retention requirements if "the information in the electronic document will be readable" and "any information that identifies the origin and destination of the electronic document and the date and time when it was sent or received is also retained."

Retention for Admissibility into Evidence

Broadly defined, evidence consists of testimony or physical items such as records that are submitted in relation to alleged facts in judicial or other legal proceedings.

The preceding section examined recordkeeping requirements specified in legal statutes and government regulations. A different, much discussed group of legal considerations involves the retention of records for use as evidence in litigation, government investigations, or other legal proceedings. The purpose of evidence is to prove or clarify points at issue in such proceedings. Evidence that a judge or jury can properly consider is termed *admissible.*

Admissibility issues are important factors in retention decisions. As previously noted, laws and government regulations that specify retention periods affect a subset of an organization's records. By contrast, any record might prove useful as evidence in litigation, and many organizations retain large quantities of records for their possible relevance to legal actions that may occur in the future. Predicting which information will be involved in and relevant for legal matters is difficult. However, obvious examples include records relating to:

- Contracts, including leases, loan agreements, insurance policies, and shareholder agreements.

- Fair employment practices or their opposite—job discrimination, wrongful termination, and sexual harassment.

- Intellectual property, including patents, copyrights, and trademarks.

- Product quality and safety, including test results and quality assurance policies, procedures, and findings.

- Accidents or other incidents that may result in illness or injury.

- Customer-related or client matters with unsatisfactory outcomes.

Evidentiary issues are principally the concerns of attorneys involved in legal matters. Records managers are responsible for planning and implementing recordkeeping systems that provide effective documentary support for possible future legal actions. In particular, records managers must ensure that evidentiary issues are considered when retention guidelines are formulated and that records are retained in a reliable manner so as not to imperil their admissibility in future legal proceedings. The following discussion provides a brief tutorial on selected evidentiary matters that records managers need to understand and consider when making retention decisions.

Authentication

In court trials, admissibility of records in evidence is determined by rules of evidence, which are embodied in legal statutes and court decisions (common law). In the United States, admissibility is guided by the Federal Rules of Evidence (FRE), which apply in federal courts; the Uniform Rules of Evidence (URE), which apply in those state courts where they have been adopted; and rules of evidence that apply in courts of other states. Similar rules of evidence apply in other countries. Examples can be found in the Canada Evidence Act and provincial evidence acts, the Civil Evidence Act and Criminal Evidence Act in the United Kingdom, the Australian Evidence Act, and the New Zealand Evidence Act, with their various amendments.

The purpose of authentication is to demonstrate the reliability of records to a court's satisfaction. To be considered reliable, a paper, photographic, or electronic record must meet the following criteria:

1. The record must have been created at or near the time of the event that is the subject of litigation.

2. The record must have been created by a person with knowledge of the event.

3. The record must have been maintained in the regular course of an organization's business.

To be admissible as evidence, a record must satisfy two foundation requirements that apply to all evidence: (1) The record's content must be relevant to the matter at issue; and (2) The record's authenticity must be firmly established— that is, the court must be convinced that the record is what its proponents claim it to be. Records managers are much more likely to be involved with authentication issues than with relevance determinations, which are case-specific and handled by attorneys.

Under FRE, URE, and many state-specific rules of evidence, certain types of records are considered self-authenticating, meaning that extrinsic support for reliability is not required for them. Examples include public records bearing the official seal of a government entity or the signature of an authorized government official, certified copies of public records, official publications of government agencies, documents accompanied by a certificate of acknowledgment executed by a notary public, and published documents such as newspapers and periodicals.

Recent changes to FRE and URE have simplified authentication requirements for many business records. Correspondence, reports, or other records relating to regularly conducted business activity are considered authentic and admissible when accompanied by a written declaration by a custodian or other qualified person that the record satisfies the criteria listed in the sidebar. A live witness is not required for authentication of such business records. In certain cases, as when a business record is maintained in a central file room or offsite storage facility operated by a records management unit, a records manager is the person best qualified to provide the required declaration. The party that offers business records in evidence must provide written notice of that intention to adverse parties and must make the record and declaration available to them for inspection and possible challenge.

Authentication principles apply to records in all formats: paper, photographic, and electronic, but special concerns have been raised about the reliability of computer records. Those concerns relate to the ease with which records stored on magnetic disks, magnetic tapes, or rewritable optical disks can be erased, edited, or otherwise altered, possibly in an undetectable manner. Word processing documents and database records can be easily overwritten with new information. Computer technology permits the undetected manipulation of electronic document images, digital photographs, computer-aided design files, video recordings, and audio recordings. In the case of electronic records maintained by networked computer systems, such alterations may be performed by a remote perpetrator, thereby circumventing physical accessibility requirements associated with the alteration of paper records. With nonelectronic recordkeeping systems, by contrast, modifications are often difficult to make and easy to detect. The alteration of an organization's paper-based accounting records, for example, may require tampering with multiple ledgers, balance sheets, invoices, and other source documents, some of which may be inaccessible to the perpetrator. As a further impediment, alterations to paper records involve physical changes, which may be detectable by specialists or even casual observers. Forensic scientists have decades of experience with the examination of suspect documents. Where records are stored on microfilm, undetectable alterations can prove particularly difficult to make.

To successfully address concerns about tampering, records managers may be expected to provide testimony and/or documentation pertaining to computer system administration, input procedures, equipment, software, security, and the competency of employees who operate the system. Computer hardware and software characteristics must be documented in a manner that fully describes the role of each component in the creation and maintenance of electronic records being submitted as evidence. The accuracy and trustworthiness of electronic records can be affirmed by thorough documentation of record creation procedures, as well as by descriptions of training given to data entry personnel, video camera operators, or other personnel responsible for creation of electronic records. Business processes that create electronic records must be documented through written procedures and work flow diagrams. Electronic records must be protected from physical damage or tampering that could impair their accuracy or raise questions about their trustworthiness. Media handling guidelines and access control procedures for electronic records and security provisions, such as password protection and privilege controls in computer-based systems, must be documented. All aspects of system operation should be audited regularly for compliance with established procedures. Audit findings and the implementation of corrective actions should be fully documented.

The foregoing discussion applies to the admissibility of records in federal and state courts. Certain legal and quasi-legal proceedings, however, are held before federal and state administrative agencies where court-oriented rules of evidence do not apply. Admissibility issues in such situations cannot be generalized. Federal administrative agencies are bound by the Administrative Procedure Act

(5 U.S. Code 500), which gives such agencies considerable discretion in determining the admissibility of records. At the state government level, the admissibility of evidence in administrative proceedings is typically governed by state administrative procedures acts and agency procedural rules. Significant variations in admissibility rules may be encountered from one state to another and, within a given state, from one agency to another.

Statutes of Limitations

Retention periods appropriate to the use of records in evidence are influenced by laws that limit the time periods for initiation of lawsuits, criminal prosecutions, or other legal actions. **Statutes of limitations**, also known as *limitations of action* or *periods of prescription*, define the time period when a person or organization can sue or be sued for personal injury, breach of contract, or other reasons. Limitations of assessment periods are the fiscal counterparts of statutes of limitations. They prescribe the period of time that a government agency can determine taxes owed.

Once the period defined by a given statute of limitations or limitation of assessment has elapsed, no legal action can be initiated for a specific matter. If the statute of limitations on personal injury lawsuits is two years in a given jurisdiction, for example, the injured party loses the legal right to sue after that time.

The time periods defined by statutes of limitations depend on the type of legal matter involved and the circumstances of the case. For a given type of legal proceeding, statutes of limitations vary from country to country and, in federated nations, from state to state. In the United States, for example, the statute of limitations for contract-related litigation ranges from 5 to 15 years, depending on the state in which the litigation is initiated. As a complicating factor for retention decisions, statutes of limitations begin when an event, such as breach of contract, occurs, not when records relating to that event are created. In the case of personal injury, the limitation period typically begins when the injured party becomes aware, or should reasonably have become aware, of the injury. Recorded information about products being developed, tested, manufactured, or sold today may be relevant for legal actions several decades in the future. In some countries, however, statutes of repose specify a maximum time period based on the date when a given product was initially introduced. For personal injuries, statutes of repose may specify a maximum time period after the events that caused the alleged damage regardless of when the claimant became aware of the damage.

Statutes of limitations and statutes of repose define the period of time that records being retained in support of an actual or possible legal action can be used for that purpose. Although they can have a significant impact on a given organization's records retention practices, the time periods specified by statutes of limitations and statutes or repose are not equivalent to retention periods. Records need not be retained for the entire time periods specified by statutes of limitations or statutes of repose, but it is often prudent to do so. If records are being retained specifically and solely to support legal actions, and they otherwise have no other business or scholarly value, retention periods longer than pertinent statutes of limitations or statutes of repose serve no purpose.

Discovery

Discovery is the investigative phase of civil litigation when the opposing parties can obtain information to help them prepare for trial. According to Rule 26(b) of the Federal Rules of Civil Procedure, discovery extends to any nonprivileged matter that is relevant to a party's claim or defense. Discovery often involves document production, which is broadly defined as a request for records in paper or electronic formats. The term "documents" in this context encompasses computer-processable data, video recordings, audio recordings, and other records that are not typically considered documents. The term "e-discovery" refers to discovery requests that involve these and other types of electronically stored information (ESI). **Pretrial discovery** is the investigative phase of litigation when the opposing party can obtain access to recorded information believed to be relevant to its case.

Parties involved in legal proceedings must comply fully and in a timely manner with document production requests. Failure to do so can have serious consequences, particularly if the requested records were destroyed without a satisfactory explanation. Destruction of requested records can lead to charges of **spoliation**—the intentional or negligent destruction of evidence in pending or reasonably foreseeable legal proceedings. Depending on the nature of the records and the party's perceived intent, the possible corrective actions include monetary sanctions; adverse inference instructions, in which a jury is allowed to infer that the destroyed records were harmful to the party that destroyed them; a default judgment in favor of the opposing party, and, at the extreme, criminal penalties for obstruction of justice.

Dozens of cases confirm these possibilities. In 1997, for example, a federal judge imposed a $1 million dollar fine on Prudential Insurance for its "haphazard and uncoordinated approach" to retention of documents subpoenaed in a class action lawsuit (In Re Prudential Insurance Company Sales Practice Litigation, 169 F.R.D. 598, D. N.J. 1997). In Applied Telematics, Inc. v. Sprint Communications Co., WL539595 (E.D., Pa, 1996), the court ordered the defendant to pay the plaintiff's costs and attorney's fees for failure to retain records. In Capellupo v. FMC Corporation, 126 F.R.D., 545, 551 (D. Minn., 1989), the court ordered the defendant to pay twice the plaintiff's costs and attorney's fees for researching and presenting motions relating to document destruction. Widely cited cases in which the destruction of records led to default judgments include Carlucci v. Piper Aircraft Corp., 102 F.R.D. 472, 475 (S.D. Fla. 1984), William T. Thompson Company v. General Nutrition, 593 F. Supp. 1443 (C.D. Cal. 1984), Teletron Inc. v. Overhead Door Corp., 116 F.R.D. 107, 126-27 (S.D. Fla. 1987), Computer Associates International, Inc. v. American Fundware, Inc., 133 F.R.D. 166 (D. Colo. 1990), and Baker by Cress v. General Motors Corp., 519 F.R.D. 519 (W.D. Mo. 1994).

In the most widely publicized criminal prosecution for destruction of business records, the U.S. Securities and Exchange Commission issued a subpoena to Arthur Andersen, a public accounting firm, in November 2001 requesting records related to work it performed for Enron Corporation, which at that time was the subject of a government investigation for possible violation of federal securities laws. The government's investigation of Enron began in October 2001, although the events leading up to it were widely reported during the preceding months. In January 2002, Andersen officials disclosed that the company had destroyed a number of records related to Enron audits. The officials said that the records were destroyed in conformity with company policy, which permitted the destruction of nonessential records relating to specific audits. Andersen officials further stated that the audit records were destroyed without criminal intent before the government investigation began and the subpoena was received. Federal prosecutors alleged, however, that Andersen destroyed the audit records after the government investigation had begun and that Andersen officials were fully aware that the company would be asked to produce the records. In March 2002, federal prosecutors charged Andersen with obstruction of justice for destroying records needed for the Enron investigation. The company was convicted of obstructing justice in June 2002. In 2005, the Supreme Court reversed that conviction, but considerable damage was done even before the guilty verdict was rendered. Many of Andersen's leading clients withdrew their business shortly after the criminal charges were announced, and the company drastically reduced its workforce and sold several of its operations to competitors.

The inability to comply with discovery orders is explainable if subpoenaed records were destroyed prior to the start of litigation in conformity with an organization's formalized retention policies and procedures. In the United States, this point is well documented in case law. Widely cited examples include Smith v. Uniroyal, Inc., 420 F.2d 438, 442-43 (Seventh Circuit, 1970), Vick v. Texas Employment Commission, 514 F.2d 734, 737 (Fifth Circuit, 1975), and Moore v. General Motors, 558 S.W. 2d 720 (Mo. Ct. App. 1977). In those cases, the courts found that adverse inferences should not be drawn where records are destroyed in conformity with an organization's established retention policies and procedures. In other words, the records must have been discarded with the intention of destroying evidence to warrant adverse jury instructions, sanctions, or other penalties.

Merely having a retention policy is not an adequate defense against destruction of evidence, however. In Lewy v. Remington Arms Co., 836 F.2d 1104 (Eighth Circuit, 1988) an influential case in which the defendant was unable to produce customer complaint records that it had reportedly destroyed after three years pursuant to the company's established retention practices, the court delineated guidelines for an acceptable retention policy. According to those guidelines, a retention policy must not be instituted in bad faith solely to dispose of potentially damaging evidence of possible relevance to future litigation. When determining retention periods, an organization must consider the frequency and magnitude of previous complaints and lawsuits that involved certain types of recorded information. The court found that a retention period of three years "may be sufficient for documents such as appointment books or telephone messages, but inadequate for documents such as customer complaints." Records that are likely to be the subject of future litigation should be retained for a longer period of time.

For records associated with certain industries or business operations, relevance for future lawsuits is always a possibility. Examples include technical reports and test results that relate to product design, manufacturing, and safety; contracts and related correspondence, which specify terms and conditions that must be fulfilled; performance evaluations and other personnel records, that document the circumstances in which employees were promoted, demoted, or dismissed; and medical records that document a patient's diagnosis and treatment. The obvious retention strategy is to keep records that are likely to be useful for possible future litigation while discarding those that do not need to be kept for other reasons, but identifying useful records to the exclusion of others is difficult. To ensure the preservation of evidence, attorneys may advise the retention of large quantities of records until all applicable statutes of limitations expire, but that approach can have unintended effects:

- *It can result in costly retention of many irrelevant records.* While some records might conceivably be useful for future litigation, most records have no evidentiary value. According to a study of discovery requests, the ratio of pages produced in response to discovery requests to pages that were actually used as exhibits in litigation exceeds 1000 to 1. In 2008, an average of 4.98 million pages of documents were produced in response to discovery orders in major cases that went to trial, but the average number of pages actually used as documentary evidence was less than 4,775 per case.[3]

- *Needless retention of large quantities of records can increase the time and effort to respond to discovery orders.* Compliance with discovery requests is a time-consuming process. The requested records must be identified, retrieved from their storage locations; reviewed for relevance and privileged information; copied to establish a reliable chain of custody; catalogued and assigned unique control numbers; recorded in an agreed-upon format on appropriate media for delivery to the requesting party; and preserved until the applicable legal proceedings are resolved. Nonresponsive and duplicate records must be eliminated. Confidential content and privileged information must be redacted. All this administrative work must be done in a legally defensible manner, often on a tight schedule. Timely compliance with discovery orders depends on the ability to identify potentially relevant records quickly, but the greater the quantity of records to be examined, the longer the process will take.

- *Needless retention of large quantities of records can give the opposing party access to information that it might not otherwise have.* Few organizations exercise effective control over the content of recorded information associated with their business operations. Memoranda, email messages, and other communications may contain ill-considered, inaccurate, and potentially damaging statements

---

[3]   Litigation Cost Survey of Major Companies, Statement Submitted by Lawyers for Civil Justice, Civil Justice Reform Group, and U.S. Chamber Institute for Legal Reform for Presentation to Committee on Rules of Practice and Procedure, Judicial Conference of the United States, 2010 Conference on Civil Litigation, Duke Law School, May 10-11, 2010. *www.uscourts.gov/file/ document/litigation-cost-survey-major-companies*

about an organization's employees, products, services, or activities. Recorded information obtained through discovery can be misinterpreted, cited out of context, or otherwise presented in court in a manner that proves damaging to an organization. The opposing party in a lawsuit can also make effective use of drafts, preliminary reports, notes taken at meetings, or other records that may not be complete or accurate.

- *Needless retention of large quantities of records increases an organization's exposure to nonparty (third-party) discovery orders for litigation in which the organization is neither the claimant nor the defendant.* Such nonparty discovery orders, which typically take the form of a subpoena, can involve requests to produce documents. They are routinely received by financial institutions, medical service providers, insurance companies, educational institutions, and companies with which a claimant or defendant has done business. Nonparty discovery requests obligate an organization to identify and produce relevant records for legal matters in which they have no direct interest. An organization may also receive a nonparty request to preserve records related to a particular matter that is the subject of actual or anticipated litigation. As a complicating factor with an adverse impact on records retention, nonparties are not necessarily informed about resolution of the litigation covered by a discovery order or preservation request. Consequently, determining when its obligations end can be difficult.

Litigation Holds

An organization must act promptly and decisively to preserve evidence by imposing a mandatory litigation hold on records deemed relevant for lawsuits, government investigations, arbitrations, or other legal proceedings. A litigation hold is a temporary suspension of destruction for records that may be relevant for litigation or government investigations. The hold must be implemented as soon as the organization receives a summons or complaint, when the organization is first on notice regarding possible legal proceedings, or when a prelitigation dispute or repeated inquiries about a specific matter suggests that legal proceedings can be reasonably anticipated. The organization's routine retention policies and practices will be temporarily suspended for records that are subject to a litigation hold. Such records will not be destroyed until the legal matters to which they relate are fully resolved and the litigation hold is rescinded, even if the records' retention periods elapse in the interim.

Although a records manager can provide advice and assistance, litigation holds are typically handled by an organization's legal department or other legal counsel, which will:

1. Determine when a litigation hold must be imposed.

2. Determine the types of records to which the litigation hold will apply and review retention guidelines for the records.

3. Identify the business units or individual employees that are likely to have relevant records in their custody and that must receive a litigation hold notice.

4. Prepare a written litigation hold notice to be sent to records custodians, formally instructing them to immediately suspend destruction of relevant records as well as any actions, such as software upgrades or replacements, that may render relevant records unusable. The litigation hold notice will:

   • Describe the legal matters for which the records are deemed relevant.

   • Explain the organization's obligation to preserve evidence.

   • List the types of records that must be preserved.

   • Provide contact information for records custodians who have questions, need assistance, or want additional information about the litigation hold.

5. Obtain a written acknowledgment of receipt of the litigation hold notice by records custodians.

6. Communicate directly with records custodians to explain the litigation hold, affirm their understanding of the organization's obligation to preserve evidence, and answer questions about the handling of specific records.

7. Issue periodic follow-up notices and reminders to ensure that all records custodians, including newly hired employees, are aware of and understand the litigation hold.

8. Monitor compliance with the litigation hold and address compliance-related problems and issues that may arise during the course of legal proceedings.

9. Ensure that routine destruction of records of departing employees does not violate a litigation hold.

10. Rescind the litigation hold upon resolution of the legal proceedings by issuing a written notice that authorizes records custodians to resume destruction for records with elapsed retention periods.

11. Create and maintain adequate documentation for all stages of the litigation hold process to demonstrate that the company has fulfilled its duty to preserve evidence.

Upon receipt of a litigation hold notice, employees who have records in their custody or under their supervision must immediately suspend destruction of records that are subject to the litigation hold. Employees must confirm that the litigation hold has been officially rescinded before resuming destruction of the records.

Operational Retention Requirements

Operational retention requirements are variously described as **administrative retention requirements** *or user retention requirements.*

As their name suggests, **operational retention requirements** are based on the perceived requirements of knowledgeable employees who rely on recorded information to support an organization's ongoing business operations or long-term

Often, operational requirements exceed retention periods based on legal parameters. For a given records series, operational and legal requirements should be defined separately. The applicable retention period is determined by the longer of the two requirements. In some organizations, as previously noted, the scholarly value of records is also considered when making retention decisions. Such records are retained permanently to support research, even though their business value has elapsed.

goals. Operational retention requirements should not be confused with the legal issues previously discussed. Even where recordkeeping regulations or evidentiary considerations warrant specific retention periods for particular records series, operational requirements must also be considered.

Determination

Like their legal counterparts, operational retention periods are usually measured in years following the occurrence of a specified event such as the end of a fiscal year or calendar year, the completion of an audit, the fulfillment of a contract, the payment of an invoice, the completion of a project, the termination of employment, the resolution of a legal case, the graduation of a student, the date of last medical treatment, or the discontinuation of a product. Operational retention criteria are based on concerns about the availability of records for long-term administrative consistency and continuity, as well as for the day-to-day operations of individual program units. Operational retention parameters are retention limits determined by the operational requirements of employees who rely on recorded information to support an organization's daily business activities or long-term goals. Operational retention decisions are based on the content and business purpose of a given records series in relation to a specific business operation, process, activity, or objective. Operational retention periods are typically negotiated through meetings or other consultation with knowledgeable employees who use the records to fulfill their assigned work responsibilities.

A fundamental records management assumption is that users of records are qualified to determine their continuing value based on their experience with a given records series and their knowledge of specific business operations, processes, activities, or objectives. Sometimes, however, users want to retain records longer than is necessary. Taking the view that long retention periods minimize the risk of discarding records that may be needed in the future, they may not recognize that retention of unneeded records entails its own risks. Through questions and discussion, records managers can help users clarify the relationship between business value and retention requirements for specific records series. A useful aid to such clarification, is to compare users' perceived retention requirements with prevailing practices as reflected in published discussions of records retention and in the retention schedules of government agencies, academic institutions, corporations, and other organizations with well-developed records management programs.

Meetings about operational retention requirements are usually attended by one or more representatives of the departments or other program units that create, maintain, and use specific records series. Often, the departmental records coordinator takes the lead in explaining the program unit's operational requirements at such meetings. Other interested parties, including administrative and managerial employees who maintain and use the records in question, may also be involved. Where records maintained by one program unit are referenced by others, employees in additional departments may also be consulted regarding retention decisions. This collaboration is the case, for example, with centralized paper files and with enterprise-wide databases, data warehouses, web pages on organizational intranets, and other computer-based information resources.

Retention and the Information Life Cycle

As discussed in the preceding chapter, a thorough inventory includes questions about reference activity and retention practices associated with specific records series. A program unit's responses to such questions provides a useful starting point for the determination of operational retention periods, which should be based on the reasonable probability that a given records series will be needed in the future for business reasons. Operational retention determinations are based on the information life cycle concept discussed in Chapter 1. The concept is important enough to bear repetition. Decades of records management theory and practice confirm that the business value of many, if not most, records vary inversely with the age of the records. Typically, records maintained by companies, government agencies, and other organizations are most valuable and are consulted most frequently for a relatively brief period of time following their creation or receipt. As the records age, their business value and reference activity diminish, either gradually or abruptly. When, and if, their business value falls to or approaches zero, the records can be discarded, assuming that they have no other value such as legal or scholarly use.

Operational retention periods are essentially estimates of life cycle duration for specific records series. Certain records, such as general administrative announcements sent to all employees in an organization or unsolicited product literature received from vendors, have very short life cycles; they are often discarded after an initial reading. Other records, such as computer-generated accounting reports, are updated by replacement at similarly brief intervals. Some business records, such as routine correspondence and budget preparation documents, may be retained for several years then discarded. Many transaction-oriented records, such as purchase orders, invoices, and insurance claims, are referenced frequently for several weeks or months following their creation or receipt, but only occasionally after the matters to which they pertain are resolved. Total retention periods for such records are strongly influenced by statutes of limitations for contract-related litigation.

Certain records are useful for much longer periods. Their retention parameters may be determined by the life cycles of objects to which the records pertain. As an example, engineering drawings, specifications, and other technical records that pertain to facilities or equipment should be retained at least as long as the facilities or equipment remain in service. Test results, statistical data, quality assurance reports, and other records that relate to products are retained as long as the products are sold and often longer, because discontinued products may remain at customer sites for years after being withdrawn from the market. Some records have continuing operational value that warrants multidecade or permanent retention.

Examples include patent files and other intellectual property records maintained by corporations; case files maintained by law firms; student transcripts maintained by academic institutions; and deeds, mortgages, birth and death certificates, marriage licenses, and court records maintained by government agencies.

In some cases, the time-dependent business value of a given records series can be established with confidence. Experience may confirm, for example, that mechanical and electrical drawings contain information essential to future building repairs and must be retained until an organization sells, demolishes, or otherwise disposes of the buildings to which they pertain. Similarly, closed contract files may have been used in the past to prepare new contracts or contract amendments. Consequently, they will likely prove useful in the future for that purpose. More often, however, the future need or lack of need for a specific records series is uncertain; therefore, some risk is inevitably associated with operational retention decisions. Because destruction is irreversible, program units may be reluctant to discard older records on the off chance that they may need them. Long retention periods are consequently established by default to allow for improbable contingencies. Such conservative retention practices entail their own risks, however. As previously discussed, such records may be subject to time-consuming and costly discovery actions. Further, long-term storage of large quantities of unneeded paper records can prove expensive. If commercial providers are utilized, storage charges will be incurred for many years or possibly indefinitely. Given the falling cost of computer storage, this appears to be less a concern for electronic records, but excessive retention of large quantities of computer-processable information can have an adverse impact on system performance.

Retention of Drafts and Other Transitory Documents

When drafts are created in the preparation of an organization's records, the final version is considered the official copy for retention purposes. Drafts should be discarded when no longer needed for the purposes for which they were created. Destruction should be done at the earliest opportunity following approval of the final version or whenever a given draft is no longer needed, whichever occurs first. In no case should drafts be retained longer than a specified short period of time—one year, for example—after approval of the final version or completion of the project or other activity to which they relate. This policy should apply to drafts in all formats.

Working papers, including outlines and notes, may be developed during the transaction of an organization's business or during the preparation of company records. Most working papers, such as notes taken at a meeting or annotations on a draft record that is ultimately superseded by a final version, have no business value that warrants retaining them beyond their moment of immediate usefulness.

The following records of transitory value should be discarded at the earliest opportunity:

1. Meeting invitations, appointment schedules, and other calendar items after they are accepted and entered onto the calendar.

2. Action items once the indicated action is taken or the event to which the action pertains has passed, including documents that report actions taken.

3. Brochures, advertisements, product catalogs, flyers, and similar publications that have no continuing reference value.

4. Travel schedules and related information for trips previously taken or canceled.

5. Documents that merely acknowledge the receipt or confirm the content of other documents such as correspondence or email messages that confirm meetings.

6. Correspondence or email messages that merely thank the recipient for taking a particular action.

7. Correspondence or email messages that merely transmit an attachment that is saved elsewhere.

8. Announcements of social events or other activities that may involve employees but that do not directly relate to the organization's business.

9. Duplicate records—that is, any records that are not considered official copies.

Items to Be Destroyed at Once

As a matter of policy, the following items, which are considered nonrecords, should be destroyed immediately when encountered:

1. Documents with sexist, racist, defamatory, abusive, obscene, or pornographic content.

2. Documents with copyrighted content where required permissions (if any) have not been obtained.

3. Digital documents, email messages, and other computer files that contain or are suspected of containing viruses or other malicious software.

4. Digital documents, email messages, and other computer files from suspicious sources.

Special Considerations for Electronic Records

Long retention periods for electronic records are complicated by the limited storage stability of certain electronic recordkeeping media and their dependence on specific configurations of computer, video, or audio hardware and/or software. Limited media stability and hardware/software dependence also have obvious and significant implications for scholarly retention criteria, which typically involve the permanent preservation of records.

In most cases, the useful lives of paper and photographic media equal or exceed the retention periods for information that such media contain. With few exceptions, the useful lives of media that store electronic records are much shorter than those of paper and photographic films. In many cases, the stable life spans of electronic media are shorter than the retention periods for information recorded on such media.

Media stability, however, is rarely the limiting factor for long-term storage of computer-processable information, audio recordings, or video images. Even if the stability of electronic media were to improve to levels comparable to those of acid-free papers or photographic films, retention periods for electronic records would still be limited by the interdependence of media, recorded information, hardware, and software. The service lives of computer storage devices are typically shorter than those of media intended for use in such devices. While magnetic tapes and optical disks may remain stable for several decades, few recording and playback devices are engineered for a useful life longer than 10 years, and most will be removed from service within a shorter time. Computer storage devices are usually replaced with newer equipment within five years. Audio and video recorders may have longer service lives, but the enhanced capabilities and attractive cost-performance characteristics of new models provide a powerful motive for replacement at relatively short intervals. In computer applications, problems of hardware dependence are compounded by software considerations. Electronic records are intended for retrieval or other processing by specific application programs that, in turn, operate in a specific systems software environment. Even more than equipment, software is subject to changes that can render previously recorded information unusable. Successor versions of a given program may not be able to read data, text, or images recorded by earlier versions.

Data migration, the process of periodically converting electronic records to new file formats and/or new storage media, is necessary to satisfy long retention requirements for electronic records. Data migration is discussed in ISO 13008, *Information and Documentation—Digital Records Conversion and Migration Process*, which defines "conversion" as a change in file format and "migration" as the movement of records from one computer platform to another without changing the format. Conversion of electronic records to new file formats will maintain the usability of recorded information when computer systems and/or software are upgraded or replaced. Conversion of electronic records to new storage media will maintain the usability of recorded information where the stable life span of a given storage medium is shorter than the retention period for recorded information or where product modifications or discontinuations render a given storage medium unusable. Data migration requirements should be determined when retention periods are defined for electronic records. The longer the retention period for recorded information, the greater the need for data migration to ensure the future usability of electronic records. A data migration plan is essential where the destruction date for electronic records is greater than five years from the implementation date of the computer system or software that maintains the records or where the total retention period for electronic records is 10 years or longer.

Data migration requirements have no counterparts in nonelectronic record-keeping systems. They may prove impractical or impossible to implement in specific situations. Where electronic records must be retained for long periods of time, periodic recopying involves a future commitment of labor and economic resources of uncertain availability. Where electronic records are designated for permanent retention, the commitment is perpetual. Where the same information exists in electronic and nonelectronic formats, or where information can be converted easily and reliably to nonelectronic formats through printing or transcription, records managers may prefer paper or microfilm for information designated for long-term retention. While conceptually unattractive, this method is easily implemented and minimizes the risk that required information will be unreadable in the future.

Implementation Issues

Retention schedules are initially prepared in draft form for review and approval by those who will be affected by them and responsible for implementing them.

Functional retention schedules are typically reviewed by a committee that represents key program units and organizational perspectives. In most cases, a functional schedule will also be circulated to selected departments for comment. Program-specific (departmental) retention schedules are reviewed by the program units for which they are prepared. All schedules are typically reviewed by other officials or departments that have an interest in records retention. Such reviewers may include, but are not necessarily limited to, the legal department, the chief financial officer, the tax department, and an archival agency. The review process may lead to changes that will be incorporated into additional drafts, which may be subject to additional reviews. This process is repeated until agreement is reached. A records retention schedule approval request form is often used to secure all required approval signatures. A sample approval request is shown in Figure 3-3.

Importance of Implementation

Once approved, an organization's records retention policies and procedures must be fully implemented by all program units. Records must be discarded when specified in the organization's retention schedules, except where destruction of specific records has been suspended for litigation, government investigation, tax audits, or other reasons specified in the organization's records retention policies. If records are not destroyed as scheduled, the preparation of retention schedules is merely a time-consuming exercise. For an organization's retention practices to be considered legally acceptable, records must be discarded in the normal course of business when their retention periods elapse.

This point is confirmed by the previously cited case of U.S. v. Arthur Andersen, LLP, which involved the destruction of audit records relating to the government's investigation of Enron Corporation's accounting irregularities. Arthur Andersen had corporate retention guidelines that authorized the destruction of correspondence, email messages, drafts, and other nonessential records when audits are completed, but apparently those guidelines were not strictly enforced. In October 2001, one of Andersen's attorneys sent an email message to employees who worked on the Enron audit in the Houston office, reminding them about the policy,

Figure 3-3

**Sample Records
Retention
Schedule
Approval
Request**

Records Retention Schedule Approval Request			
Internal Memorandum			

DATE: _____

FROM: _____

TO: _____

Please review the attached revised Records Retention Schedule for the _____ Department.

If you agree with the information, please sign below in the space provided and forward to the Tax Department.

TAX DEPARTMENT – Please approve in the space provided. Please forward this RRS to the Law Department.

LAW DEPARTMENT – Please approve in the space provided. Please forward this RRS to the Corporate Secretary.

If any approver has an issue, please discuss it with the Records Coordinator or call _____.

Thank you for your cooperation.

Approvals	Printed Name	Signature	Date
Records Manager			
Records Coordinator			
Department Head			
Tax Department			
Law Department			
Corporate Secretary			

(*Source:* Sample Forms for Archival & Records Management Programs, *published by ARMA International and the Society of American Archivists*)

but federal prosecutors argued that the reminder was an instruction to destroy potentially damaging evidence relating to an impending government investigation. The reminder would not have been necessary, of course, had Andersen routinely monitored its business operations for routine compliance with retention policies. At trial, witnesses testified that, after becoming aware that a government inquiry into Enron's financial irregularities had begun, Andersen executives discussed the need for its Enron auditing team to conform to the company's retention policy. Andersen's lead partner on the Enron account subsequently pled guilty to obstruction of justice, admitting that he had authorized the destruction of audit records after becoming aware that the government had begun investigating Enron's accounting practices.

Discretionary deviations from approved retention schedules are not acceptable. If, for any reason, a program unit cannot comply with an approved retention period for a given records series, it must notify the organization's records management program immediately to request a re-evaluation of the retention period for the records series in question. The request must clearly state the reason that the prescribed retention period does not satisfy the organization's requirements. The program unit should suggest a more appropriate retention period if one can be determined. Destruction of the records series will be temporarily suspended while the retention period is re-evaluated.

Implementation Principles

An organization's implementation plan for a new or revised records retention schedule and related policies should be based on the following principles:

- **Reasonable Expectations.** The ultimate objective of the implementation effort is adoption of the new retention schedule and related policies by all program units in all locations, but an overly ambitious implementation timetable is unlikely to succeed in an organization with multiple locations and a complex structure. The implementation plan must be realistic and, from the perspective of organizational change, it must be executable with minimal disruption of departmental operations and employee productivity.

- **Guided Implementation.** The new retention schedule can be consulted as needed by any employee to determine whether and when specific records are eligible for destruction. However, a systematic, structured implementation plan will be required to fulfill the principal objectives of the organization's records retention program: the preservation of records needed to satisfy legal and operational requirements on the one hand and the timely destruction of **obsolete records** to reduce recordkeeping costs on the other.

- **Phased Implementation.** To increase the likelihood of a successful enterprise-wide implementation of the new retention schedule, a phased rollout at a measured pace is strongly recommended. In a large organization, an enterprise-wide implementation may take several years to complete.

- **Collaborative Effort.** The new retention schedule must not be imposed on program units. The records manager must work closely and cooperatively with departmental coordinators and other knowledgeable persons in individual program units to be certain that the retention schedule is well understood, to address questions and concerns raised by employees, and to ensure that implementation issues and problems are appropriately resolved.

Implementation Actions

To implement retention schedules, program units must identify records series in their custody that are eligible for retention actions and apply the appropriate actions. Possible retention actions include but are not necessarily limited to:

1. Destruction of records with elapsed retention periods

2. Transfer of inactive paper or photographic records to offsite storage

3. Transfer of inactive electronic records from hard drives to lower cost online storage

4. Transfer of inactive electronic records from on-premises hard drives to cloud-based storage providers

5. Transfer of inactive electronic records from hard drives to removable media for offline or offsite storage

6. Scanning or microfilming of records followed by destruction of paper copies

7. Scanning or microfilming of records followed by transfer of paper copies to offsite storage

Records management coordinators are typically responsible for organizing and supervising retention initiatives in their program units. Prior to implementing retention schedules, records management coordinators should take the following actions and precautions:

1. Conduct one or more training sessions to inform program unit employees about the organization's records retention policies and procedure.

2. Ensure that all program unit employees who will participate in retention initiatives have access to the latest version of the organization's retention schedules.

3. Determine that program unit employees who will participate in retention initiatives are able to accurately identify records series, correctly interpret retention periods for records in their custody, and take appropriate retention actions in conformity with the organization's retention schedules.

4. Consult with the organization's records management program to determine whether destruction of specific records has been suspended for litigation, government investigation, tax audits, or other reasons.

Paper and photographic records eligible for retention actions must be located and removed from file cabinets or other containers. Electronic records must be located in directories and subdirectories or on offline media. This process, which must be performed manually, is time-consuming. In some cases, folders or documents must be individually inspected to determine whether their retention periods have elapsed. To simplify the identification of records eligible for retention actions, records series should be subdivided chronologically whenever possible and practical. This practice is known as *breaking files*. It involves the closing or cutting off of a folder at the end of a calendar or fiscal year and the establishment of a new active folder. A file of purchase orders and supporting documentation, for example, might be arranged by year then by purchase order number. If the organization's retention schedule specifies that purchase orders are to be kept for two years in the purchasing department's office and five more years offsite, records that are eligible for disposal or transfer to offsite storage in a given year will be grouped together and easily identified.

Chronological file breaks are best suited to accounting records, purchasing records, customer order records, and other transaction records. Case files, contract files, project files, and similar files can be cut off when the matters to which they pertain terminate or are resolved, at which time they should be moved to a closed category that is subdivided by calendar or fiscal year.

Secure Destruction

Records that contain nonconfidential information can be discarded by any method consistent with an organization's waste management practices and with the waste removal requirements of the locality where the records will be discarded. Records with confidential or sensitive information about persons, organizations, research and development activities, strategic plans, products, prices, or other matters must be destroyed in an irreversible manner that completely obliterates their contents and renders them unreadable and unusable. Locked bins or other secure containers should be used to collect these records for disposal.

Shredding is the most common method of secure destruction for paper documents. Shredding can also be used to destroy photographic media and removable electronic media. Shredders are rated according to security levels defined in DIN 66399-1 *Office Machines—Destruction of Data Carriers—Part 1: Principles and Definitions*, and DIN 66399-2 *Office Machines—Destruction of Data Carriers—Part 2: Requirements for Equipment for Destruction of Data Carriers*, which were issued by the Deutsches Institut fuer Normung in 2012. The DIN 66399 standards define shredding requirements for recorded information at seven security levels ranging from illegibility to pulverization. Depending on the device, a shredder may produce strips or particles; the higher the security level, the smaller the remnants. At the lowest protection level (P-1), remnants have a maximum surface area of 2,000 square millimeters (3.1 square inches). At the highest protection level (P-7), remnant particles have a maximum surface area of just 5 square millimeters (0.0078 square inches).

Incineration and chemical disintegration are possible alternatives to shredding for secure destruction of paper documents and photographic media, but they may be prohibited by local ordinances. Recycling is not an acceptable method of secure destruction because recycling contractors may store records in unsupervised areas while awaiting recycling.

Although it may permit the recovery of information, file deletion is the only practical method of destroying confidential electronic records stored on hard drives that will remain in service following destruction of the information. A hard drive that previously contained confidential information should be reformatted then physically destroyed when it is taken out of service. Secure methods of destroying confidential electronic records stored on magnetic tapes, floppy disks, or other removable magnetic media include degaussing (bulk erasure) or reformatting, followed by physical destruction of the media. Special shredders are available for that purpose. Secure methods of destroying confidential electronic records stored on optical disks, including CDs and DVDs, including cutting, crushing, pulverizing, and chemical disintegration.

Organizations may have adequate in-house facilities to shred small quantities of confidential records, but secure disposal of a large volume of records will often require the services of a commercial provider that specializes in records destruction. A number of companies offer plant-based and mobile services of this type. If an organization contracts with a commercial provider for destruction of records, the contractor must:

1. Specify the destruction method to be used for confidential and nonconfidential records.

2. Specify the amount of time that will elapse between pickup of records from an organization's location and their destruction.

3. Allow the organization's representatives to observe all stages of the destruction process from pickup of records to disposal of remnant material following destruction of records.

4. Demonstrate safeguards for confidential information at all stages in the destruction process.

5. Complete a **certificate of destruction** as specified by the organization.

6. Provide proof of destruction of records in the manner specified by the organization.

7. Assume full liability for breaches of confidentiality involving records while they are in the contractor's custody.

The National Association for Information Destruction (NAID), a not-for-profit trade association, has developed a security certification program for records destruction contractors and facilities. A sample records destruction authorization and certificate is shown in Figure 3-4a. A sample certificate of destruction is shown in Figure 3-4b.

Training Requirements

To support its retention initiatives, an organization must develop and conduct training sessions for departmental records coordinators and for other employees, including those who may be hired in the future. At the inception of the implementation initiative, departmental records coordinators should attend a half-day training session that will cover the following topics:

- Definition and ownership of the organization's records

- Retention principles for records in relation to legal and operational requirements

- Records retention responsibilities of departmental coordinators

- Purpose and characteristics of the retention schedule with detailed instructions for its application to specific types of program records

- Questions and issues likely to arise during implementation

- Procedures for requesting revisions to the retention schedule

- Procedures for destruction of records

Post-implementation, departmental records coordinators should receive additional training annually to reinforce their understanding of the retention schedule and to discuss implementation-related issues. As time passes, a records and information management program will need to develop a supplemental training

Figure 3-4a

Records Destruction Authorization and Certificate

Records Destruction Authorization and Certificate		

Department, Unit, Name, Address	Department Manager
	Date

The records listed below are now eligible for destruction according to the approved records retention schedule. Please indicate your approval for the destruction unless reasons to delay exist. Your signature below attests that no unresolved (1) audit questions, (2) investigations, (3) civil suits or criminal prosecutions, or (4) other reasons for holding up the destruction exist. If the destruction is to be delayed, please give the reason in the space indicated and provide a revised destruction date.

Schedule Item No.	Series Title, Inclusive Dates, and Total Volume	Scheduled Destruction Date	Revised Destruction Date

Reason for Continued Retention

Security Destruction ☐ Yes ☐ No	Department Manager (Signature)	Date

Certificate of Destruction

This completed and signed form certifies that the records listed above have been destroyed on the date shown below.

If Security Destruction, Witnessed By (Signature)	Date
Records Center Manager (Signature)	Date

(Source: Sample Forms for Archival & Records Management Programs, *published by ARMA International and the Society of American Archivists*)

initiative for new departmental coordinators; that is, for those individuals who replace previously designated coordinators or coordinators designated for newly formed departments.

Program unit managers must understand the scope and purpose of the records retention initiative in order to support their departmental coordinators and ensure

Figure 3-4b

Certificate of Destruction

Certificate of Destruction
Company:
Department:
Records Coordinator:	Phone:
FAX:	E-mail:
Schedule Issue Date:

Records Disposed Of:

Records Code	Records Title	Date/Alpha Range

On _____, destruction of the above records was made by means of :

☐ Incineration   ☐ Shredding   ☐ Other _____

Total # Of Boxes Destroyed: _____

Name

Signature | Date

(Source: Sample Forms for Archival & Records Management Programs, published by ARMA International and the Society of American Archivists)

compliance. All employees will require a basic understanding of the organization's records management policies and retention schedule at a level sufficient to implement prescribed retention periods for records in their custody. This training can be accomplished through a 60-to-90-minute in-person training session or through a computer-based learning component of equivalent duration. In either case, employee training should cover a subset of topics presented in the training session for departmental records coordinators:

- Definition and ownership of the organization's records
- Retention principles for records in relation to legal and operational requirements
- The purpose and characteristics of the retention schedule and related policies
- Procedures for destruction of records

New employees should receive this training at the time they are hired as part of the organization's orientation process.

Compliance

In most organizations, individual program units are responsible for implementing retention schedules for records in their possession. The records management staff should provide training for that purpose and be available to interpret retention guidelines as needed. Departmental records coordinators play a key role in the implementation process. Some organizations designate annual review periods or cleanup days for destruction of records with elapsed retention periods or transfer of inactive records to offsite storage in conformity with retention schedules. Department managers may be required to sign a certificate of compliance attesting that the annual review has been completed and that retention guidelines have been properly implemented.

Regular or unscheduled physical audits of selected departments are recommended to confirm these self-assessments. The authority to conduct or commission such audits should be clearly established when a records management program is established. A **records retention audit** involves a sampling of records in one or more series that may be performed by the records management department or by a compliance-oriented organizational unit such as an internal audit or quality assurance department. In the latter case, the records management department typically provides a checklist of recordkeeping characteristics to be examined for compliance with organizational policies and procedures. In addition to conformity with retention schedules, an audit may consider the security of records, appropriate methods for destroying confidential information, backup protection for vital records, efficient use of available storage space, or other matters.

To be effective, of course, audit findings must be taken seriously. In most organizations, audit reports, which indicate compliance problems and present recommendations for corrective action, are initially discussed with line management in the departments involved. A return visit is then scheduled to confirm that appropriate corrective actions have been taken. Continuing problems should be referred to executive management for resolution.

Revision of Retention Schedules

Like all policy and procedural documents, retention schedules are subject to changes in legal, regulatory, and organizational requirements. Retention schedules must be reviewed periodically and revised as necessary to add or delete records series or to change retention periods. Program units should be instructed to notify the organization's records management program when any of the following occurs:

- A new records series is created.

- A records series was overlooked when the organization's retention schedules were initially prepared or last revised.

- The organization obtains one or more records series through a merger or acquisition.

- The organization's retention schedules do not conclusively identify an existing records series.

- The title or form number for an existing records series is changed.

- An existing records series is divided into multiple series, each having different retention requirements.

- An existing records series is combined with another records series that has a different retention period.

- A records series listed in the organization's retention schedules is discontinued.

- The retention period prescribed for a given records series is not clear.

- Legal or regulatory developments warrant reconsideration of retention periods for specific records series.

Revisions to retention schedules typically apply retroactively. If a revision decreases the retention period for a given records series, records that would have been kept under the old retention schedule must be destroyed at the earliest opportunity in conformity with the new retention period.

Summary of Major Points

☑ A retention schedule is a list of records series maintained by all or part of an organization. It specifies the period of time that each records series is to be kept. Retention schedules are the core component in a systematic records management program. By preparing retention schedules, an organization acknowledges that systematic disposition of recorded information is a critical activity to be governed by formalized operating procedures rather than the discretion of individual employees.

☑ Retention decisions are based on the content and purpose of records. Retention periods are determined by legal, operational (administrative), and scholarly (research) criteria.

☑ Legal criteria may be defined by laws or government regulations that mandate the retention of records for specific periods of time. Where legally mandated recordkeeping requirements apply to an organization's records, they must be incorporated into retention guidelines. For records managers, assessing legal compliance is one of the most important aspects of professional practice. Reliable determination and careful analysis of recordkeeping requirements is a critical component of systematically developed retention initiatives.

☑ A broader group of legal considerations is concerned with the admissibility of records as evidence in trials and other legal proceedings. Statutes of limitations prescribe the time periods within which lawsuits or other legal actions must be initiated. If records are being retained specifically and exclusively to support legal actions and they otherwise have no operational or scholarly value, retention periods longer than pertinent statutes of limitations serve no purpose.

☑ Operational retention criteria are based on the continued need for specific records series to support an organization's mission, the public interest (in the case of government records), or owners' or stockholders' interest (for records of private or publicly held companies, including sole proprietorships and partnerships). Such criteria are concerned with the availability of records for long-term administrative consistency and continuity, as well as for an organization's day-to-day operations.

☑ Retention of records for their scholarly value is principally the concern of archival administration rather than records management. Such determination requires specialized knowledge about the scholarly disciplines and research activities for which particular records may be relevant.

☑ Where a given record exists in multiple copies, the copy that will satisfy an organization's legal and administrative retention requirements is termed the *official copy*. The program unit that maintains the official copy is designated as the office of record for retention purposes. Other copies are considered duplicate records.

☑ For an organization's retention practices to be considered legally acceptable, records must be discarded in the normal course of business when their retention periods elapse, except where destruction of specific records has been suspended for litigation, government investigation, tax audits, or other reasons specified in the organization's records retention policies.

☑ In most organizations, individual program units are responsible for implementing retention schedules for records in their custody. The records management unit should provide training for that purpose and be available to interpret retention guidelines as needed. Departmental records coordinators play a key role in the implementation process.

☑ Retention schedules require periodic revisions to add or delete records series or to change retention periods.

Chapter 4

Records Centers

A **records center** is a specially designed, warehouse-type facility that provides safe, economical, warehouse-type storage for records that are consulted infrequently but that must be retained for legal or operational reasons.

Records centers are often characterized as offsite storage facilities because they are located apart from an organization's office locations. Properly organized and operated, a records center is an important component in a systematic records management program and a critical resource for cost-effective storage of records that are in the inactive portion of the information life cycle.

A records center may be operated by a company, government agency, university, cultural institution, or other organization for its own use. Such in-house records centers are an important component of some records management programs. The U.S. National Archives and Records Administration, for example, opened the first Federal Record Center in 1950. It now operates 17 regional records storage facilities, which collectively house 27 million cubic feet of federal agency records. Similarly, the Regional Service Centres operated by the Library and Archives of Canada provide warehouse-type storage for Canadian government records. As an alternative to in-house operations, many organizations contract with commercial records centers that charge predetermined fees for storage and related recordkeeping services. When measuring the quantity of records, the contents of a container with interior dimensions of 10 inches high by 12 inches wide by 15 inches deep is one **cubic foot**. Worldwide, commercial records centers store hundreds of millions of cubic feet of records for organizations of all types and sizes. These two approaches are not mutually exclusive. Some organizations use commercial storage providers to supplement their in-house records centers for specific types of records or in selected geographic locations.

Whether in-house or outsourced, records center operations are typically integrated with and provide essential support for an organization's records retention initiatives. In some organizations, retention guidelines specify which records are to be transferred to a records center by specific program units and when the transfer should occur. Retention guidelines also identify records to be discarded rather than sent to offsite storage. These instructions may be included in retention schedules or presented in separate procedural documents. Alternatively, the decision to transfer inactive records to offsite storage may be left to the discretion of individual program units. In either case, preparing records for transfer by removing them from file cabinets, packing them in appropriate containers, and inventorying their contents is an important aspect of schedule implementation. These activities are typically considered when program units are audited for compliance with retention policies and procedures. Figure 4-1 shows a records transfer list that may be affixed to a records container when it is transferred to offsite storage.

Most records centers will destroy records, subject to required approvals, when their retention periods elapse. Some organizations limit records center storage to inactive records that have a specified destruction date—within 15 or 20 years from the date of transfer, for example. Records center storage, where conveniently available and compatible with a program unit's access requirements, is almost invariably the best practice for cost-effective management of such records. As discussed elsewhere in this book, scanning or microfilming may be a more economical alternative for large quantities of inactive records with longer retention periods, although the cost of these approaches must be carefully compared on a case-by-case basis.

The business case for records centers is straightforward: Expensive office space and filing equipment should be reserved for records that will be consulted frequently and that must be available immediately when needed. Inactive records should be stored elsewhere, provided that they can be retrieved on demand within a reasonable period of time. In office areas, where records are stored in conventional file cabinets, wide aisles are required to accommodate extended file drawers and the air space above cabinets is wasted. The resulting cubic-foot-to-square-foot ratio—the ratio of records to floor space, an important indicator of storage efficiency and economy—rarely exceeds 1:1. A typical letter-size vertical filing cabinet has base measurements of 1.25 feet wide by 2.5 feet deep for an approximate footprint of three square feet. An additional three square feet of installation space is required for the extended drawer plus a minimum of three square feet in front of the extended drawer for a user to stand while inserting and removing files. When moderately full, a four-drawer, letter-size vertical filing cabinet contains six to eight cubic feet of records (10,000 to 12,000 pages) but requires at least nine square feet of installation space, including floor space that must be allocated for the extended drawer and for a user to stand. The resulting cubic-foot to square-foot storage ratio ranges from 0.68:1 to 0.89:1.[4]

Assuming that a well-constructed filing cabinet suitable for daily use in a business office costs $400 and has a 10-year useful life and that office space in a

---

[4]   Adding a fifth drawer to a vertical cabinet will bring the ratio closer to 1:1. By eliminating space for extended drawers, shelf-type filing cabinets offer better space utilization but, even then, the cubic-foot to square-foot storage ratio is constrained by the height of the cabinet, which rarely exceeds 4.5 feet. To fully utilize available floor space, a filing area must be configured with floor-to-ceiling shelving, which is not practical in some office settings.

Figure 4-1

**Records
Transfer List**

<table>
<tr><td colspan="4" align="center">**Records Transfer List**</td></tr>
<tr><td colspan="3"></td><td>Date Prepared:</td></tr>
<tr><td>Dept. Name</td><td>Dept. No.</td><td>RRS No.</td><td>Location:
☐ _____ ☐ _____</td></tr>
<tr><td colspan="2">Bar Code Label Number (6 Middle Digits):</td><td colspan="2">Contact Name/Tel No. / E-mail Address:</td></tr>
</table>

Records Title & Description From Records Retention Schedule	Records Dates From – To	Destruction Year

Affix Bar Code Label Here: ☛

1. Contact Records Coordinator to arrange pickup.
2. Make 4 Copies of Form: Place Bar Code Label on Copy 1.
   Give Copies 1 & 2 to Driver. Copy 3 to Records Coordinator.
   Copy 4 Retained by User.

(Source: Sample Forms for Archival & Records Management Programs, *published by ARMA International and the Society of American Archivists)*

Class A building, as explained in Chapter 1, rents for $30 per square foot per year, the annual cost of records storage is $38.75 to $51.66 per cubic foot, calculated as follows:

- The cost of the cabinet ($400) is divided by a 10-year useful life, which equals an effective annual cost of $40 per year.

- The file cabinet occupies nine square feet times $30 per square foot, which equals $270 per year.

- The total cost of filing cabinet and floor space is $310 per year.

- That amount divided by six cubic feet of records equals $46.67 per cubic foot. Divided by eight cubic feet of records, the cost per square foot is $38.75.

In a records center, by contrast, storage density is maximized by combining floor-to-ceiling shelving with standardized containers. Cubic-foot-to-square-foot ratios routinely exceed 4:1 within records storage areas (as opposed to administrative areas in the same facility) and are often substantially higher. Based on rates charged by commercial records centers, the resulting annual storage costs range from $2 to $5 per cubic foot, which is a fraction of the cost of in-office storage.

A records center thus functions as a less costly extension of an organization's office space. Individual program units retain full authority over the records they transfer to a records center, which serves as a physical custodian for such records. In this respect, records centers differ from archival agencies, which usually assume full authority over records transferred to their custody. More significantly, records centers and archives differ in their missions; archival agencies are principally concerned with the preservation of records of scholarly value or long-term policy or administrative value, while records centers support an organization's business objectives through safe, economical recordkeeping. In practice, the relationship between records centers and archives is complementary rather than competitive. In government and academic institutions, in-house records centers may be operated by archival agencies, as with the examples previously cited. In some organizations, a records center provides intermediate storage for permanent records that will eventually be transferred to an archival agency.

Although they were originally developed for paper documents, records centers can and do store recorded information in any format. Many records centers provide vault areas for environmentally controlled storage of microforms as well as for computer tapes, video tapes, optical disks, or other electronic media. Regardless of media, records centers are intended for inactive records or, in the case of electronic media and microforms, backup copies that require secure storage. Records center storage is not suitable for active records, which are subject to urgent retrieval demands to support ongoing business operations. Depending on a records center's location, retrieval requests can take a half a day or longer to fulfill. Frequent retrieval demands also increase staffing requirements for records center operations with a resulting increase in costs. Where commercial records centers are used or where in-house records centers charge back their services to individual program units, retrieval charges for active records can mount up quickly.

While they provide economical storage space, records centers are not mere warehouses. They are designed and equipped specifically for records storage and related services. Records centers should not be used for library books, undistributed inventories of publications, product samples, or other nonrecord materials discussed in Chapter 1.

This chapter surveys records center characteristics and components, including records storage containers, shelving, fire protection requirements, and environmental controls. It also describes retrieval operations and other services that support records storage. The chapter concludes with a discussion of commercial records centers. The discussion emphasizes factors that records managers must consider when planning, implementing, and operating in-house records centers and when evaluating the facilities and capabilities of commercial storage providers. The discussion draws on requirements and recommendations presented in standards and related documents, including ANSI/ARMA TR-01, *Record Center Operations*; 36 CFR 1228, *Subpart K—Facility Standards for Record Storage Facilities*; *Standard for the Storage of Archival Records*, issued by the National Archives of Australia; FC no. 311 (M), *Standard for Record Storage*, issued by the fire commissioner of Canada; *Identifying and Specifying Requirements for Offsite Storage of Physical Records*, issued by the National Archives of the United Kingdom; and ISO 11799, *Information and Documentation—Document Storage Requirements for Archive and Library Materials*.

Features and Functions

A records center's economic advantages over in-office storage are based on a combination of location and storage density.

Records centers seldom occupy prime real estate. In cities and well-developed suburbs where office space is costly, records centers may be located in semi-industrial areas away from major business districts, on the perimeters of office parks or academic campuses, or in other relatively inexpensive, sub-prime locations that are safe for records storage but generally unacceptable for office use. Some commercial records centers, for example, are located in former warehouses or factory buildings that have been refurbished for secure records storage but are not suitable for other business purposes. Alternatively, a records center may be located in outer suburbs or rural areas at some distance from the offices where active records are maintained. The distance must be compatible with responsive service, however.

General Characteristics

The ideal records center is a standalone structure used exclusively for records storage and related functions. If such a facility is not possible, activities conducted in other parts of the building must not endanger stored records. The records storage area must be physically separated from other business functions by a four-hour firewall. As its name implies, a *firewall* is a fire-resistant barrier designed to keep fire from spreading to adjacent areas of a structure. A firewall is rated by the period of time that it will contain a fire in the compartment of origin. A four-hour rating is required for protection of paper records.

Whether it is a standalone or shared facility, a records center must occupy a safe location above flood plains and away from known, avoidable hazards such as seismic faults, chemical factories, oil refineries, high voltage electrical power transmission lines or other sources of electromagnetic radiation, contaminated landfill sites, airports, transportation routes for dangerous materials, and strategic installations or symbolic sites that could be a target of terrorist attack or armed conflict. A records center's location should be within a short response time of police and fire services. The records center's perimeter should be well lighted and free of landscaping or large objects that obscure the building.

A records center is a utilitarian structure. It may be built specifically to house records or adapted for records storage from a structure originally intended for other purposes. In either case, a records center building must be fire-resistant and solidly built, preferably of concrete or steel, with structural members composed of noncombustible materials. It must be well insulated, preferably windowless but well ventilated with high ceilings, adequate lighting, and, where necessary, firewalls to separate records storage areas from hazardous substances in adjacent rooms or buildings. Some archival agencies have published guidelines for the location and construction of records storage facilities to be used by government agencies subject to their authority. Such guidelines typically prohibit or strongly discourage self-service storage in basements, closets, or other unsupervised areas.

A records center building must comply with the International Building Code, a model building code developed by the International Code Council, and with applicable local building, electrical, plumbing, and other codes. The building's structural characteristics must be appropriate for records storage. In particular, floors above ground level must be engineered to bear the substantial weight of large quantities of records, shelving, and related equipment. Floor loads of 300 to 500 pounds per square foot are typical in records storage areas as compared with about 150 pounds per square foot in office areas. Refurbished structures will often require floor reinforcement. The records center building must be able to withstand strong storms, lightning strikes, and other extreme weather conditions. Because weather can affect electrical systems, emergency power systems should be installed to maintain lighting and environmental controls.

A records center must be kept clean and in good repair. Storage areas and shelving should be inspected regularly. Because insects and rodents are a threat to records, building maintenance plans should include pest management measures, as discussed later in this chapter. Building entrances should be well controlled and supervised during operating hours. An intrusion detection and notification system linked to a local law enforcement agency should be installed on all doors and windows to protect records while the building is unoccupied. Intruder alarms should comply with the UL 1076 standard, *Proprietary Burglar Alarm Units and Systems*, issued by Underwriters Laboratories. If a records center shares a building with other organizations or business functions, access to records storage areas must be restricted to records center personnel.

Within a records center, some space is reserved for administrative offices and work areas where records are accessioned, prepared for shelving, and housed temporarily while awaiting destruction or delivery in response to retrieval requests. Some records centers also provide a reference room where records can be examined by authorized persons. Most of the interior space, however, is dedicated to and optimized for records storage. A combination of floor-to-ceiling shelving and standardized containers yields high cubic-foot-to-square-foot storage ratios. As a general guideline, subject to variation with ceiling height and other building characteristics, the amount of floor space required for records storage will be one-fourth to one-fifth the number of cubic feet of records to be stored. Thus, 4,000 to 5,000 square feet of floor space will be required to store 20,000 cubic feet of records, which is equivalent to 10,000 to 13,000 letter-size file drawers.

Records Storage Containers

Records centers store records in cardboard containers rather than in metal cabinets. The containers must be an appropriate size for the records to be stored. The most widely used records storage container has interior dimensions of 10 inches high by 12 inches wide by 15 inches deep. Its external measurements, which affect shelving configurations and capacity, are 10.5 inches high by 12.5 inches wide by 16.5 inches deep. (See Figure 4-2a.)This container is routinely available from a number of manufacturers and office supply companies. Widely described as a *cubic-foot container* or *records center box*, it can store approximately one cubic foot of records. (The container requires about 1.25 cubic feet of shelf space, but its interior space is just slightly greater than one cubic foot.) This container can accommodate letter-size folders and pages packed along the 12-inch side and legal-size folders and pages packed along the 15-inch side. Computer printouts measuring 11 inches by 14 inches can be stacked from top to bottom. Such printouts were commonplace in the 1960s and 1970s. Many examples remain in storage, but the devices that produce those printouts are seldom encountered.

Larger containers, sometimes described as *transfer cases*, measure 10 inches high by 12 inches wide by 24 inches deep. (See Figure 4-2b.) They can store the entire contents of a letter-size file drawer, but they are heavier than cubic-foot containers,

Figure 4-2a

Cubic-foot Storage Container

(Source: Fellowes)

Figure 4-2b

File Transfer Box

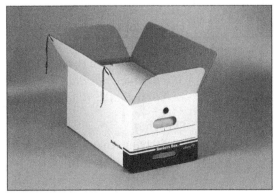

(Source: Fellowes)

require deeper shelves, and often prove less durable when handled frequently. Their use is consequently discouraged.

Properly packed, a records center container can also store index cards and other small documents, as well as microforms and certain electronic media such as computer tape cartridges, videotape cassettes, audiocassettes, and optical disks. Containers densely packed with such media may be heavier than comparably sized containers that store paper documents. Special containers are available for other records, including bank checks, x-rays, bound computer printouts, engineering drawings, architectural plans, and maps. Whenever possible, large documents should be stored flat rather than rolled. If flat storage is not possible, the document should be rolled around the outside of a paper tube to provide support then inserted into a tube-shaped container for protection.

When filled with paper documents, a cubic-foot container weighs 25 to 35 pounds. Side openings serve as handles for easy portability. Containers must be strong enough to protect records during handling and storage. In the event of sprinkler activation, they must also be able to absorb moisture without collapsing. Products with double-wall (two-ply) construction on the sides and bottom are recommended, particularly where several containers will be stacked in staging or storage areas. Some shelving arrangements stack containers to reduce costs. Because they are durable, double-wall containers can often be reused when their contents are destroyed in conformity with retention schedules.

Conventional records center containers are constructed of wood pulp. They are adequate for business records with medium-term retention periods. For permanent records, so-called archival containers conform to requirements presented in ANSI/NISO Z39.48, *Permanence of Paper for Publications and Documents in Libraries and Archives*; ISO 9706, *Information and Documentation—Paper for Documents—Requirements for Permanence*; ISO 11108, *Information and Documentation—Archival Paper—Requirements for Permanence and Durability*; and ISO 16245, *Information and Documentation—Boxes, File Covers and other Enclosures, Made from Cellulosic Materials, for Storage of Paper and Parchment Documents*. Available in cubic foot and other sizes, archival containers are constructed of acid-free materials buffered with calcium or magnesium carbonate as an alkaline reserve to protect valuable records. As might be expected, these containers are several times more expensive than conventional records center boxes. Before they are packed in acid-free containers, records should be transferred into acid-free folders or envelopes. Folder specifications are covered in ANSI/ASTM D3301, *Standard Specification for File Folders for Storage of Permanent Records*, which was withdrawn in 2010 but remains useful.

Shelving

Shelving characteristics are covered in ANSI MH28.1, *Specifications for the Design, Testing, Utilization and Application of Industrial Grade Steel Shelving*; ANSI/NISO, Z39.73, *Single-Tier, Steel Bracket Library Shelving*; Australian Standard AS 2143, *Industrial and Commercial Steel Shelving*; and European Standard 15635,

Steel Static Storage Systems—Application and Maintenance of Storage Equipment.
Shelving for records storage must be constructed of noncombustible, noncorrosive metal such as coated steel, stainless steel, or anodized aluminum. Most records centers employ steel shelving or pallet rack units with open backs and sides that are braced for stability and lateral rigidity under full load. Conventional shelving units are suitable for low-volume in-house records centers operated by corporations, government agencies, and other organizations. They resemble their library counterparts, but shelf widths are designed specifically for cubic-foot containers. A 42-inch shelf, for example, provides a clear opening for easy insertion and removal of three cubic-foot containers along their 12-inch sides.

In commercial records centers and other high-volume installations, pallet racks are preferred to conventional shelving for cost and capacity. Pallet racks feature steel uprights and beams that create a frame for decking on which records storage containers are placed. Steel is the preferred decking material for strength and fire safety. Rack units with particleboard or plywood decking are less expensive than all-steel units, but flammable components are not suitable for records storage.

Shelving units must be strong enough to bear the weight of wet records and containers in case fire sprinklers are activated. Wet paper weighs about 2.5 times as much as dry paper. Gauge is a measure of the thickness of steel shelving; the lower the gauge, the heavier and stronger the shelving but the higher the cost. Most manufacturers recommend 18-gauge or 20-gauge steel for records center shelving, but well-constructed 22-gauge shelving units may also be suitable for records storage.

A records center's storage capacity depends on the shelving layout, which is determined and constrained by the dimensions of the storage area. Shelving configurations and storage density are obviously affected by ceiling height. As previously noted, records centers employ floor-to-ceiling shelving for maximum density, although bottom shelves are usually about three inches off the floor to allow for flooding and the top shelves must provide sufficient space between containers and sprinklers as specified in local building codes. Very high ceilings permit multilevel storage with mezzanines and catwalks supported by the shelving units. These structures must comply with regulations established by the Occupational Safety and Health Administration.

Aisles between rows of shelving must be wide enough to allow easy passage of wheeled carts, platform ladders, and other equipment but not so wide as to compromise storage density. Typical aisle widths range from 30 to 36 inches, although main corridors are usually wider. To increase storage density by minimizing the number of aisles between shelving units, containers may be stored two or three rows deep on shelves or rack decking. To reduce cost by minimizing the number of required shelves, containers may be stacked two or three high as well as two or three deep. Such multicontainer stacking is typical in pallet rack installations. Because multiple boxes must be moved, however, additional time and labor will be required to retrieve and replace containers located in interior rows or bottom layers. This effort can be reduced by reserving top layers and outermost rows for records likely to be retrieved, but future reference activity for inactive records is difficult to predict.

Mobile shelving units that roll along a floor-mounted track can maximize storage density by drastically reducing the amount of floor space required for aisles, but such units are much more expensive to purchase and install than their static counterparts. As discussed in Chapter 7, mobile shelving units are usually installed in offices rather than records centers. Within a records center, mobile shelving is more likely to be installed in vault areas than in open warehouse space.

Material Handling Equipment

Records centers must have material handling equipment to transport containers of records to and from shelves when they are initially accessioned, requested by authorized persons, or removed for destruction. Examples of useful devices include, but are not limited to, the following:

- **Platform ladders.** A platform ladder is a movable stairway with handrails, a platform at the top for placing cartons, and spring wheels that make the ladder stationary when in use. It is rolled from aisle to aisle within a records storage area to access containers stored on upper shelf levels. Platform ladders are well suited to ceiling heights up to 15 feet. If boxes are stacked 14-feet high, the ladders will need to be a little over 11 feet from the floor to the top platform rail, and about 8.5 feet from the floor to the top step. A 10-step platform ladder will satisfy this requirement. As with shelving, metal construction is recommended for sturdiness and fire resistance. Platform ladders must conform to Occupational Safety and Health Administration (OSHA) requirements specified in 29 CFR 1910.29, which covers the design, construction and use of manually propelled mobile ladder stands and scaffolds. Pneumatic tires are required in catwalk installations. The applicable international standard is ISO 14122-3, *Safety of Machinery—Permanent Means of Access to Machinery—Part 3: Stairs, Stepladders and Guard-Rails.*

- **Motorized filing equipment.** Forklifts or other motorized lifting equipment may be required for heavy loads or very high shelving units. These devices are covered by 29 CFR 1910.178 and ANSI/ITSDF B56.1, *Safety Standard for Low Lift and High Lift Trucks.*

- **Raised platforms.** To avoid the risk of water damage, records should never be stored on the floor. While awaiting shelving, delivery, or reshelving, containers should be placed on raised pallets or other platforms. Pallet jacks are wheeled devices that can move single pallets of records storage cartons from place to place within a records center.

- **Dollies.** Dollies can be used to move a small quantity of cartons from place to place within a records center or to and from delivery vehicles for pickup and retrieval service.

- **Platform trucks.** Four-wheel, nonmotorized platform trucks can move cartons of records from loading docks and processing areas to and from storage areas or within the storage area itself. A useful size for these units is 30 inches by 72 inches, with sides that are 4 feet high. This size and type of platform truck can transport up to 40 cubic-foot containers.

- **Table-top carts.** These carts are used for retrieval and interfiling tasks in records storage areas. They must be small enough to maneuver between rows of shelving.

- **Vans or trucks.** Some in-house records centers operate one or more cargo vans or trucks for records pickup and delivery. Alternatively, a records center may rely on transport services provided by other departments within their organizations, such as general services or facilities management, that operate fleets of vehicles.

Environmental Controls

Heat accelerates chemical reactions that can damage paper, photographic, and electronic media. High humidity, in combination with heat, promotes the growth of mold, fungi, and other contaminants. The temperature and relative humidity in records storage areas must consequently be controlled, but the nature and extent of required control depends upon the retention periods for records to be stored. Generally, the shorter the retention period, the less stringent the environmental controls need to be. Records centers store many records that will be retained for 15 years or less. Such records are typically stored in open warehouse areas. These areas should be well ventilated to prevent stagnant air. Air conditioning is not required, but the temperature should be less than 80 degrees Fahrenheit (27 degrees Celsius) with a relative humidity below 60 percent.

Many records centers provide one or more storage vaults for permanent paper records, photographic films, or electronic media that require special environmental controls, security, or, as discussed in a later section, fire protection. All authorities advocate cool, dry storage conditions for permanent records, but specific recommendations vary with the physical composition of records media. For combined storage and user areas, NISO TR-01, *Environmental Guidelines for Storage of Paper Records*, recommends a maximum temperature of 70 degrees Fahrenheit (21 degrees Celsius) with relative humidity ranging from 30 to 50 percent. For storage areas where users are excluded, the recommended maximum temperature is 65 degrees Fahrenheit (19 degrees Celsius). Daily fluctuations must not exceed two degrees Fahrenheit for temperature and three percent for relative humidity. Air within vault areas should be filtered to remove dust and other particulate matter as well as gaseous pollutants, such as sulfur dioxide and ozones, that can promote acid formation.

ISO 18911, *Imaging Materials—Processed Safety Photographic Film—Storage Practices*, specifies maximum temperatures and acceptable relative humidity for extended-term (permanent) and medium-term storage of microforms. For black-and-white microforms that contain permanent records, the extended-term storage recommendation specifies the following combinations of temperature and relative humidity:

- A maximum temperature of 70 degrees Fahrenheit (21 degrees Celsius) with relative humidity of 20 to 30 percent

- A maximum temperature of 60 degrees Fahrenheit (15 degrees Celsius) with relative humidity of 20 to 40 percent

- A maximum temperature of 50 degrees Fahrenheit (10 degrees Celsius) with relative humidity of 20 to 50 percent

These recommendations apply to all types of microfilms, including camera original and duplicating films, as discussed in Chapter 5. They also apply to other black-and-white photographic films such as medical x-rays. As with paper records, low temperatures and low humidity promote stable storage of photographic films. Lower temperatures can compensate for high humidity, but the relative humidity cannot exceed 50 percent in microform storage areas. Relative humidity below 20 percent is not recommended because low humidity extracts moisture from photographic emulsions, which can lead to brittleness and curling of microfilms. Humidity must be controlled within the specified ranges; variations must not exceed five percent in 24 hours. The recommended environmental conditions can be maintained within individual microform housings or within the storage area that contains such housings.

For extended storage of color microforms and other color photographic films, the ISO 18911 standard recommends a maximum temperature of two degrees Celsius (36 degrees Fahrenheit) with relative humidity of 20 to 30 percent. At lower temperatures, a broader range of relative humidity is permissible. Color films should be stored in two heat-sealed foil bags for moisture protection and to limit exposure to air. Some commercial storage companies offer cold or frozen storage for long-term preservation of color photographic media, including negatives, prints, slides, and microforms. Cold storage is defined as 40 degrees Fahrenheit (4 degrees Celsius) or lower. Frozen storage is defined as 32 degrees Fahrenheit (zero degrees Celsius) or lower.

The ISO 18911 standard defines medium-term storage conditions as suitable for preservation of microforms and other photographic films for at least 10 years. For medium-term storage, environmental requirements are much less stringent than those cited above. The maximum temperature should not exceed 77 degrees Fahrenheit (25 degrees Celsius). Storage temperatures below 70 degrees Fahrenheit (21 degrees Celsius) are preferable. The peak temperature for short periods in medium-term storage areas can reach 90 degrees Fahrenheit (32 degrees Celsius), but short-term cycling of temperature must be avoided. Depending on the records center, these conditions may be satisfied outside of a vault environment. Relative humidity for medium-term storage can range from 20 to 50 percent. Humidity variations must not exceed 10 percent per day. Prolonged exposure to higher humidity conditions, as previously discussed, promotes bacterial growths and accelerates the harmful effects of residual processing chemicals.

Temperature and humidity conditions recommended in the ISO 18911 standard are similar to those specified in ISO 18923, *Imaging Materials—Polyester Base Magnetic Tape—Storage Practices.* That standard specifies medium-term storage conditions, which are suitable for the preservation of recorded information for a minimum of 10 years, and extended-term storage conditions, which are suitable for the preservation of recorded information of permanent value. The standard does not state or imply, however, that magnetic tapes have permanent keeping properties. For medium-term storage of magnetic tapes, the maximum temperature is 73 degrees Fahrenheit (23 degrees Celsius) with a relative humidity of 20 to 50 percent. Temperature variations in the storage area must not exceed four degrees Fahrenheit (two degrees Celsius) over a 24-hour period. Humidity variations must not exceed 10 percent over a 24-hour period. Rapid cycling of temperature and humidity can damage binder materials and media substrates.

For extended-term storage of magnetic tapes, the ISO 18923 standard, like its counterpart for photographic films, specifies the following combinations of temperature and relative humidity:

- A maximum temperature of 68 degrees Fahrenheit (20 degrees Celsius) with relative humidity ranging from 20 to 30 percent

- A maximum temperature of 59 degrees Fahrenheit (15 degrees Celsius) with relative humidity ranging from 20 to 40 percent

- A maximum temperature of 50 degrees Fahrenheit (10 degrees Celsius) with relative humidity ranging from 20 to 50 percent

For both medium- and extended-term storage, the ISO 18923 standard notes that an air-conditioned facility is usually necessary to maintain temperature and humidity within approved limits. A vault environment may be required to maintain low temperatures within the specified humidity ranges. Where air conditioning is not practical or required, as in underground storage areas with naturally low temperatures, dehumidification is often necessary.

According to ISO 18925, *Imaging Materials—Optical Disc Media—Storage Practices*, the preferred environment for long-term storage of compact discs is a maximum temperature of 74 degrees Fahrenheit (23 degrees Celsius) with relative humidity ranging from 20 to 50 percent. Similar storage conditions are specified in ISO/IEC 10995, *Information Technology—Digitally Recorded Media for Information Interchange and Storage—Test Method for the Estimation of the Archival Lifetime of Optical Media*; ISO 18926, *Imaging Materials—Information Stored on Magneto-Optical (MO) Discs—Method for Estimating the Life Expectancy Based on the Effects of Temperature and Relative Humidity*; and ISO 18927, *Imaging Materials—Recordable Compact Disc Systems—Method for Estimating the Life Expectancy Based on the Effects of Temperature and Relative Humidity*. ISO 18934, *Imaging Materials—Multiple Media Archives—Storage Environment*, recommends temperature and humidity conditions for repositories that store a combination of safety-base photographic films, nitrate-base motion-picture films, photographic plates, reflection prints, magnetic tape, and optical storage media. The recommendations are based on the corresponding ISO standards for those media.

Temperature and humidity conditions in storage vaults and other environmentally controlled areas must be monitored using devices that are tested regularly and recalibrated as necessary. To avoid damage associated with abrupt changes in environmental conditions, a records center should include a staging area for items moved into and out of vault storage. Photographic films and computer media can be housed in the same storage vault, but they should not be comingled in file drawers, boxes, or other containers.

Fire Protection

In 1973, a fire in a government-operated storage facility in St. Louis destroyed many records of discharged U.S. Army and U.S. Air Force personnel. Between 1996 and 2006, fires in commercial storage facilities in the United States and in the United Kingdom destroyed several million cubic feet of stored records. In 2015, a fire in a commercial records center in Brooklyn, New York, destroyed almost one million cubic feet of records.

While records center fires are alarming, they represent a very small percentage of industrial fires, and they have not resulted in civilian deaths or injuries. Given the large number of boxes housed in commercial and in-house records centers, the odds that any given box will be destroyed by fire are immeasurably low. Several thousand records storage facilities exist worldwide but only a handful have experienced a fire. The fires that have occurred underscore the importance of fire protection in the design and operation of records storage facilities.

The problem is obvious: Paper ignites at 451 degrees Fahrenheit (230 degrees Celsius). That temperature is quickly reached in a fire, which may originate in the records center building or spread from neighboring structures. Large quantities of paper documents stored at high density in cardboard containers are a powerful source of fuel for any fire. The high ceilings and catwalks encountered in many records centers provide open space for the uninterrupted upward flow of flames, heat, and smoke. Steel shelving can collapse during prolonged exposure to temperatures encountered in uncontrolled fires. Once started, records center fires can be long burning. Total burnouts have occurred.

NFPA 232, *Protection of Records*, issued by the National Fire Protection Association, provides the most thorough and informative review of fire protection principles, issues, and requirements for records storage. NFPA 232 notes that ensuring total fire protection in records storage facilities is not possible, but certain measures can limit the potential destruction of records. In particular, fire control depends on precautionary measures to avoid potential causes of fire and rapid detection and suppression when a fire occurs. Recommended precautionary measures include:

1. Comply completely with international and local fire codes and ordinances, which typically mandate heat and smoke detectors, fire alarms connected to a local fire department, portable fire extinguishers, standpipes and hoses, and automatic sprinkler systems or other fire suppression systems in storage and work areas.

2. Prohibit smoking and flammable materials in the records storage facility.

3. Conduct personnel screenings to include complete background checks for criminal behavior, previous involvement with fires, or other problems. These background checks should be performed at initial hiring of employees and periodically thereafter.

4. Implement physical security measures, including access controls, intrusion detection, and surveillance of storage areas.

5. Maintain close supervision of employees, contractors, and visitors to the records center.

6. Engage in regular safety inspection and close monitoring of gasoline-powered and electrical vehicles and equipment, such as battery chargers, employed in or near the records storage facility.

7. Separate boiler rooms, generators, and related equipment from records storage areas by four-hour firewalls and regularly inspect them.

8. Require periodic inspection of the records storage facility by a licensed fire protection engineer.

9. Install heat and smoke detectors in storage and work areas and periodically test them for rapid detection and suppression of a fire.

10. Install automatic sprinkler systems, portable fire extinguishers, hoses, stand-pipes, and other fire suppression equipment and periodically test them.

11. Connect fire alarms to a local fire department.

12. Locate the records storage facility in a reasonable proximity to a trained fire department.

To limit the spread and destructive potential of fires, a records center may be divided into two or more compartments separated by firewalls with a minimum three-hour fire resistance rating. As specified in 36 CFR 1228 Subpart K, records centers utilized by U.S. government agencies must not store more than 250,000 cubic feet in a single compartment. NFPA 232 specifies a maximum capacity of 1.2 million cubic feet per compartment.

Properly constructed fire-resistant vaults and safes provide additional protection against total burnout in one or more records storage compartments. While often confused, vaults and safes have different characteristics:

- *A vault is a sealed room-size storage enclosure that is incorporated into a structure, either at ground level or on one of the upper floors.* A vault's walls, roof, and doors should have a minimum fire resistance rating of four hours. To limit the quantity of records exposed to fire and to reduce the possibility of fire originating within the vault itself, the NFPA 232 standard recommends that vault size be limited to 5,000 cubic feet with a maximum ceiling height of 12 feet.

- *A safe is a fire-resistant, theft-resistant container for valuable items.* A safe may be a freestanding chest or installed in a wall. Safes vary in size, capacity, and construction. As specified in UL 72, *Standard for Tests for Fire Resistance of Record Protection Equipment,* Underwriters Laboratories rates safes for the period of time, in hours, that the interior temperature will remain below 350 degrees Fahrenheit (175 degrees Celsius) with a relative humidity below 85 percent when exposed to fire temperatures up to 1,700 degrees Fahrenheit (920 degrees Celsius). Safes that pass the test are described as Class 350 products. Underwriters Laboratories' impact test confirms that a safe will remain intact and protect its contents when exposed to high temperatures for 30 minutes then dropped onto concrete rubble from a height of 30 feet. Safes are also placed into an oven at 2,000 degrees Fahrenheit (1,085 degrees Celsius) to confirm that they will not explode. Underwriters Laboratories imposes more stringent fire resistance requirements for safes that store electronic media and photographic films. Intended for electronic media, Class 125 safes must maintain an interior temperature below 125 degrees Fahrenheit (53 degrees Celsius) with a relative humidity below 80 percent. Class 150 safes, which are intended for photographic films, must maintain an interior temperature below 150 degrees Fahrenheit (66 degrees Celsius) with a relative humidity below 85 percent.

- *Automated sprinkler systems can help confine a fire to a limited area, but records in a much wider area will become wet and possibly damaged in the process.* As might be expected, water exposure is greatest for containers on high shelves, which are closest to sprinkler heads. High-quality records center containers can absorb some water. In some cases, the fire will be extinguished before wet containers collapse.

- *Alternative fire suppression technologies, which use inert gases and chemical agents, prevent water damage and simplify salvage operations.* These technologies are covered by NFPA 17, *Standard for Dry Chemical Extinguishing Systems*, and NFPA 2001, *Standard on Clean Agent Fire Extinguishing.* Examples include systems that use sodium bicarbonate or other chemical powders; high-compression foam, which consists of air-filled bubbles that smother a fire and suppress the release of flammable vapors, and carbon dioxide systems, which deprive a fire of oxygen. Because these technologies are more expensive than conventional sprinkler systems, they are often limited to vault installations that house microfilm, electronic media, and high-value paper records. Halon extinguishes flames through chemical interaction, but it can decompose into toxic byproducts and depletes the earth's ozone layer. Halon products are no longer manufactured in the United States, Canada, and some other countries. In the United States, organizations can continue to use existing halon systems for fire suppression, but the Environmental Protection Agency encourages their replacement.

Pest Control

Paper records can be damaged by rodents and insects, including termites, cockroaches, crickets, and silverfish, which are attracted to dark spaces and feed upon cellulose, starches, adhesives, and other organic substances found in paper. Exclusion and extermination of vermin is the most effective way to prevent such damage. Storage and work areas should be inspected periodically for pest infestation, which may indicate possible openings under doors, around windows and service ducts, or in the records center structure. Good housekeeping procedures are essential. Records storage and work areas must be kept clean to remove dust, which provides breeding ground for vermin. Food and potted plants should be prohibited in records storage areas. Traps and gaseous or chemical pest extermination should be employed when necessary, but care must be taken to avoid damage to records or cardboard containers. Trash should be removed promptly from storage and office areas, and trash containers should be located away from the entrance to the records center building.

Services

A records center provides safe, economical storage for inactive records that must be retained for legal or administrative reasons. Records centers also provide a variety of related services. Such services include, but are not necessarily limited to, the following:

1. Picking up records from program units or client sites.

2. Entering data and indexing for newly accessioned containers.

3. Retrieving records requested by authorized persons.

4. Delivering requested records to program units or client sites.

5. Reshelving previously retrieved records when returned to storage.

6. Destroying records when their retention periods elapse.

All records center operations depend on accurate packing, labeling, and inventorying of containers. A records center must provide clear, detailed instructions for these tasks, which are usually performed by personnel in the program units where the records reside. Records centers operated by corporations, government agencies, and other organizations typically supply cubic-foot containers to program units or make arrangements for program units to purchase approved containers from authorized suppliers. Commercial records centers sell containers, but clients can usually obtain them from other sources provided that they meet the records center's specifications.

In either case, a container inventory lists the contents of each container in a given shipment in sufficient detail to identify the records when they need to be retrieved. Depending on the nature of the records and anticipated retrieval requirements, the inventory may provide a summary description of the contents of each container or a detailed listing of individual folder titles, reports, microforms, electronic media, or other items in each container. Depending on records center procedures, inventory information may be prepared on a special transmittal form or entered online. Records centers increasingly support the latter option. When packing, inventorying, and labeling are completed, the program unit notifies the records center, which will arrange to pick up the records. Some records centers support electronic vaulting in which computer-generated records are transmitted to the records center's computer via the Internet or other networking arrangements. The records center then copies the transferred information onto file servers, magnetic tapes, or other media for storage.

At the records center, transmittal forms are matched against containers, and information about newly received records is logged into a computer database or other index. Depending on records center procedures, the computer database may contain detailed inventory information or a summary description of each container. Control numbers assigned by the records center when shipments are received identify each container to the exclusion of others, including containers in previous shipments from a given program unit or client. Containers may be barcoded to simplify tracking. Some records centers provide barcode labels to program units, which affix them to containers when records are being prepared for transfer.

Shelf locations are determined based on space availability. All containers in a given shipment or from a given program unit may be stored contiguously, but this practice becomes increasingly difficult to achieve as a records center fills up. Large shipments may consequently be dispersed for storage. Many in-house records centers and all commercial storage providers rely on software to assign control numbers, store inventory information, determine space availability, and keep track of container locations. The software, which may be custom-developed or purchased from one of the companies that specialize in such products, also supports retrieval operations, container tracking, and other services.

Records sent to a records center are presumably inactive and, if properly scheduled, should experience little retrieval activity, but some items must occasionally be consulted. A records center is a custodial facility not a reference library. As previously explained, individual program units retain full authority over the records they transfer to a records center, which merely serves as the physical custodian for such records. All retrieval requests must be authorized by the program unit that transmitted the records. Typically, the originating program unit gives the records center a list of approved requesters. Other requests must be approved on a case-by-case basis. Access restrictions are rigorously enforced. Confidential records receive the same degree of protection that they would in the program units that sent them to the records center.

Depending on records center procedures, requests may be submitted by telephone, by email, by fax, by interoffice or conventional mail, or in person. Records center personnel are not reference librarians. They are not familiar with the contents of records in their custody and are not qualified to interpret retrieval requests or otherwise assist customers in determining which records they need. Consequently, requests for records must be unambiguous. The requestor must accurately identify desired container(s). This container identification is done by consulting the descriptive information in container inventory forms or online inventory lists associated with specific shipments.

When a retrieval request is received, the records center consults a database or other index to determine the shelf location(s) for the requested container(s). Inventory details determine the types of retrieval requests that a records center can accommodate. Where inventory information is limited to container summaries, the most common retrieval requests involve the temporary removal of entire containers for return to the program units or clients that transmitted them to the records center. If inventory information is sufficiently detailed, some records centers will retrieve individual file folders, documents, or other items from within containers. In either case, software keeps track of containers or individual items charged out to specific clients and will check them back in when they are returned to storage. In this respect, a records center operates much like a circulating library.

In some records centers, returned containers are replaced into their original shelf locations and placeholders may reserve the empty spaces for that purpose. Some records centers, however, allocate shelf space dynamically. Newly accessed records may be assigned to spaces previously occupied by charged-out containers, which will be assigned new shelf locations on their return. Where large numbers of records are charged out at any given time, dynamic allocation makes productive use of shelf space that would otherwise sit empty. Like library circulation control systems, some records center software will generate periodic reminder notices for charged-out containers or items.

Most in-house records centers will deliver requested records within a reasonable period of time—one or two days in most cases. Commercial records centers typically offer next-day delivery as a standard service with same-day delivery at an extra cost for urgently needed records. Pickup of requested records by authorized persons is also an option. Where inventory information includes detailed item lists, specified pages may be photocopied for or faxed to requestors. Commercial records centers increasingly offer a scan-on-demand service by which specified pages are digitized and the resulting images transmitted to requestors as email attachments. For financial audits, litigation support, or other activities that require lengthy examination of large quantities of information, some records centers provide workrooms where authorized persons can examine records. In-person examination may also be needed to locate specific records where container contents cannot be verified by consulting inventory information.

Among other services, some records centers will add records to previously transmitted containers. Most records centers will also destroy records, subject to client approval, when their retention periods elapse. They may be equipped with shredders, incinerators, or other equipment for destruction of confidential records. Some records centers have paper recycling arrangements for discarded documents, but recycling is not suitable for destruction of confidential information. Recycling facilities manually examine records to remove unacceptable papers or other materials. Acceptable papers may be stored under unsecured conditions for long periods of time while they await recycling.

Records Center Software

Records center software is a special purpose computer application designed to inventory, track, and service physical records (paper records and media) in warehouse storage locations operated by an organization or a commercial provider.

Some records center software can also manage records in departmental file rooms or other active records repositories. Records center software may be custom-developed by an organization, but it is typically purchased as a pre-written application. Pre-written records center software is a well-established, highly functional product group that is widely implemented in both in-house and commercial storage facilities. Available products support the following capabilities:

- **Acquisition and Data Entry.** Records center software maintains a database of information about containers, folders, or other items sent to the records center or maintained in a file room or other active records repository. Database records typically include a combination of predefined and customer-defined fields. Authorized persons can check in containers or other items and enter descriptive information about them when they arrive at the center. Most products support formatted data entry screens and editing capabilities for this purpose. In some cases, specific field values, such as names of originating departments, can be selected from drop-down lists defined by the customer.

- **Records Tracking.** Records center software will allocate space and track the specific shelf locations of items in storage. It can display a map, listing, or other representation of the storage area that indicates available space for a given quantity of records. The software can also track containers that are relocated from one shelf to another.

- **Database Searching.** Authorized persons can search database records for information about specific containers or other items in storage. Some products support advanced retrieval capabilities such as Boolean operations, relational expressions, root word searching, wildcard characters, and full-text searching of item descriptions.

- **Circulation Control.** Records center software supports check-out and return functionality to track containers, folders, or other items sent to authorized users in response to retrieval requests or are otherwise removed from offsite storage locations. The software will create and maintain an audit trail and circulation history for all containers or other items requested and returned by authorized users.

- **Retention Functionality.** Records center software can maintain customer-defined retention periods for specific records series and associate that information with containers or other items in storage. The software will calculate destruction dates based on the designated retention periods. The calculated destruction dates are inserted into database records for specific items. The software can identify records with elapsed retention periods and prepare notices of impending destruction for submission to and review by authorized persons. Authorized persons can suspend destruction of records that are relevant for litigation, government investigations, audits, or other legal or quasi-legal proceedings.

- **Records Destruction.** Records center software can create and maintain documentation to identify containers, folders, or other items destroyed in conformity with an organization's retention policies and schedule.

- **Report Generation.** Records center software can generate a variety of preformatted and ad hoc reports, including records control sheets; transportation work orders; barcode labels; pick lists; statistical summaries of records in storage; retrieval activity reports for specific time periods, program units, or items; lists of items in circulation by program unit, date, or other parameters; lists of records destroyed by program unit; and lists of records subject to holds for litigation, audits, or other purposes.

Commercial Records Centers

A commercial records center is a for-profit company that provides fee-based storage and related services for records of multiple clients.

The membership of PRISM International, a not-for-profit trade association for the records storage industry, ranges from relatively small, privately-owned companies that operate in a single location to large publicly traded companies with hundreds of storage facilities throughout the world. Commercial records centers obviously compete with in-house warehouses or other records storage arrangements operated by companies, government agencies, and other organizations, but many organizations lack secure, economical in-house storage arrangements for their inactive records. Rather than constructing warehouses or refurbishing inadequate facilities, purchasing shelving and material handling equipment, and hiring records center employees, such organizations may find that outsourcing their records storage requirements is cheaper and more convenient.

Even where in-house records storage facilities are effective and economical, commercial records centers can provide complementary or supplementary services. Some large corporations, for example, have in-house storage facilities for records generated at a headquarters location but rely on local commercial records centers to serve branch offices, manufacturing facilities, and other geographically dispersed operations. Similarly, a company, government agency, or other organization may limit its in-house records center to warehouse-type storage of paper documents and use commercial providers for electronic media or confidential records requiring vault storage or other special security arrangements.

Commercial records centers are subject to the same evaluative criteria as in-house storage facilities:

- The records center building must be appropriately constructed, fire-resistant, and secure, with shelving and environmental controls appropriate to the types of records to be stored.

- Access to the building should be limited to employees and other authorized persons.

- Provisions for fire protection must conform to local building codes and to the NFPA 232 standard previously discussed.

- The records storage facility should be located in close proximity to a trained fire department.

- Vault space must be available for confidential records or records that require special environmental controls.

- The records center's staff must be large enough and appropriately skilled for the services to be provided.

- Operating procedures must be well organized and effectively administered.

- Computer systems, including any software provided to clients, must be reliable, efficient, and capable of tracking shelf locations for containers transferred by a given client, the movement of records within the records center, charge-out and return of records to storage, destruction of specific containers, and other operations.

- Many commercial records centers support web-based access for entry and searching of inventory information, as well as for online initiation of records retrieval requests by authorized persons at a customer's site.

Services and Costs

A commercial records center's services and fee structure depend upon several factors, including geographic location and the clientele served. As a defining characteristic, all commercial records centers provide fee-based storage, usually for a specified monthly rate per cubic-foot container for paper documents. Per-item storage charges may be imposed for microforms, x-ray films, electronic media, or large-format paper records such as engineering drawings and maps. Storage charges per cubic foot or item usually vary inversely with the quantity of records stored by a given customer.

Typically, the records of different customers are comingled in a commercial records center's open warehouse area. If this situation is unacceptable, customers may be offered reserved shelving areas or dedicated storage rooms at extra cost. Some commercial records centers also offer shelf-type filing cabinets, of the type described in Chapter 7, for semi-active folders that are not packed in containers. Vault storage, where available, commands a premium price.

Commercial records centers also charge for the following services on a per-incident basis:

- Records pick up, including new shipments and previously retrieved records being returned to storage

- Inventory data entry for newly accessioned records, including key-entry as well as conversion of computer-processible inventory data provided by clients

- Records retrieval, including entire containers or individual files, when requested by authorized persons

- Delivery services for retrieved records, including normal and rush delivery where available

- Photocopying records requested by authorized persons

- Faxing or scan-on-demand services for records requested by authorized persons
- Reshelving or refiling records returned to the records center
- Interfiling records to be added to containers previously sent to the records center
- Records destruction when authorized, including confidential destruction when requested by the client
- Periodic or special report preparation about records storage and retrieval activity

Basic records center charges typically apply to services provided during normal business hours, as defined by the commercial records center. After-hours retrieval and delivery services may be available at a higher rate. Some records centers will provide these services around the clock, 365 days per year.

Terms, conditions, and per-incident charges for records center services are specified in customer contracts, to which rate schedules are customarily appended. Customers can expect to incur a charge any time their records are handled, whether they are being accessioned, retrieved, transported, reshelved, or destroyed. While costs usually depend on the volume of records affected by a particular service, minimum charges may apply to certain services such as pickup and delivery of records.

Commercial records centers produce a variety of periodic and customized reports for clients. Possibilities include, but are not limited to, the following:

1. Inventory proof lists

2. Lists and statistical tabulations of records in storage by media type

3. Lists and statistical tabulations of records in storage by the transmitting program unit, which can be used for charge back or other cost control measures

4. Lists of records scheduled for destruction on specific dates

5. Lists and statistical tabulations of records destroyed as authorized by the client

6. Transaction histories by date or program unit

7. Lists of records removed from storage and not yet returned

8. Lists of records permanently removed from storage

9. Billing summaries by activity and period

10. Lists and statistical tabulations of per-incident charges; reports may be printed or delivered to clients via email or on electronic media.

In some cases, commercial records centers impose per-container charges for the permanent removal of records from storage, whether through destruction of records when directed by the customer or because the records will be moved to a competitor or to an in-house records storage facility. These termination charges are commonly described as *exit fees* or *out-charges*. Where present, they are usually equal to about one year's storage fee for the container being removed. The customer must also pay retrieval and delivery charges for the removed containers.

Some customers refuse to accept contracts that include termination charges. In such cases, the customer may be charged slightly higher monthly storage fees to offset the loss of revenue when service is terminated.

Safekeeping for valuable information resources is an often claimed and much advertised advantage of commercial records centers, but fire and other calamities—as previously discussed—have occurred. Records center contracts indicate insurance coverage and reimbursement amounts for records that are lost, damaged, or destroyed by fire, natural disaster, or accident while in the records center's custody. Such reimbursements are typically nominal. Often based simply on the replacement value of cubic-foot containers, they do not reflect the adverse consequences that an organization may incur if needed records are unavailable. By signing the contract, however, customers presumably accept the specified amount as sufficient compensation for any losses. Most contracts further state that the commercial storage provider will not be liable for the cost of recreating lost records, for lost profits or revenues, or for any other consequential or incidental damages based on tort, contract, or any other legal theories unless the loss or damage resulted from the storage provider's failure to exercise reasonable care that would have prevented the loss or damage. A commercial records center may offer additional insurance coverage at extra cost. Customers also have the option of purchasing "valuable papers" coverage from insurance companies.

Cloud-based Records Storage

Going beyond their traditional focus on warehouse storage for paper records, some commercial storage providers offer cloud-based repositories for retention of electronic records. Sometimes characterized as *digital records centers*, these repositories offer an outsourced, easily implemented alternative to in-house retention of semi-active and inactive electronic records. Web-based access to computing services, including storage of databases, digital documents, and other electronic records, is known as **cloud computing**. Utilizing content management or records management application software of the type discussed in Chapter 8, digital records centers operate on the same principles as storage facilities for paper records. They supplement or replace an organization's in-house storage capabilities. The commercial storage provider is the physical custodian of the records. Customers specify retention periods and access privileges for the stored records.

Digital records centers can store electronic records in most formats, including digital documents, video recordings, and audio recordings. As a convenient feature, digital records centers support self-service capabilities for input and retrieval operations. Customers upload and request electronic records via the Internet. The records and their associated metadata are stored on file servers operated by the commercial storage provider. Customers are typically charged by the quantity of electronic records stored and the number of authorized users. The records are available at any time for immediate access from any location with an Internet connection. Security arrangements protect the records from unauthorized access. The commercial storage provider is responsible for backing up the records for disaster recovery and uninterrupted access. Customers can authorize the removal or secure destruction of records with elapsed retention periods

Summary of Major Points

☑ A records center is a specially designed, warehouse-type facility that provides safe, economical, high-density storage for inactive records that must be retained for legal or operational reasons.

☑ The business case for offsite storage is straightforward: Expensive office space and filing equipment should be reserved for records that will be consulted frequently and that must be available immediately when needed. Inactive records should be stored elsewhere, provided that they can be retrieved on demand within a reasonable period of time.

☑ For a given quantity of inactive records, offsite storage is much less expensive than in-office storage. A records center's economic advantages over office storage are based on a combination of location and storage density. Records centers seldom occupy prime real estate, while a combination of floor-to-ceiling shelving and standardized containers maximizes storage density.

☑ The most widely used records center container stores approximately one cubic foot of records.

☑ In addition to storing paper documents, many records centers provide vault areas for environmentally controlled storage of microforms as well as for computer tapes, videotapes, optical disks, or other electronic media.

☑ Records center buildings must conform to local fire codes and ordinances, which typically mandate heat and smoke detectors, fire alarms connected to a local fire department, portable fire extinguishers, standpipes and hoses, and automatic sprinkler systems or other fire suppression systems in storage and work areas.

☑ Records centers should be inspected periodically for pest infestation. Good house-keeping procedures are essential. Records storage and work areas must be kept clean to remove dust, which provides breeding ground for vermin.

☑ In addition to storage facilities, records centers provide a variety of related services, including records pickup and delivery, data entry and indexing for newly accessioned records, retrieving records required by authorized persons, reshelving previously retrieved records when returned to storage, and destroying records when their retention periods elapse.

☑ All records center operations depend on accurate packing, labeling, and inventory-ing of containers. A records center must provide clear, detailed instructions for these tasks, which are usually performed by personnel in the program units where the records originate.

☑ Some government agencies, companies, and other organizations operate their own records centers. Others contract with commercial providers who charge predetermined fees for records storage and related recordkeeping services. These two approaches are not mutually exclusive. Commercial storage providers may supplement in-house records centers for specific types of records or in specific geographic locations.

☑ Commercial records centers range from relatively small, privately-owned warehouse installations in a single location to large publicly traded companies with hundreds of storage facilities throughout the world. Commercial records centers are subject to the same evaluative criteria as in-house storage facilities. They must be appropriately constructed, fire-resistant, and secure, with shelving and environmental controls appropriate to the types of records to be stored. The records center's staff must be large enough and appropriately skilled for the services to be provided.

☑ Cloud-based repositories offer an outsourced, easily implemented alternative to in-house retention of semi-active and inactive electronic records.

Chapter 5

Document Imaging

As described in the previous chapter, records centers minimize storage costs for inactive records by moving them from expensive office space to more economical offsite locations where they are kept until their retention periods elapse. Digital document imaging and micrographics take a different approach to space management. They create miniaturized images of documents for compact storage in offices or elsewhere. Depending on the application, the source documents may be business correspondence, financial records, technical reports, legal case files, patient records, insurance claim files, customer service records, student records, engineering drawings, maps, or scholarly research materials. These and other documents are scanned or microfilmed every day by government agencies, banks, insurance companies, manufacturing companies, scientific laboratories, professional services firms, hospitals, schools, libraries, and other organizations.

Micrographics[5] has been an important component of records management practice for more than half a century. Digital document imaging, sometimes described as *optical document imaging* or *electronic document imaging*, was introduced in the 1980s. Its use—initially as a micrographics alternative and subsequently as a solution to records management problems for which micrographics technology was never intended—has increased steadily and significantly since that time. As an alternative to paper documents, both imaging technologies can drastically reduce storage requirements and costs for inactive records that must be kept for long periods of time. As discussed in Chapter 6, scanning and microfilming can also be used to create backup copies of vital records for disaster recovery.

---

[5] The term "micrographics" was introduced in the 1970s as a broader, more meaningful alternative to the then-current term "microfilm," which is just one of several micrographic formats described later in this chapter. Used as a singular noun, micrographics denotes the technology itself as well as the professional specialty that applies micrographics technology to records management problems. Used as an adjective, micrographics—or, less commonly, micrographic—describes products and services offered by equipment manufacturers, media suppliers, service bureaus, consultants, and others. In recent years, the micrographics industry has adopted the alternative phrase "film-based imaging" to obtain a closer identification with digital imaging technology.

During the 1970s and 1980s, micrographics technology was used to facilitate retrieval, distribution, and handling of active records. Indeed, certain micrographics products and methods—such as self-threading microfilm cartridges, microfilm jackets, and computer-assisted microfilm retrieval—were developed specifically for applications involving files that were frequently consulted and updated. While some of these approaches remain in use, micrographics is no longer a recommended technology for active records management. It is best suited to long-term retention or permanent preservation of inactive records.

When combined with document management software and appropriate indexing, digital imaging can provide convenient online access to active records. That aspect of digital imaging is discussed in Chapter 8.

For cost-effective management of inactive records, digital imaging and micrographics technology must be judiciously implemented in the context of a systematic retention program that identifies appropriate storage solutions for specific types of recorded information. A comprehensive records management program will combine digital imaging and micrographics with selective destruction and offsite storage of inactive records. Destruction rather than scanning or microfilming is obviously recommended for obsolete records that have no continuing value for business or scholarly purposes. Offsite storage, where available and appropriate, will usually prove more economical than scanning or microfilming for inactive records that are retained for less than 15 to 20 years and in some cases longer. After that time, accumulated annual charges for offsite storage will exceed scanning or microfilming costs.

Digital imaging and micrographics technologies produce document images in different ways:

- **Digital imaging is a computer technology.** Digital images are created by scanning paper documents or, less commonly, by scanning microform images. In either case, the scanners are specially designed computer input devices, and the resulting images are digitally recorded on computer storage media.

- **Micrographics is a photographic technology.** In the most widely encountered approach, known as **source document microphotography**, specially designed cameras equipped with reducing lenses take pictures of paper documents, recording them as miniaturized images on high-resolution photographic film. Alternatively and less commonly, a variant form of computer printing technology records computer-generated information in human-readable form directly onto microfilm. That method is known as **computer-output microfilm (COM)**.

Among their professional responsibilities, records managers identify candidate applications for scanning or microfilming, plan and implement digital imaging and micrographics systems, and prepare cost estimates and justifications for scanning and microfilming projects. Some records management departments are responsible for in-house digital imaging or microfilming operations. Where scanning or microfilming is outsourced, records managers typically prepare specifications for the work to be done, evaluate the qualifications and capabilities of imaging service companies, and inspect the work performed. This chapter examines the distinctive characteristics and advantages of digital imaging and micrographics for storage, retrieval, handling, and retention of recorded information. The discussion emphasizes factors that records managers must consider when evaluating and implementing these technologies.

Document Preparation

Document preparation is the essential first step in creating digital or micrographic images.

In most cases, source documents are prepared for scanning or microfilming in batches. Batch size is determined by application characteristics. In low-volume imaging applications, newly created or received documents may be prepared at a specific time each day or when a sufficient number of pages accumulate. In high-volume imaging installations, document preparation is often a continuous activity; multiple workers may be assigned to document preparation, while others operate scanners or microfilm cameras or perform related production tasks such as image inspection.

The purpose of document preparation is to make source documents "scanner ready" or "camera ready"; that is, to put documents into a condition and sequence appropriate for scanning or microfilming. Well-prepared source documents are critical to efficient operation of document scanners and microfilm cameras, effective deployment of scanning and microfilming labor, and consistent production of usable images.

While all source documents require some preparation, specific work steps depend on application requirements, file organization, the physical condition and other attributes of source documents, the type of scanner or microfilm cameras to be used, and other factors. At a minimum, correspondence, memoranda, project reports, case files, and other records must be removed from file cabinets, folders, or other containers; unfolded if necessary; and stacked neatly in the correct sequence for scanning or microfilming. Some document scanners and **microfilm cameras** require removal of staples and paper clips from source documents. Even when not required, removal of such fasteners is generally advisable; it improves the productivity of scanner or camera operators and enhances the appearance of document images.

Some source documents are more difficult or time-consuming to prepare than others. Older office records, for example, may be crowded into boxes that must be retrieved from warehouses, basements, closets, or other storage areas and properly identified prior to scanning. Engineering drawings, architectural plans, maps, charts, and other large documents can be awkward to handle. Often rolled for storage, they must be flattened before scanning or microfilming. Older drawings and maps may be in poor condition from years of repeated reference. Brittle or otherwise fragile documents must be handled carefully. Torn pages must be mended or photocopied prior to scanning or microfilming them.

Where significant, post-it notes attached to documents may be taped in place or affixed to separate pages. Small sheets of paper, such as message slips, should likewise be taped to larger pages. Very thin pages may need to be photocopied for scanning or microfilming by the sheetfed devices described in the next section. For best image quality and operator productivity, books, reports, catalogs, and other bound documents should be unbound prior to scanning or microfilming. If that process is impractical or impossible (as with rare books, for example), specially designed book scanners and cameras are available, but they are expensive. Intended for libraries, some models feature automatic page turning; even then, scanning or microfilming bound volumes requires more time and effort than scanning or microfilming unbound pages.

In certain applications, specially prepared separator sheets must be inserted between documents to identify related groups of pages. This practice is often the case, for example, with individual patient files in medical records applications; individual student files in educational applications; individual case files in legal applications; and books, reports, or other multipage documents. Sometimes, the separator sheets identify double-sided pages or instruct the scanner or camera operator to treat multiple pages as a unit for recording on specific media. Alternatively, divider sheets called "targets" may contain identifying information to be scanned or microfilmed before the pages to which they pertain. In a medical records application, for example, a target may indicate the name of the patient whose file is being scanned or microfilmed, the date the scanning or microfilming was performed, and the number of pages in the file. Depending on the software utilized, separator pages may contain barcodes that change equipment settings or initiate specific scanner or camera actions without operator intervention.

Special requirements and precautions aside, preparation of source documents is one of the most time-consuming and labor-intensive aspects of image production. Unlike other activities described in this chapter, document preparation tasks must be performed manually. Their efficient execution depends on the skill, attentiveness, and motivation of workers to whom they are assigned. Clear procedures and appropriate supervision are essential. Even when preparation is limited to removal of staples and paper clips, sustained operator productivity will rarely exceed 1,000 pages per hour for office records in good condition. At that rate, the contents of one file cabinet drawer (approximately 2,500 pages) will require about 2.5 hours of preparation time. As previously noted, older source documents may be in more variable condition than newer office records. They consequently take longer to prepare; 750 to 800 pages per hour are maximum productivity expectations for such documents. Thus, preparation of a one million-page backfile of older records packed in boxes will require at least 1,250 hours of labor.

These estimates of preparation effort are based on the assumption that source documents will be scanned or microfilmed without misfile detection, rearrangement, purging of unneeded records, or other evaluation of files or documents for correctness or completeness. If the sequence of pages within a file must be changed or if files must be checked for misplaced or missing pages prior to scanning or microfilming, preparation time will escalate dramatically. At first glance, purging files of unneeded records prior to scanning or microfilming may seem advisable. Many files contain multiple copies of documents as well as drafts and other records that do not need to be kept. Purging these items can lower image production costs by reducing the number of documents to be scanned or micro-filmed. Labor requirements and supply consumption will be correspondingly reduced for image inspection, data entry, and recording.

Often, however, purging unneeded records increases preparation time without increasing value. To justify purging, any savings that result from the elimination of unneeded records must exceed the labor cost to identify and remove those records, but the required savings may not be attainable. In many applications, knowledgeable persons must examine source documents individually to determine whether they should be imaged or purged. Document content must be evaluated for relevance and future utility, ideally in conformity with predefined retention guidelines. Even the identification of duplicate records can be complicated by the presence of potentially important annotations on one or more copies. This evaluation of individual documents is a time-consuming process. It is also a potentially wasteful activity: If a document is evaluated for purging but retained for scanning or microfilming rather than discarded, nothing is gained. In such situations, the greater preparation labor associated with document evaluation increases total image production costs. Purging of source documents prior to scanning or microfilming should consequently be limited to those files that are known to contain a large percentage of readily identifiable, easily removable duplicates or other unneeded records.

Digital Imaging

Document **scanners** *are computer input devices that create digital images of paper documents.*

Source documents may be typed, printed, handwritten, or hand-drawn. They may contain textual or graphic information in black and white, gray tones, or color. While characteristics and capabilities of specific devices vary, a document scanner divides a page into a grid of small, scannable units that are variously called *picture elements*, *pixels*, or simply *dots*. Using optical and photosensitive components, the scanner measures the amount of light reflected by successively encountered pixels within the page. It then generates a corresponding electrical signal that is converted into digital bit patterns.

Digital images consist of predetermined sequences of "zero" and "one" bits that represent the tonal values of individual pixels. The simplest scanning operations involve office records and engineering drawings that contain dark (usually black) text or line art on a light (usually white) background. Such documents are described as bi-tonal. When digitizing them, document scanners use a single zero bit or one bit to encode each pixel as white or black, depending on their relative lightness or darkness. Multibit coding is used to digitize photographs, drawings with shaded areas, and other documents where meaningful grayscale or color content must be accurately reproduced in digitized images.

Document Scanners

As a computer input device, a document scanner is one component of a scanning workstation that also includes a personal computer and software that initiates and controls scanning operations. Depending on the system configuration, digital images may be stored temporarily on a hard drive within the scanning workstation pending inspection or other action. In most cases, the scanning workstation ultimately transmits digital images to storage devices located elsewhere on a computer network to which the scanning workstation is itself connected.

Since the early 1990s, document scanners have improved steadily and significantly in product availability, variety, and functionality. Most manufacturers offer a range of models with different cost/performance attributes to address specific customer requirements:

- **Sheetfed vs. Flatbed Scanners.** With sheetfed scanners, pages to be scanned are inserted into a narrow opening and transported across a scanning mechanism that includes optical and photosensitive components. Most models are configured with automatic feeders that can accept stacks of pages. Depending on equipment design, the scanned pages are ejected at the top, back, or bottom of the machine. A flatbed scanner, by contrast, features a flat exposure surface on which pages are individually positioned for scanning. Most models feature a glass platen on which pages are placed face down. Much less commonly, flatbed scanners may employ an overhead design in which individual pages are positioned face up for digitization by optical and photosensitive components positioned at the top of a vertical column. Compared to flatbed scanning, sheetfed operation is faster and yields higher labor productivity, but flatbed scanners are necessary for bound volumes or fragile documents. For maximum flexibility, some document scanners support both sheetfed and flatbed input methods. An operator can remove or lift the scanner's page feeding mechanism to reveal a flat glass surface on which bound volumes or fragile documents can be positioned.

- **Input Sizes.** All document scanners impose restrictions on the sizes of pages they can accept. Among scanners for office applications, most models can accommodate pages up to A3-size (approximately 11 inches by 17 inches), the largest paper size routinely employed for business records. Pages larger than A3-size require a large-format scanner. Such devices are principally intended for engineering drawings, architectural schematics, maps, charts, and other large documents.

- **Scanning Resolution.** Resolution is an important quality determinant that denotes the capability to capture fine details in document images. A scanner divides a source document into a grid of pixels, each of which is sampled for its light reflectance characteristics. The scanning resolution denotes the specific pattern and number of pixels sampled during the scanning process.[6] Scanning resolution is usually measured and expressed as the number of pixels or dots

---

[6]   The meaning of resolution in digital imaging and micrographics is explained in ANSI/AIIM TR26, *Resolution as It Relates to Photographic and Electronic Imaging.*

per inch or millimeter within a scanned page—200 dots per inch (dpi) or 8 dots per millimeter, for example. Most scanners support multiple resolutions. Possibilities range from less than 50 dots per inch to more than 1,200 dots per inch. For records management work, 200 dots per inch is the minimum scanning resolution required for consistently legible reproduction of most office records and engineering drawings. Some government regulations specify a minimum scanning resolution of 300 dpi for digital imaging implementations that involve certain public records.[7]

- **Grayscale and Color Scanning.** Multibit coding is used to capture grayscale or color information. The number of gray shades that a given scanner can reproduce depends on the number of bits used to encode each pixel. Eight-bit scanners, the most popular configuration, can differentiate 256 shades of gray. Depending on the model, color scanners use 24 or 36 bits to encode each pixel, which can reproduce millions of different colors.

- **Scanning Speed.** A scanner's rated speed is the elapsed time required to convert one page to a digitized image from the moment the page is positioned for scanning until digitization is completed. The rated speed of a given scanner depends on the device's mechanical characteristics, as well as such application-specific factors as digitization mode, scanning resolution, and page size. In their technical specification sheets, manufacturers of document scanners indicate rated speeds in seconds per page, pages per minute, or, occasionally, inches per second at a specified resolution, typically 200 dots per inch. Mid-range scanners, which are suitable for workgroup or departmental installations, can digitize a letter-size page in two or three seconds. High-volume scanners, which can digitize a letter-size page in 1.5 seconds or less, are designed for production-intensive work environments such as document imaging service bureaus and centralized scanning departments within large organizations. Rated speed, however, measures just one part of the scanning process—the time required to sample pixels within a scanned page. Scanning throughput, by contrast, measures the total time required to produce a serviceable digitized image from a scanned page. Scanning throughput is affected by various factors, including the scanning workstation's host computer, software characteristics, and operator efficiency. As a general guideline, the attainable and sustainable throughput for a given scanner will be about one-half of the rated speed.

---

[7] Document characteristics that influence the choice of resolution are described in ANSI/AIIM MS52, *Recommended Practice for the Requirements and Characteristics of Original Documents Intended for Optical Scanning*, and ISO 10196, *Document Imaging Applications—Recommendations for the Creation of Original Documents*. Drafting practices that may affect the scanning of engineering drawings are discussed in ISO 3098-1, *Technical Product Documentation—Lettering—Part 1: General Requirements*; ISO 3098-2, *Technical Drawings—Lettering—Part 2: Latin Alphabet, Numerals, and Marks*; ISO 5457, *Technical Product Documentation—Sizes and Layout of Drawing Sheets*; and ASME Y14.2, *Line Conventions and Lettering*. ISO 6428, *Technical Drawings—Requirements for Microcopying*, was written specifically for microfilming but is useful for other types of reproductions.

- **Simplex vs. Duplex Scanners.** Simplex scanners can digitize one side of a page at a time. Double-sided pages must be turned over and repositioned for scanning. Duplex scanners, by contrast, can digitize both sides of a double-sided page at the same time. Such devices typically feature two sets of optical and photosensitive components located on opposite sides of the scanner's paper path. All duplex scanners are sheetfed in operation. While duplex scanners can optionally operate in the simplex mode, intermingling of single- and double-sided pages can pose problems. During document preparation, single- and double-sided pages can be grouped for scanning in batches. The appropriate scanning mode can be activated manually or by specially-coded *separator sheets* inserted between batches. Alternatively, software can detect and automatically delete blank images produced by duplex scanning of single-sided pages.

- **Multifunctional Scanners.** Multifunctional devices combine scanning with printing, copying, and faxing capabilities. They are best suited to installations with occasional or low-volume scanning requirements. A specialized group of multifunctional imaging peripherals combines document scanning with microfilming capabilities. Such devices, which are variously termed scanner/filmers or camera/scanners, produce both digitized images and photographically reduced microfilm images in a single operation.

Quality control is discussed in ISO 12653-1, *Electronic Imaging—Test Target for the Black-and-White Scanning of Office Documents—Part 1: Characteristics*; ISO 12653-2, *Electronic Imaging—Test Target for the Black-and-White Scanning of Office Documents—Part 2: Method of Use*; ISO 12653-3, *Electronic Imaging—Test Target for Scanning of Office Documents—Part 3: Test Target for Use in Lower Resolution Applications*, and ISO 29861, *Document Management Applications—Quality Control for Scanning Office Documents in Colour*. Sample-based image inspection is discussed in ANSI/AIIM TR34, *Sampling Procedures for Inspection by Attributes of Images in Electronic Image Management (EIM) & Micrographics Systems*.

Quality Control

Inspection is necessary to ensure that digital images are sufficiently legible and usable for their intended purposes. Possible problems include excessive page skewing, double-feeding or other problems of page feeding and alignment, pages scanned upside down or backwards, pages with folded corners, obliteration of information within pages, insufficient clarity or contrast, blotches or other blemishes, and curved or jagged lines within images. Inspection may encompass all digital images or be limited to a predetermined sample. Careful inspection of all images is critical if paper documents will be discarded following scanning.

Image Formats

Digital images are made up of encoded pixels that represent the tonal values of specific pages. These images, variously described as bit-mapped images or raster images, are recorded as computer files for storage and retrieval. The two most popular image formats are the tagged image file format (TIFF) and the portable document format (PDF). Both formats are compatible with single- and multi-page documents and with binary (black-and-white), grayscale, and color scanning modes.

The TIF format was originally created for desktop publishing. Version 6, the last update of the TIFF specification, was published by Adobe Systems in 1992, and it has been widely used in **digital document imaging** implementations since that time. TIFF is covered by several standards, including ISO 12639, *Graphic Technology—Prepress Digital Data Exchange—Tag Image File Format for Image Technology (TIFF/IT)*, and ISO 12234-2, *Electronic Still-Picture Imaging—Removable Memory—Part 2: TIFF/EP Image Data Format*. A TIF image file includes a header that describes the file's contents, size, and other characteristics. TIF images are often saved in compressed form, which conserves storage space and reduces bandwidth requirements for transmission of images over computer networks. Image compression concepts and methods are discussed in ISO/TR 12033, *Document Management—Electronic Imaging—Guidance for the Selection of Document Image Compression Methods*. TIF images can be read by a variety of computer programs, including viewer software supplied with many personal computers. Plug-ins are available for web browsers.

The PDF format provides excellent functionality for document display, page navigation, printing, and security. It is standardized by ISO 32000-1, *Document Management—Portable Document Format—PDF 1.7*, and ISO 32000-2, *Document Management—Portable Document Format—Part 2: PDF 2.0*. Other standards apply to specialized subsets of PDF. Examples: ISO 19005-1, *Document Management—Electronic Document File Format for Long-Term Preservation—Part 1: Use of PDF 1.4 (PDF/A-1)*; ISO 19005-2, *Document Management—Electronic Document File Format for Long-Term Preservation—Part 2: Use of ISO 32000-1 (PDF/A-2)*; ISO 19005-3, *Document Management—Electronic Document File Format for Long-Term Preservation—Part 3: Use of ISO 32000-1 with Support for Embedded Files (PDF/A-3)*. PDF/Archival (PDF/A) is a subset of PDF intended specifically for long-term retention of digital documents. PDF files are viewed with the Adobe Reader® program, which is supplied with most personal computers and can be downloaded from Internet sites without charge. Use of PDF for engineering documents is covered by ISO 24517-1, *Document Management—Engineering Document Format Using PDF—Part 1: Use of PDF 1.6 (PDF/E-1)*, and ISO 24517-2, *Document Management—Engineering Document Format Using PDF—Part 2: Use of 32000-2 Including Support for Long-Term Preservation (PDF/E-2)*.

Media Stability

Digital document images may be saved on any computer storage medium. In the early to mid-1980s, when digital imaging systems were initially commercialized, hard drives were expensive and their capacities were too low for voluminous imaging applications. As a result, digital images were typically recorded on optical disks, which were characteristically slower and less convenient than hard drives, but they offered higher capacity at lower cost. Since that time, however, hard drive capacities have improved dramatically, and their prices have plunged. They are now the storage media of choice for high performance in most digital imaging implementations. Optical disks, where they are used at all, are typically reserved for offline storage of backup copies or preservation copies.

The stability of a given information storage medium depends on several factors, including the medium's chemical composition and the conditions under which it is stored and used. While optical disks and magnetic tapes are sometimes described as *archival media*, they do not offer the permanence implied in that description. On the contrary, optical disks and magnetic tapes are vulnerable to significant time-dependent degradation that eventually will render them unsuitable for accurate retrieval of recorded information. Such changes may be induced by environmental effects or by defects associated with media manufacturing. Further, information recorded on optical disks and magnetic tapes can be damaged by improper media handling.

A digital image is as stable as the medium on which it is recorded. Stability estimates, also termed *lifetime estimates* or *life spans*, define the time periods during which a given medium will support reliable retrieval of recorded information. With electronic storage media, reliability is determined by the preservation of signal strength and the absence of permanent read/write errors during recording and playback of information. Stability estimates are limited to storage copies; working copies of any medium can be damaged by use. Stability estimates are further limited to removable media such as optical disks and magnetic tapes. While hard drives can provide rapid, convenient access to actively referenced documents, they are, in effect, working media. Consequently, they cannot be considered stable. Incorporated into computer hardware, hard drives are replaced at relatively short intervals and, while in use, are subject to damage from various equipment malfunctions. For secure retention and disaster recovery, digital images must be replicated onto other hard drives or copied onto removable media for offline storage. Such storage copies should be referenced as little as possible.

Available magnetic and optical storage products employ a variety of technologies, each involving different recording materials, substrates, processes, and equipment. Manufacturers claim lifetime estimates of 75 to 200 years for their recordable compact discs and DVD media. Stability periods for other types of optical disks range from 10 to 40 years, with 30 years being a typical claim. Because most optical disks have been in existence for less than these time periods, stability estimates cannot be based on direct observation of media in prolonged storage. Instead, stability claims are based on accelerated aging tests, which are discussed in ISO 18924, *Imaging Materials— Test Method for Arrhenius-type Predictions.*

Published research and manufacturers' claims support lifetime estimates of 10 to 30 years, depending on format, for most magnetic tapes. Typically, newer formats, such as LTO Ultrium and digital linear tape, have longer lifetime estimates than older formats such as nine-track magnetic tape on reels.

While these media lifetime estimates are compatible with multidecade retention requirements, the continued usability of digital images over time will be impacted by other factors. Computer storage media are designed for use with specific hardware and software components that usually have shorter service lives than the media themselves. A given optical disk or magnetic tape may retain playback stability for multiple decades, but no historical precedent has been set for computer storage devices remaining in use for that length of time. Most optical disk drives and magnetic tape units are engineered for a maximum service life of 10 years, and the frequency of repair and high maintenance costs associated with aging equipment will typically necessitate replacement before that time. The availability of new models with improved cost-performance characteristics, coupled with changing application requirements, also encourage replacement at relatively short intervals—within five years or less in many cases. To preserve the utility of previously recorded media, new optical disk drives and magnetic tape units may offer backward compatibility for reading purposes; that is, they can retrieve information from media recorded by predecessor models in a given manufacturer's product line. While such backward compatibility is customary, manufacturers do not guarantee that it will be continued in all future products. On the contrary, the history of computer storage peripherals suggests that, at best, backward compatibility provides a bridge between two or three generations of equipment. Eventually, support for older storage media formats will be phased out. As an additional complication, digital documents are saved in file formats associated with specific software, which may be updated or otherwise changed in a manner that can render previously recorded information unusable.

Usability of digital images can be extended indefinitely by periodically converting them to new file formats or media as discussed in Chapter 3. The use of such data migration to satisfy retention requirements is based on the assumptions that: (1) digital images can be conveniently and reliably transferred from one computer storage medium or file format to another, (2) the cost of such transfer is not prohibitive, and (3) the required media and format migrations can be incorporated into an organization's work routines and prioritized at a sufficiently high level to ensure its completion at scheduled intervals. The time and effort to accomplish the periodic transfer of digital documents to new file formats or media should not be trivialized. In most digital document implementations, the migration effort will be pyramidal. As the number of digital documents increases, successive data migrations will involve greater volumes of information and will require more time to complete.

Image Organization and Retrieval

Where paper files are logically organized, digital images can replicate the existing arrangement of source documents. If a public school district is scanning student files that are arranged alphabetically, for example, an electronic folder can be created for each student, and source documents for individual students will be scanned into the appropriate folders as TIFF or PDF images. The folders will be labeled with the students' names and saved in a designated directory on a local or network drive. Within the hard drive directory, folders can be arranged alphabetically by student name, like their paper counterparts in filing cabinet drawers. To retrieve a specific document, an authorized user opens the desired student folder and browses through digital images. To facilitate this process, images can be labeled by the document type—reports, correspondence, immunization forms, and so on. When the desired image is selected, a TIFF or PDF viewer is launched.

Replication of existing folder-oriented filing arrangements is best suited to records requested by a single identifier, such as a student's name, in situations where an entire folder will be retrieved at one time. To satisfy more demanding retrieval requirements, document management software can index digital images by multiple parameters. In addition to or instead of grouping related documents in folders, an index database keeps track of digital documents with specific characteristics. Student records, for example, can be indexed by the student's name, identification number, document type, date, or other attributes. Retrieval software can execute complex search commands to conclusively identify the exact documents needed for a given purpose. If digital images are processed by optical character recognition (OCR) software, full-text indexing will permit retrieval of documents by words that they contain. This approach to digital document imaging is discussed in Chapter 8.

Micrographics

Micrographics is a document imaging technology that is concerned with the creation and use of microforms as storage media for recorded information.

A **microform** is a photographic information carrier that contains highly miniaturized document images. The images, which are termed **microimages**, require magnification for eye-legible viewing or printing. This requirement distinguishes microforms from optically reduced photocopies, which are smaller than the documents from which they were made but can be read with the unaided eye. Microimages, by contrast, are drastically reduced, which is their defining characteristic. As previously noted, microimages can be produced from source documents or from computer-processable information that would otherwise be printed on paper.

Reduction

Reduction is a measure of the number of times a given linear dimension (one of the sides) of a document is reduced through microphotography. This measure is expressed as 15x, 24x, 48x, and so on, where the reduced linear dimension is 1/15, 1/24, or 1/48 the length of its full-size counterpart. Alternatively, reduction can be expressed as a ratio that represents the relationship between a given linear dimension of a source document and the corresponding linear dimension of a microimage made from that document—for example, 15:1, 24:1, or 48:1.

The reduction used in a specific situation depends on several factors, including the characteristics of the source documents being microfilmed, the type of microform, and the capabilities of available equipment for image production, display, and printing. Higher reductions are attractive because they increase the number of images that can be recorded on a particular type of microform and correspondingly reduce the number of microforms necessary to store a given document collection, thereby simplifying filing, duplication, and other handling of microforms. The reduction selected, however, must be suitable for recording a specified group of documents without loss of information. The reduction must also support the production of legible duplicate microforms through the required number of generations. Some quality is lost in duplication, hence the need for very high-quality camera original microfilms. Further, legibility is important where camera original microfilms or duplicates will be scanned for conversion to digital formats.

Following long-standing industry practice, reductions below 15x are termed *low*. They are most often utilized in library and archival applications that involve historical manuscripts, newspapers, and books of marginal legibility. Office records and engineering drawings are typically microfilmed at medium reductions, which range from 15x to 30x. Common examples are 24x for U.S. letter-size (8.5 inches by 11 inches) and international A4-size pages, and 27x to 29x for U.S. legal-size and international B5-size pages. Reductions of 30x to 32x, which fall just outside the medium range, are used to microfilm U.S. computer printout-size (11 inches by 14 inches) pages and their international B4-size counterparts. Engineering drawings, architectural renderings, maps, and other large-format documents up to D-size (24 inches by 36 inches) or international A1-size can be microfilmed at 24x. E-size (36 inches by 48 inches) and international A0-size drawings are usually microfilmed at 30x.

High reductions, which range from 30x to 60x, are typically reserved for computer output microfilm (COM), which is produced from computer-processable information rather than source documents. With COM technology, type fonts, character sizes, image density, and other factors that affect legibility can be optimized for microreproduction. The most widely encountered reduction in COM applications is 48x. Very high reductions (60x to 90x) and ultra-high reductions (90x and above) play no role in records management. They were principally utilized in the 1960s and 1970s for publishing applications ranging from legal reference books to automobile parts catalogs, but they have since been supplanted by computer databases that provide online access to the same information.

Types of Microforms

Microforms can be categorized, by their physical shape, into two broad groups: roll microforms and flat microforms. Roll microforms are ribbons or strips of microfilm that are wound onto plastic or metal reels or loaded into self-threading cartridges. Flat microforms, by contrast, consist of sheets or pieces of film that contain one or more microimages. Flat microforms include microfiche, microfilm jackets, and aperture cards.

Unexposed microfilm is supplied on rolls in 16mm, 35mm, and 105mm widths. The most common film lengths are 100 and 215 feet. Following exposure and development, microfilm rolls may be converted to other formats as described in this section.

Microfiche is created from 105mm microfilm that is usually cut into 148mm lengths. Individual frames, cut from developed rolls of 35mm microfilm, may be inserted into aperture cards. Strips of developed 16mm or 35mm

Applicable standards are ISO 6148, *Photography—Micrographic Films, Spools and Cores—Dimensions*, ISO 6199, *Micrographics—Microfilming of Documents on 16 mm and 35 mm Silver-Gelatin Type Microfilm—Operating Procedures*; and ISO 24537, *Micrographics—Dimensions for Reels Used for 16mm and 35mm Microfilm.*

film may be inserted into **microfilm jackets**. Often, however, processed 16mm and 35mm microfilm is simply wound onto plastic or metal reels for viewing, printing, or storage.

Since the inception of commercial microphotography, 16mm has been the preferred microfilm width for office documents measuring up to 11 inches by 17 inches in size. The image capacity of a given reel of 16mm microfilm depends on several factors, including page size, reduction, image positioning, film length, and camera characteristics. For letter-size documents reduced 24x, a 100-foot reel of 16mm microfilm can store about 2,500 pages—the approximate contents of one file cabinet drawer. A 215-foot reel can store about 5,400 pages. The 215-foot length is the more economical choice for storage-oriented records management applications. Compared to 100-foot film, it provides more than twice the image capacity but does not cost twice as much to purchase. It also reduces the number of reels required for a given set of documents. Thus, a one-million-page collection of paper documents that occupies 400 reels of 100-foot microfilm would require just 185 reels of 215-foot microfilm.

Applicable standards include ISO 3272-1, *Microfilming of Technical Drawings and Other Drawing Office Documents—Part 1: Operating Procedures*; ISO 3272-4, *Microfilming of Technical Drawings and Other Drawing Office Documents—Part 4: Microfilming of Drawings of Special and Exceptional Elongated Sizes*; ISO 12650, *Document Imaging Applications—Microfilming of Achromatic Maps on 35mm Microfilm*; ISO 408, and *Micrographics—Microfilming of Newspapers for Archival Purposes on 35mm Microfilm*.

With its larger image area, 35mm microfilm permits the legible reproduction of engineering drawings, architectural plans, maps, and other large documents at medium reductions. The principal records management applications for 35mm microfilm are larger documents. A 100-foot reel of 35mm microfilm can store about 700 D-size (A1-size) engineering drawings reduced 24x. Common uses for 35mm microfilm are preservation microfilming by libraries, archives, historical agencies, and other cultural organizations.

Regardless of width, microfilm reels are usually the least expensive microforms to create from a given collection of source documents. They are consequently preferred for inactive records that are microfilmed for long-term retention and compact storage. Microfilm reels are also well suited to vital records protection, where microform copies of mission-critical documents will be stored in offsite locations. As their principal disadvantage, microfilm reels require cumbersome film handling for display or printing. They are consequently recommended for storage copies only. For working copies, 16mm microfilm should be loaded into self-threading cartridges, which offer the economy and capacity of microfilm reels but are much easier to use. A standardized cartridge format, introduced in the mid-1970s, is described in ISO 7761, *Micrographics—Single Core Cartridge for 16mm Processed Microfilm—Dimensions and Operational Constraints*.

As a group, flat microforms have lower capacities than roll microforms. Microfiche, the best known example, is a sheet of film that contains multiple microimages in a two-dimensional grid of rows and columns. Microfiche characteristics are covered by ISO 9923, *Micrographics Transparent A6 Microfiche—Image*

Arrangements, which specifies external dimensions of 105mm by 148mm. Within a given microfiche, individual images are arranged in a grid of rows and columns. An area at the top of each fiche, equivalent to one row of frames, is reserved for eye-legible title information.

Microfiche formats are identified by numeric designations that indicate the reduction utilized and the number of images each microfiche contains. The 24/98 format is the most common format for microfiche made from source documents. It provides 7 rows and 14 columns for a total of 98 images. The recommended reduction is 24x for letter-size pages. Lower reductions are possible for smaller documents. Alternatively, several small documents can be combined in a single frame. Larger pages must be microfilmed at higher reductions or, less desirably, in sections that occupy several frames. Legal-size pages, for example, are typically filmed at 29x. The 48/270 format is the most common format for microfiche produced from computer output. It provides 15 rows and 18 columns for a total of 270 images. Based on 11-inch by 14-inch computer printouts, the 48/270 format is intended for landscape-mode pages that are wider than they are tall. The reduction is 48x. An older microfiche format, designated 42/208, predated the commercial availability of 48x COM technology. It provides 13 rows and 16 columns for a total of 208 11-inch by 14-inch pages. The reduction is 42x.

In active paper-based filing systems, new documents are routinely added to and removed from individual folders. Microfilm jackets, which resemble microfiche, were developed for such situations. As described in ISO/TR 10593, *Micrographics— Use of Microfilm Jackets*, a **jacket** is a transparent acetate or polyester carrier with one or more sleeves, channels, or chambers designed to hold flat strips of 16mm or 35mm microfilm. The strips are cut from microfilm rolls. In most implementations, camera original microfilm rolls are duplicated, and the copies are cut into strips for insertion into jackets. The original rolls are retained as storage copies for retention or security purposes. While microfilm strips can be inserted into jackets by hand, a motorized device called a *viewer-inserter* is customarily used.

Jacket dimensions and other basic characteristics are described in ISO 8127-1, *Micrographics—A6 Size Microfilm Jackets—Part 1: Five Channel Jacket for 16 mm Microfilm.* In the United States, the most popular jacket configuration measures four and one-eighth inches high by six inches wide (approximately 103mm by 152mm). It features five channels for the insertion of 16mm microfilm strips. For letter-size pages reduced 24x, a six-inch strip of 16mm microfilm will contain 12 or 14 images, which yields a maximum capacity of 60 or 70 pages per five-sleeve jacket. If space is available in one of the sleeves, new images can be added to a given jacket. Similarly, obsolete images can be removed. Microfilm jackets can also be used as alternatives to microfiche for miniaturization of closed files. As their principal disadvantage, microfilm jackets are time-consuming and labor-intensive to create, especially in high-volume file conversions. Multiple work steps involving several pieces of equipment are required.

An **aperture card** is a tabulating-size (86 by 187 mm) card with an opening (aperture) that contains one frame of 35mm microfilm. As with microfilm jackets, the frame is usually cut from a roll of microfilm. Aperture card characteristics are specified in ISO 3272-3, *Microfilming of Technical Drawings and Other Drawing Office Documents—Part 3: Aperture Card for 35mm Microfilm*. Aperture cards are the most widely used microforms for engineering drawings, architectural plans, and maps. An aperture card provides ample paper space for eye-legible information that identifies and describes the microfilmed document. This information may be handwritten, typed, or computer printed. The front and back of an aperture card can be custom printed to accommodate special requirements. Cards can be ordered in various colors or with color striping to differentiate portions of a document collection.

Microfilm Cameras

Microfilm cameras are special-purpose photographic devices that produce highly miniaturized reproductions of source documents. While early models required many operator decisions that could only be made by specially trained technicians, later model microfilm cameras are designed for operation in an office environment by nontechnical personnel with little or no knowledge of photography. Focus and film advance mechanisms are invariably automatic. Simplified control panels, pushbutton operation, informative operator displays, and attention to ergonomics are the rule. Warning lights and audible alarms alert the operator to the approaching end of a roll of film, improper film loading, burned-out lamps, and other problems. Automatic exposure controls compensate for variations in color, texture, contrast, and other document characteristics.

Cameras for source document microfilms are typically categorized by the types of microforms they produce and their mode of operation:

- *Rotary cameras are the micrographic counterparts of sheet-fed scanners.* Source documents inserted into a narrow opening are quickly transported past a lens and a light source where they are recorded onto 16mm microfilm. The applicable standard is ISO 10198, *Micrographics—Rotary Camera for 16mm Microfilm—Mechanical and Optical Characteristics*. Input is limited to single sheets of paper with all staples, paper clips, and other fasteners removed. Depending on the model, rotary cameras can accept documents that measure 12 to 14 inches wide by any reasonable length. To avoid double-feeding, skewing, and jamming, letter-size pages and other office documents are usually inserted into the rotary camera's transport mechanism by hand. A moderately skilled operator can sustain filming rates of 800 to 1,000 letter-size pages per hour, assuming that the pages are properly prepared. Automatic page feeders permit rapid microfilming of stacks of bank checks and other small documents. Their mechanical operating speeds can exceed 500 checks per minute.

- *Planetary, or flatbed, microfilmers combine a camera unit, a flat exposure surface, a light source, and various operator controls into a tabletop or free-standing device.* The camera unit contains a lens system, a film supply, and a film advance mechanism. With an overhead planetary microfilmer, the most common type, source documents are individually positioned, face-up, on a flat copyboard for microfilming by a camera unit mounted onto a vertical column. With the inverted planetary microfilmer, the camera unit and light source are located below or behind a glass exposure surface on which source documents are positioned face down for microfilming. Depending on the model, planetary cameras produce 16mm or 35mm microfilm. Special models are available for engineering drawings, architectural plans, and other large documents. Rotary cameras microfilm documents while they are moving, which can degrade image quality. Planetary cameras, by contrast, film stationary documents, which yields excellent image quality but compromises productivity. When source documents are properly prepared, an experienced planetary camera operator can sustain filming rates up to 500 letter-size pages per hour, but large pages, fragile documents, or bound volumes can take much longer to film. Engineering drawings, for example, may take several minutes each to position, expose, and remove.

- *Step-and-repeat cameras create microfiche by recording source documents onto 105mm microfilm in a predetermined format of rows and columns.* A step-and-repeat camera is loaded with unexposed 105mm roll film, which is cut to microfiche size following exposure and development. Depending on the model, a step-and-repeat camera may require manual positioning of individual pages or have an automatic page feeder.

Computer-output Microfilm

Like any other documents, voluminous computer printouts can be microfilmed to save space, but computer-output microfilm (COM) technology addresses this problem at its source: It records computer-processable information on microforms instead of, rather than after, printing it. A **COM recorder**, the device that produces computer-output microfilm, combines the functionality of a computer printer and a microfilm camera. Like a computer printer, a COM recorder converts the results of computer processing to human-readable form. Like a microfilm camera, a COM recorder produces page images that require magnification for viewing or printing.

COM gained popularity in the 1960s and 1970s as an efficient technology for storage and distribution of long reports to be distributed to many users and updated frequently. For the most part, such voluminous printed reports have been supplanted by online access. While COM is no longer a widely utilized technology, it remains an effective alternative to paper or electronic media for computer-generated information to be archived for long-term retention or permanent preservation as discussed in ISO 11506, *Document Management Applications—Archiving of Electronic Data—Computer Output Microfilm (COM)/Computer Output Laser Disc (COLD)*.

COM production begins with computer-processable information that would otherwise be printed on paper. The information, appropriately formatted, is transferred to a COM recorder, which creates microimages that resemble miniaturized versions of printed pages. Most COM recorders produce microfiche, although devices that record information on 16mm or 35mm roll microfilm are also available. Alphanumeric COM recorders print alphabetic characters, numeric digits, punctuation marks, and other symbols commonly encountered in textual documents. They are suitable for accounting reports, customer lists, and other straight-forward business documents. Graphic COM recorders have full alphanumeric capabilities. They can also print engineering drawings, charts, graphs, plots, circuit diagrams, maps, and medical imagery. A special group of COM recorders, collectively described as "archive writers," produces microfilm copies of digital images created by document scanners.

Microfilm Processing and Inspection

Exposed microfilms contain latent (invisible) photographic images that require development—a work step that has no counterpart in digital imaging implementations. Microfilm processing equipment applies physical and chemical treatments that make latent images visible and stable. Exposed microfilm is removed from a camera and carried to a processing device in a light-tight canister. Microfilm processors are available in tabletop and floor-standing models that vary in capability and complexity.

The purpose of image quality inspections is to ensure that microimages are sufficiently legible for their intended purposes, which may include viewing, printing paper copies, duplication to create working or storage copies, or scanning for facsimile transmission or input to a digital document management application. Unlike digital image inspections, which are limited to visual examination, micro-image inspections involve technical procedures that require special equipment. Quality determinations are usually based on resolution and density measurements, which compare specific microimages to predetermined values for images of acceptable quality.

Resolution, which roughly equates to image sharpness, measures the ability of microfilm equipment and photographic materials to render fine detail visible within a microimage. Resolution is measured by examining a microimage of a specially designed test target that is recorded on a roll of microfilm or microfiche. The test targets are described in ISO 3334, *Micrographics—ISO Resolution Test Chart No. 2—Description and Use*; ISO 10550, *Micrographics—Planetary Camera Systems—Test Target for Checking Performance*; and ISO 10594, *Micrographics— Rotary Camera Systems—Test Target for Checking Performance*. Image density tests measure the contrast between information and noninformation areas within microimages. A densitometer is used for this test. High contrast between line and background densities is desirable for microimages that contain textual information or line art. The applicable standard is ISO 6200, *Micrographics—First Generation Silver-gelatin Microforms of Source Documents—Density Specifications and Method of Measurement*.

Processed microfilm must also be inspected for stability. With silver gelatin microfilms, the type used in microfilm cameras, latent images are developed by a chemical agent that converts exposed silver grains to black metallic silver.

Development is followed by the application of a fixing bath that converts unexposed silver grains to silver thiosulfate compounds, making them water-soluble so that they can be washed out of the film. If left on the film, thiosulfate will darken on exposure to light. Adequate film washing is consequently essential for microforms that contain permanent records. Guidelines are presented in ISO 18901, *Imaging Materials—Processed Silver-Gelatin Type Black-and-White Film—Specifications for Stability*. The methylene blue test is the best known and most widely applied of several methods of confirming adequate removal of thiosulfate during microfilm processing. It should be performed each time film, chemicals, or the microfilm processor are changed. Stability test methods are covered by ISO 18917, *Photography—Determination of Residual Thiosulfate and Other Related Chemicals in Processed Photographic Materials—Methods Using Iodine-Amylose, Methylene Blue and Silver Sulfide.*

Microform Duplication

Microform duplication is used to make additional microform copies for storage, reference, or distribution. The microform being duplicated is called the *master*. It may be a camera original microform or a copy that is one or more generations removed from it. Unlike original microphotography, which is an optical process, microform duplication relies on contact printing methodologies. Microfilms intended for duplication are termed *copy films*, *duplicating films*, or *print films* to distinguish them from camera films. Copy films are available in three types: silver gelatin, diazo, and vesicular. The films differ in their technical characteristics, which determine the records management applications for which they are suitable:

- *Diazo microfilms are intended exclusively for duplication.* They are not suitable for use in cameras. Diazo copy films are exposed to ultraviolet light and developed with ammonia fumes. The resulting copies have excellent viewing properties and are scratch-resistant. Diazo technology produces a negative-appearing copy of a negative-appearing master microform and a positive-appearing copy of a positive-appearing master microform. As a result, diazo duplication is most widely used in source document microfilm applications where master microforms are usually negative-appearing and negative-appearing working copies are desired.[8]

- *Vesicular microfilms are exposed to ultraviolet light and developed by heat, without chemicals or fluids.* As its principal advantages, vesicular technology is convenient, fast, odorless, and completely dry. It produces a positive-appearing copy of a negative-appearing master and a negative-appearing copy of a positive-appearing master. As a result, vesicular duplication is most widely used in COM applications where master microforms are often positive-appearing

---

[8] Microform users often prefer negative-appearing working copies, which hide scratches and mask uneven illumination in certain microform display devices. Sometimes, a specific polarity is required to produce a meaningful microimage; for example, with microimages of x-rays, which must be negative-appearing, and microimages of photographs, which must be positive-appearing.

and negative-appearing working copies are desired. Vesicular copies are easily identified by their distinctive beige, gray, or light blue color.

- *Silver gelatin copy films are typically reserved for applications that require permanent microform storage copies.* When properly processed and stored, silver gelatin print films have the same stability characteristics as silver gelatin camera films. Copies made from silver gelatin print films may be either positive-appearing or negative-appearing, depending on the type of print film used.

Microform copies must be inspected for legibility and technical characteristics. The latter are discussed in ISO 8126, *Micrographics—Duplicating Film, Silver, Diazo, and Vesicular—Visual Density—Specifications and Measurement.*

Media Stability

Decades of scientific research confirm that microfilm offers excellent physical and chemical stability for long-term retention and archival preservation of valuable documents. Microfilm offers superior stability attributes when compared to many types of paper and electronic media. These attributes are important enough to warrant a more detailed explanation.

International standards specify the stability characteristics of photographic films, including microfilms. The scope and content of standards that specify the stability characteristics of silver gelatin microfilms have changed significantly since the 1970s. Earliest versions emphasized the preservation of information of permanent value. They specified the conditions under which silver gelatin microfilms must be manufactured, processed, and stored for permanent stability. Silver gelatin microfilms that conformed to those standards were characterized as "archival" quality. Films that did not meet archival specifications were often categorized as "commercial" quality. Standards issued in the early 1980s retained the archival specifications for permanent preservation of information, while recognizing two shorter periods of microfilm stability: long-term (100 years) and medium-term (10 years).

Since 1991, standards for stability of photographic media have replaced the archival, long-term, and medium-term categories with life expectancy (LE) designations for specific media under recommended storage conditions. The LE designation is a prediction of the minimum life expectancy, in years, for a given medium. For example, a life expectancy of LE-100 represents a stability period of at least 100 years. Among its principal objectives, this stability nomenclature is designed to minimize confusion resulting from differing uses of the term "archival" in information management. In records management, for example, the term implies permanence. In computing, however, the archival designation is broadly applied to magnetic tape and other removable media that are suitable for offline storage of inactive information, an activity termed "data archiving." No implication of media stability is associated with such data archiving.

Under the standard designations, the life expectancy is 100 years (LE-100) for silver gelatin microfilms with cellulose triacetate base material and 500 years (LE-500) for silver gelatin microfilms with polyester base materials. In each case, the media must be manufactured, processed, and stored in conformity with pertinent international standards cited above. International standards specify a life expectancy of 100 years (LE-100) for thermally processed silver microfilms, which are utilized by some COM recorders, and for diazo and vesicular microfilms, which are utilized for microform duplication. The applicable standards are ISO 18905, *Imaging Materials—Ammonia-Processed Diazo Photographic Film—Specifications for Stability*; ISO 18912, *Imaging Materials—Processed Vesicular Photographic Film—Specifications for Stability*; and ISO 18919, *Imaging Materials—Thermally Processed Silver Microfilm—Specifications for Stability*. As with silver gelatin microfilms, appropriate storage conditions are assumed.

Where microforms will be used for long-term retention or permanent preservation of recorded information, storage copies, which are used to produce one or more working copies and seldom handled thereafter, need to be distinguished from working copies, which are intended for display, printing, distribution, or other purposes. The life expectancies previously discussed apply to microform storage copies only. Microform working copies, which may be referenced frequently, are imperiled by use, and their life expectancies are invariably compromised. Typically stored in office locations rather than in controlled environments, working copies may be exposed to high temperatures and relative humidity. They may be scratched during viewing, printing, duplication, filing, or distribution. Working copies may also be contaminated by airborne particles, smoke residues, skin oils, fingerprints, and spilled liquids.

Unlike digital imaging, micrographics implementations have minimal hardware dependencies. Microimages, like paper documents, contain human-readable information, but they require magnification for eye-legible display or printing of recorded information. The system components needed for that purpose are straightforward, however. Microform display and printing devices remain available, although the number of suppliers has decreased in recent years. Given the large installed base of microforms in companies, government agencies, and other organizations throughout the world, however, complete discontinuation of such products is unlikely. Unless computer databases are used to index microimages, micrographics implementations have no software dependencies.

Micrographics technology has a long history of standardization, which offers exceptional compatibility and interchangeability of recorded information among the products of different vendors. Users can exchange microforms worldwide with confidence that recorded information will be viewable and printable by available equipment. Similarly, micrographics equipment offers superior backward compatibility. Assuming appropriate magnification, newly manufactured micrographics equipment can display or print microimages created in the past. Similarly, micrographics users can have a high degree of confidence that microimages created today will be compatible with display and printing equipment to be introduced in the future. In this respect, micrographics enjoys an important competitive advantage over computer technologies, such as electronic document imaging, for long-term retention or permanent preservation of recorded information.

Microform Display and Printing

Most micrographics applications involve storage copies and working copies. Storage copies are kept in a safe, environmentally controlled location to satisfy retention or backup requirements. Working copies, by contrast, are designed to be consulted for business or other purposes. User acceptance of microforms in such situations depends on the convenient and reliable ability to display, print, or otherwise process microimages when needed. Several types of devices are available for those purposes:

- A **microform reader** *projects magnified microimages for viewing.* When evaluating microform readers for specific records management applications, the main considerations include the type of microforms accepted, the availability of appropriate magnifications, and the size and orientation of the reader's screen. Important technical and operational considerations involve the image projection method, the quality of displayed images, the film transport mechanism, equipment design and construction, and ease of use. ISO 6198, *Readers for Transparent Microforms—Performance Characteristics,* and ISO 7565, *Readers for Transparent Microforms—Measurement of Characteristics,* define essential attributes and minimum performance expectations.

- **Microform reader/printers** *can display magnified microimages on a screen and make paper copies of displayed images on demand for reference, distribution, or other purposes.* In effect, a reader/printer is a microform reader with an integral photocopier. ISO 10197, *Micrographics—Reader-Printers for Transparent Microforms—Characteristics,* delineates essential equipment attributes. Reader/printers are more accurately characterized as locator/printers. Unlike readers, they are rarely used for prolonged microform viewing. Typically, users display microimages briefly on a reader/printer's screen to confirm their identity and properly align them to make paper copies. All newly manufactured reader/printers employ xerographic technology, which prints enlarged microimages on plain (uncoated) paper. They can produce legible, high-contrast enlargements that are well accepted by microform users.

Microform Scanners

Microform scanners digitize microimages for computer processing, storage, retrieval, printing, or distribution. A microform scanner combines the attributes of a microfilm densitometer and a document scanner. It operates like the document scanners described previously, but the pages it scans are highly miniaturized film images.

Microfilm scanners are available in production-level and low-volume versions. Production-level devices can scan large quantities of microimages at relatively high speed with little or no operator intervention. Their principal role in records management is scanning of microform backfiles for input to digital document management systems, computer-aided design software, or other computer applications. Depending on the model, a production-level microform scanner may be able to digitize microimages recorded on 16mm or 35mm microfilm reels, 16mm microfilm cartridges, microfiche in various formats, microfilm jackets, and aperture cards.

For low-volume scanning requirements, a reader/scanner combines the capabilities of a microform reader and an image digitizer. It produces electronic document images from magnified microimages that are displayed on a screen. Significant operator involvement is required; microimages must be individually located, displayed, focused, and positioned for scanning. Reader/scanners are best suited to selective scanning of microimages for printing, facsimile transmission, attachment to email messages, or input to computer software. When connected to a laser printer, a reader/scanner can operate as a digital reader/printer.

Retrieval of Microimages

Many micrographics applications involve logically arranged source documents that are recorded on 16mm or 35mm microfilm reels in their original filing sequence. As an example, engineering drawings for a construction project may be microfilmed in drawing number sequence. Similarly, personnel files for employees who retire in a given year may be microfilmed in alphabetic order by employee name. Each microfilm reel will be labeled with its inclusive contents. To facilitate retrieval, specially prepared target pages may be inserted between files or alphabetic groupings. Information on the target pages may be handwritten or typed in large characters that will be visible and immediately recognizable when a user browses through a microfilm reel.

The possibility of automated microimage retrieval was discussed in the mid-1940s and implemented in the 1950s. Pre-computer examples recorded index codes on microfilm adjacent to the document images to which they pertained. Introduced in the 1960s, computer-assisted microfilm retrieval systems used a computer database to index microimages. In most implementations, documents were recorded onto 16mm microfilm, which was loaded into self-threading cartridges to simplify handling and speed retrieval. Documents were microfilmed by cameras that placed small rectangular marks, called *blips* or *image count marks*, beneath all or selected microimages. Specially designed reader/printers counted the blips and in so doing counted the images. A computer database linked index terms to microimages identified by their cartridge and image addresses. That approach proved effective and reliable at a time when completely computerized approaches to document storage and retrieval were not practical, but it has been supplanted by electronic document management technology.

Imaging Service Companies

Any or all image production work steps can be performed in-house or outsourced.

An imaging service company is a business that performs one or more imaging services to customer specifications using the customer's own documents, computer data, or other source material. A service bureau may offer any combination of image production and support services, including consulting for application selection and systems design, document preparation, source document scanning or microfilming, COM data preparation and recording, microform scanning, microfilm processing, image inspection, stability testing of processed microfilm, duplication of microforms or digital images, microform reformatting, and preparation of microfilm jackets and aperture cards.

Outsourcing arrangements are increasingly popular in records management operations. While in-house scanning is commonplace, some organizations use service bureaus for all microform production requirements, and many in-house micrographics operations contract with service companies for at least one phase of microform production. For example, imaging service companies often process, inspect, and duplicate microfilm exposed by an in-house micrographics operation. Imaging service companies are particularly useful for high-volume work that must be completed in a short time or for tasks, such as microform scanning, that require special equipment, software, or technical expertise that are unavailable in-house.

> Depending on the service bureau and customer requirements, imaging services may be performed at the service bureau's facilities or at the customer's location, although onsite implementations are more costly and may limit the types of services to be offered. Some service bureaus also sell scanners, document management software, microform readers and reader/printers, and other imaging equipment or supplies.

Service company capabilities and rates vary. The nature and acceptability of services to be rendered must be negotiated between the customer and the service company's management. Critical criteria for service company selection include a demonstrated understanding of the customer's requirements, technical resources and expertise appropriate to the tasks to be performed, the ability to provide high-quality service within customer-specified deadlines, and a record of satisfactory performance in similar applications. A tour of the service company's facilities prior to contract award is strongly recommended.

Legal Acceptability

In the United States, the legal acceptability of digital images and microimages is based on their status as duplicate records; that is, true copies of the documents from which they are made.

A true copy is one that accurately reproduces an original document. An existing body of laws and legal cases addresses the legal acceptability of copies. In the United States, pertinent statutory provisions include the Uniform Photographic Copies of Business and Public Records as Evidence Act—commonly abbreviated as the Uniform Photographic Copies Act, or simply, the UPA—as well as the Uniform Rules of Evidence (URE) and its counterpart, the Federal Rules of Evidence (FRE).

Written in 1949, the Uniform Photographic Copies of Business and Public Records as Evidence Act permits the substitution of photographic copies for original documents for all judicial or administrative proceedings. The UPA applies to any copying process that "accurately reproduces or forms a durable medium for so reproducing" original documents. Similar provisions are contained in 28 U.S. Code 1732. As its title indicates, the UPA applies to copies of public records maintained by federal, state, and local government agencies. It also applies to business records maintained by corporations, partnerships, sole proprietorships, not-for-profit institutions, and other nongovernmental organizations. In every case, the copies must be accurate reproductions of original documents, and they must have been produced in the regular course of business, as part of an organization's established operating procedures.

The UPA permits, but does not mandate, the destruction of original documents, thereby allowing organizations to rely solely on copies for whatever purpose the originals were intended. Destruction is prohibited, however, where preservation of the original documents is specifically required by law. Some states have added a clause to the UPA that prohibits destruction of original documents held in a custodial or fiduciary capacity. Examples include case files, account files, and other client records maintained by law firms, public accountants, and other professional service firms. In such situations, the owner's permission is required for destruction of original documents following scanning or microfilming.

Rule 1003 of the Uniform Rules of Evidence and Federal Rules of Evidence permits the admission of duplicate records in evidence as substitutes for original documents unless serious questions are raised about the authenticity of the original records or, in specific circumstances, it is judged unfair to admit a copy in lieu of an original. Unlike the UPA, Rule 1003 of the URE/FRE does not require that duplicate records be produced in the regular course of business. The URE and FRE do not authorize destruction of original records, nor do they prohibit it.

The UPA applies to any copying process that "accurately reproduces or forms a durable medium for so reproducing" original documents. It specifically mentions microfilming as a method of document reproduction. Rule 1001(4) of the URE/FRE defines a duplicate as "a counterpart produced by the same impression as the original, or from the same matrix, or by means of photography, including enlargements and miniatures, or by mechanical or electronic re-recording, or by chemical reproduction, or by other equivalent techniques which accurately reproduces the original." Digital document images satisfy the requirements of these broad definitions.

The UPA and Rule 1003 of URE/FRE can counteract objections to the admissibility of digital document images under the best evidence rule, which requires the introduction of an "original writing" into evidence unless its absence can be satisfactorily explained. Where paper documents are destroyed in the regular course of business following scanning and recording, digital images or printouts made from them may be admissible as trustworthy copies. Unless fraud is suspected, destruction of original records in conformity with an organization's established business practices is typically considered a satisfactory explanation for the substitution of a trustworthy copy in evidence. Even where the original paper documents remain available, the UPA and Rule 1003 support the admissibility of digital images in evidence as substitutes for originals in most cases. They place the burden of argument on the party seeking to exclude digital images rather than the party seeking to admit them.

Like other uniform laws cited in this book, the Uniform Photographic Copies Act and Uniform Rules of Evidence apply only in those legal jurisdictions where they have been adopted. One or both of the laws have been adopted by 88 percent of the states. In other situations, state-specific statutes may permit or restrict the admissibility of digital image or microform copies or their suitability for retention in specific circumstances. In developments likely to be repeated in other legal jurisdictions, several states have modified their existing laws concerning duplicate records to more specifically encompass digital images of documents. As an example, the definition of a duplicate record contained in section 8.01-391(F) of the Virginia Code Annotated has been changed to include "copies from optical disks" along with photographs, photostats, and microfilm. While copies of digital images stored on magnetic media are not mentioned specifically, the definition broadly embraces "any other reproduction of an original from a process which forms a durable medium for its recording, storing, and reproducing." Similarly, Section 109.120 of the Missouri Revised Statutes addresses reproduction of documents by "photographic, video, or electronic processes." The resulting copies must be "of durable material" and "accurately reproduce and perpetuate the original records in all details." Section 44.139(B) of the Louisiana Revised Statutes gives an "electronically digitized copy" equivalent evidentiary status with microfilm as a duplicate record. When properly authenticated, such copies are admissible in evidence in all courts and administrative proceedings in the jurisdictions governed by such law.

Similar legal considerations apply in other countries. As discussed in Chapter 3, many countries have passed electronic transaction laws that apply to digital document images as a type of electronic record. Canadian national standard CAN/CGSB 72.11, *Microfilm and Electronic Images as Documentary Evidence*, provides rules and guidelines relating to legal admissibility of document images as accurate reproductions of source records in relation to the Canada Evidence Act and provincial evidence acts and ordinances. The legal status of digital document images is also supported by Sections 42 and 47 of the Canadian Personal Information Protection and Electronic Documents Act, which states that electronic documents can satisfy requirements for original documents or copies of documents. British Standard 100008, *Evidential Weight and Legal Admissibility of Electronic Information: Specification*, and BIP 0008, *Evidential Weight and Legal Admissibility of Information Stored Electronically: Code of Practice for the Implementation of BS 10008*, specify principle requirements for legal acceptability of electronic documents, including digital document images. In Australia, the Commonwealth Evidence Act provides for the admissibility of digital and microfilm images.

Summary of Major Points

☑ Micrographics technology has been an important component of records management practice for more than half a century. Digital document imaging technology was introduced in the 1980s, and its use—initially as a micrographics alternative and subsequently as a solution to recordkeeping problems for which micrographics technology was never intended—has increased steadily and significantly since that time. As an alternative to paper documents, both imaging technologies can drastically reduce storage requirements and costs for inactive records that must be kept for long periods of time. Digital imaging can also improve retrieval of active records.

☑ For cost-effective management of inactive records, digital imaging and micrographics technology must be judiciously implemented in the context of a systematic retention program that identifies appropriate storage solutions for specific types of recorded information. A comprehensive records management program will combine digital imaging and micrographics with selective destruction and offsite storage of paper records.

☑ Preparation is the essential first step in creating document images. Its purpose is to make source documents "scanner ready" or "camera ready"; that is, to put documents into a condition and sequence appropriate for scanning or microfilming. Well-prepared source documents are critical to efficient operation of document scanners and microfilm cameras, effective deployment of scanning and microfilming labor, and consistent production of usable images.

☑ The simplest scanning operations involve office records and engineering drawings that contain dark (usually black) text or line art on a light (usually white) background. In such situations, document scanners use a single zero bit or one bit to encode each pixel as white or black, depending on their relative lightness or darkness. Multibit coding is used to digitize photographs, drawings with shaded areas, and other documents where meaningful grayscale or color content must be accurately reproduced in digitized images.

☑ While digital document images may be recorded onto any computer storage medium, hard drives have replaced optical disks as the storage media of choice in most digital imaging implementations.

☑ Computer storage media are designed for use with specific hardware and software components that usually have shorter service lives than the media themselves. The usability of digital images can be extended indefinitely by periodically converting them to new file formats or media, a process termed *data migration*.

☑ Micrographics is a document imaging technology that is concerned with the creation and use of microforms. A microform is a photographic information carrier that contains highly miniaturized document images. The images, which are termed *microimages*, require magnification for eye-legible viewing or printing.

☑ Source document microphotography is the oldest and most easily understood method of microform production. Computer-output microfilm (COM), the other method of microform production, is a variant form of computer printing technology that records computer-generated information in human-readable form directly onto microfilm.

✓ Micrographics technology offers significant advantages for the inactive stages of the information life cycle. In addition to compact storage, it provides superior stability, minimal system dependence, excellent product compatibility, and legal acceptability. Micrographics is also a useful technology for vital records protection.

✓ Imaging service companies offer image production and support services, including consulting for application selection and systems design, document preparation, source document scanning and microfilming, image inspections, COM data preparation and recording, microfilm processing, stability testing of processed microfilm, media duplication, and microform reformatting.

✓ The legal acceptability of digital images and microimages is based on their status as duplicate records; that is, true copies of the documents from which they are made. A true copy is one that accurately reproduces an original document. In the United States, the Uniform Photographic Copies Act permits the substitution of photographic copies for original documents for all judicial or administrative proceedings. Rule 1003 of the Uniform Rules of Evidence and Federal Rules of Evidence permit the admission of duplicate records in evidence as substitutes for original documents. Similar provisions apply in other countries.

Chapter 6

Vital Records

Vital records, as briefly defined in preceding chapters, contain information that is essential to an organization's mission. All organizations have certain business operations that they must perform. Such operations are characterized as mission-critical because they directly relate to an organization's reason for existing. A failure or inability to perform **mission-critical operations** will have an adverse impact on an organization's most important initiatives and, in extreme cases, the organization's continued viability. Vital records contain information needed for mission-critical business operations. All mission-critical business operations depend to some extent on recorded information. If a vital record is lost, damaged, destroyed, or otherwise rendered unavailable or unusable, such operations will be curtailed or discontinued, with a resulting adverse impact on the organization.

Vital records protection is one of the most important components of a systematic records management program. Recognizing this, ISO 15489-1, *Information and Documentation—Records Management—Part 1: General*, the international records management standard, includes risk assessment and protection of records among the requirements for records management operations. The importance of protecting vital records is treated in ANSI/ARMA 5, *Vital Records Programs: Identifying, Managing, and Recovering Business-Critical Records*. Vital records protection is an aspect of the broader fields of business continuity, the ability of an organization to maintain essential business operations following a disaster, and information security, which deals with the protection of information technology and assets. These fields are covered by many international standards, including ISO 22301, *Societal Security—Business Continuity Management Systems—Requirements*; ISO 22313, *Societal Security—Business Continuity Management Systems—Guidance*; ISO/PAS 22399, *Societal Security—Guideline for Incident Preparedness and Operational Continuity Management*; ISO/IEC 24762, *Information Technology—Security Techniques—Guidelines for Information and Communications Technology Disaster Recovery Services*; ISO/IEC 27000, *Information Technology—Security Techniques—Information Security Management Systems—Overview and Vocabulary*;

ISO/IEC 27001, *Information Technology—Security Techniques—Information Security Management Systems—Requirements*; ISO/IEC 27002, *Information Technology—Security Techniques—Code of Practice for Information Security Controls*; ISO/IEC 27003, *Information Technology—Security Techniques—Information Security Management System Implementation Guidance*; ISO/IEC 27014, *Information Technology—Security Techniques—Governance of Information Security*; ISO/IEC 27031, *Information Technology—Security Techniques—Guidelines for Information and Communication Technology Readiness for Business Continuity*; and ISO/IEC 27040, *Information Technology—Security Techniques—Storage Security*.

Properly conceived and administered, a vital records program can make an indispensable contribution to business effectiveness. For many organizations, information contained in vital records is their most important asset. Without vital records:

- Equipment manufacturers will be unable to build, market, deliver, or repair their products.

- Pharmaceutical companies will be unable to develop, test, or prove the safety and efficacy of chemical compounds.

- Utility companies will be unable to operate and maintain their facilities.

- Local government agencies will be unable to document property ownership, determine tax assessments, evaluate zoning applications, or issue building permits.

- Hospitals and clinics will be unable to provide effective medical care.

- Social services agencies will be unable to help those in need.

- Schools and colleges will be unable to document the attendance or academic achievements of students.

- Insurance companies will be unable to determine policy coverage, collect premiums, or process claims.

- Financial institutions will be unable to document customer account balances, evaluate loan applications, or collect debts.

- Lawyers, engineers, architects, accountants, and other professionals will be unable to serve their clients.

In many cases, the loss of recorded information can have more devastating consequences for continuation of an organization's operations than the loss of physical plant, inventory, or raw materials, which are often replaceable and insured.

Vital records are considered vital specifically and exclusively for the information they contain and the relationship of that information to an organization's mission-critical operations. Vital record status is not necessarily related to other record attributes. Physical format is immaterial; vital records may be paper documents, photographic films, or electronic media. Vital records may be active or inactive, originals or copies. Vital record status is similarly independent of retention designations. Vital records need not be permanent records; some vital records may, in fact, be retained for brief periods of time and replaced at frequent intervals. Furthermore, some records may be considered vital for only a portion of their designated retention periods. Invoices, billing documentation, and other accounts receivable records, for example, are vital until the matters to which they pertain are paid, although they are usually retained for several years following receipt of payment for legal reasons, internal audits, or other purposes.

Specific record attributes aside, a vital records program is a set of policies and procedures for the systematic, comprehensive, and economical control of adverse consequences attributable to the loss of mission-critical information. Many businesses, government agencies, and other organizations have developed contingency plans for the protection of personnel, buildings, machinery, inventory, and other assets in the event of fire, weather-related disasters, or other unplanned calamitous events. Protection of recorded information essential to mission-critical business operations has long been recognized as an indispensable aspect of such emergency preparedness and disaster recovery initiatives. Since the 1950s, for example, U.S. laws have mandated the identification and protection of vital operating records of federal government agencies. According to 36 CFR 1223, the management of vital records must be part of each agency's plan for continuity of business operations in the event of emergencies. Similar regulations apply to protection of government records in other countries.

Various government regulations mandate protection for vital records associated with specific business activities. Among the many examples that might be cited:

1. 45 CFR 164.308, which implements the Health Insurance Portability and Accountability Act (HIPAA), requires regulated entities and their business associates to establish and implement procedures to create and maintain "retrievable exact copies" of electronic protected health information.

2. As specified in 21 CFR 211.68, pharmaceutical companies must maintain backup copies of drug manufacturing data. According to Annex 11 of Rules Governing Medicinal Products in the European Union, manufacturing data must be backed up.

3. Financial institutions insured by the FDIC are required to have organization-wide disaster recovery and business continuity plans for their computer installations. Review of financial institutions' business continuity plans is a well-established component of examinations performed by the Federal Financial Institutions Examination Council (FFIEC), which prescribes principles and standards for federal examination of financial institutions. Its examination procedures include detail questions about the development, implementation, testing, and oversight of disaster recovery policies and procedures, including provisions for data backup and offsite storage. Other regulatory bodies that require contingency plans for depository institutions include the Comptroller of the Currency, the Federal Home Loan Bank Board, the Office of Thrift Supervision, and the National Credit Union Administration.

4. Some Middle Eastern countries specify protection requirements for vital records maintained by financial services companies. In Bahrain, banks must store copies of vital records offsite as soon as possible after they are created. In Israel, banks must be able to reconstruct information from backup copies, which must be stored at a safe distance from the original storage location. In Saudi Arabia, financial services companies must have backup arrangements to support disaster recovery. The United Arab Emirates specifies retention periods of 7 to 10 years for backup copies of certain records maintained by securities companies and insurance companies.

5. Among South American countries, Uruguay requires banks to have sufficient backup copies to reconstruct their accounting operations and financial statements.

Traditionally, records management has emphasized the protection of vital records against accidental or willful damage, destruction, or misplacement; the last of these events encompasses a spectrum of inadvertent or malicious events ranging from misfiling to theft of records. An organization may also be harmed, however, by misuse of, alteration of, or unauthorized access to vital records. In the case of computer records, these considerations have been widely discussed by public policy analysts and legal scholars, but they also apply to nonelectronic records. Protection against unauthorized or unintentional disclosure of records is maintained by various privacy statutes. Among U.S. laws, the Privacy Act of 1974 (5 U.S. Code 552A) is the best known example. Other federal statutes with privacy provisions for recorded information include the Fair Credit Billing Act (15 U.S. Code 1637); the Fair Credit Reporting Act (15 U.S. Code 1681); the Family Educational Rights and Privacy Act (20 U.S. Code 1232); the Right to Financial Privacy Act (12 U.S. Code 3401); the Financial Services Modernization Act (15 U.S. Code 6801), the Electronic Communications Privacy Act of 1986 (18 U.S. Code 1367), the Drivers Privacy Protection Act of 1994 (18 U.S. Code 2721), the National Information Infrastructure Protection Act of 1996 (18 U.S. Code 1030), and the Children's Online Privacy Protection Act of 1998 (15 U.S. Code 6501-6505). Similar privacy laws have been passed by various states. Medical records and adoption records, in particular, are subject to state-specific privacy legislation.

Other countries have privacy and data protection legislation that restricts access to recorded information. Examples include the Canadian Privacy Act and Canadian Personal Information Protection and Electronic Document Act, the various European data protection laws modeled on European Community Data Protection Directive 95/46/EC, the Australian Privacy Act, the New Zealand Privacy Act, the Israeli Protection of Privacy Law, the Japanese Act on Protection of Personal Information, the Philippines Data Privacy Act, the Singapore Personal Data Protection Act, and the Taiwan Personal Information Protection Act.

Whatever the threat, vital records programs provide formalized procedures to help an organization withstand and limit the impact of adverse events, enabling it to continue information-dependent business operations—though possibly at a reduced level—following a disaster. A vital records protection program includes the following components:

1. Formal endorsement of the program by a directive from an organization's senior management with responsibility and authority for protection of vital records assigned to the records management activity, to be coordinated, where appropriate, with related contingency planning activities.

2. Identification and enumeration of vital records.

3. Risk analysis to determine the extent to which specific vital records are threatened by hazards and to calculate exposures.

4. The selection of appropriate loss prevention and records protection methods.

5. Employee training, implementation, and compliance auditing.

These program components conform closely to the multistep process defined in ISO/IEC 27002, *Information Technology—Security Techniques—Code of Practice for Information Security Controls.* That standard emphasizes security measures to protect computer-based information assets, including databases and their associated software, but its principles and practices are broadly applicable to recorded information in all formats. The following sections explain and discuss vital records protection requirements and program work steps in greater detail.

Establishing the Program

Citizens have a reasonable expectation that government agencies will safeguard essential records.

In U.S. law, the determination of negligence is based on a straightforward principle: if precautionary measures cost less than the losses they are intended to prevent, then the precautionary measures should be taken.

Similar expectations apply to corporate shareholders, to a financial institution's customers, to an insurance company's policyholders, to a professional services firm's clients, to medical patients, to students, and to any other persons or organizations that are affected by the record-keeping practices of others. These expectations are based on the legal concept of "standard of care," which is the degree of caution that a reasonable, prudent person would exercise in a given circumstance to prevent injury to another. Failure to do so constitutes negligence.

Vital Records Protection as a Management Responsibility

While the standard of care is most often discussed in the context of medical malpractice, it is relevant for other professional disciplines, including records management. As discussed in Chapter 1, an organization's records are assets. In any organization, senior management has ultimate responsibility for protection of assets, including the formulation and implementation of risk management and business continuity plans. It follows, then, that senior management is ultimately responsible for the protection of records as assets. Effective leadership and decisive action by senior management can mitigate the impact of adverse events. If the destruction or misuse of vital records results in the interruption of critical business operations, senior management must accept responsibility for the ensuing financial losses or other consequences. This idea is forcefully stated in Corpus Juris Secundum, a comprehensive legal encyclopedia that presents the principles of U.S. law as derived from legislation and reported cases. According to Volume 19, Section 491, corporate officers "owe a duty to the corporation to be vigilant and to exercise ordinary or reasonable care and diligence and the utmost good faith and fidelity to conserve the corporate property; and, if a loss or depletion of assets results from their willful or negligent failure to perform their duties, or to a willful or fraudulent abuse of their trust, they are liable, provided such losses were the natural and necessary consequences of omission on their part."

Senior management's responsibility for protecting vital records is explicitly acknowledged or implied in laws and government regulations. For example:

- Within the U.S. federal government, 36 CFR 1236.12 makes agency heads responsible for protecting vital records, which are defined as records needed to meet operational responsibilities under emergency conditions or to protect the legal and financial rights of the government and those affected by government activities.

- As specified in the Federal Information Management Security Act (FISMA) of 2002 (44 U.S. Code 3541-3549), U.S. government agencies must develop information security protection "commensurate with the risk and magnitude of the harm resulting from unauthorized access, use, disclosure, disruption, modification, or destruction of (i) information collected or maintained by or on behalf of the agency and (ii) information systems used or operated by an agency or by a contractor of an agency or other organization on behalf of an agency." As defined by FISMA, information security must provide safeguards against improper destruction of information and ensure timely and reliable access to information.

- OMB Circular A-130, issued by the Office of Management and Budget, defines policies to secure information maintained by federal government agencies. While many of its provisions are concerned with privacy protection and prevention of unauthorized access to computer systems, Circular A-130 requires U.S. government agencies to ensure that "information is protected commensurate with the risk and magnitude of the harm that would result from the loss, misuse, or unauthorized access to or modification of such information."

- The Foreign Corrupt Practices Act (FCPA) of 1977 (15 U.S. Code 78dd-1) imposes significant fines and penalties for failure to preserve records and other information pertaining to certain accounting transactions and disposition of assets. Originally intended to prevent the destruction of records in order to conceal bribery or other crimes, FCPA's recordkeeping provisions apply to all domestic and foreign companies that list their securities on U.S. exchanges.

Violations of recordkeeping provisions can be enforced or prosecuted without regard to any violation of the FCPA's anti-bribery provisions. The FCPA was amended in 1998 by the International Anti-Bribery and Fair Competition Act, which implemented provisions of the Organization for Economic Cooperation and Development's Convention on Combating Bribery of Foreign Public Officials in International Business Transactions.

Vital Records Protection as Insurance

A vital records protection program is, in effect, an insurance policy for essential information. Like any insurance policy, vital records protection can be difficult to sell to decision-makers. Vital records protection is costly and makes no direct contribution to revenues, product development, or improvement of services. It provides no benefits unless and until a disaster occurs.

Many threats to vital records have a low probability of occurrence. Senior management may consequently ignore them in favor of more pressing business concerns. The purpose of insurance, of course, is to provide protection against the adverse impact of improbable events. Insurance protection is usually unavailable for probable events. Like all insurance policies, vital records protection must be justified by the intolerable consequences that follow an improbable but adverse event.

Senior management must be made to appreciate the potential for tangible and intangible damages associated with the loss, destruction, or misuse of vital records, however unlikely that loss, destruction, or misuse may seem. Examples of such damages include, but are by no means limited to:

- Loss of customers due to inability to fulfill orders and contracts, support products, or provide services.

- Loss of revenue or disruptions of cash flow due to lack of accounts receivable records and resulting inability to reconstruct amounts to be billed to specific customers or to process payments.

- Loss of opportunity because information needed for contracts, partnerships, joint ventures, or other business agreements is unavailable.

- Fines or other penalties for failure to provide records needed for government investigations.

- Penalties for late payment of payroll or other taxes for which records are unavailable.

- Increased assessments, plus penalties and interest, following tax audits due to inadequate documentation of business expenses, depreciation, and other deductions, allowances, and tax credits.

- Delayed compliance with governmental reporting requirements for public companies.

- Lawsuits due to inability to pay employees and document pension benefits to retirees.

- Lack of records needed for litigation or other legal proceedings.

- Inability to document insurance claims with resulting delay or reduction in settlements.

- Reduced employee productivity due to longer completion times for product development, design, testing, marketing, support, and other information-dependent business operations.

- High labor costs to reconstruct recorded information from alternative sources, assuming that reconstruction is possible.

- Tarnished reputation and loss of customer good will.

Further, an organization may be sued for damages resulting from its failure to protect essential operating records from accidental or willful loss or destruction. A hospital's failure to protect medical records, for example, could complicate treatment and damage a patient's health. A university's failure to protect academic transcripts could place its graduates at a disadvantage when competing for employment or seeking further education. An organization's failure to protect its personnel records could result in incorrect determination of retirement eligibility or calculation of pension benefits. Loss of revenue resulting from a public company's failure to protect essential business records could lower the value of the company's stock, provoking shareholder lawsuits. Destruction of birth, death, marriage, or property records maintained by state or local government agencies can have actionable consequences for individuals and organizations.

Legal actions related to an organization's failure to protect recorded information may have occurred but gone unreported because they were settled out of court. Arguments in favor of liability for failure to protect records are based on the previously discussed concept of standard of care. Arguments that vital records protection plans are not required by law or not pervasive in a given industry are no defense. The Hooper Doctrine, which dates from a 1928 incident in which a company was held liable for the sinking of barges because it did not equip its tugboats with radio receivers, established the principle that an organization can be held liable for failing to take reasonable precautionary measures, even where such measures may be widely ignored by others.[9]

An organization's senior management bears ultimate responsibility for safeguarding mission-critical information assets, but its involvement is typically and properly limited to delegating authority for the creation, implementation, and operation of a systematic vital records program. To formalize a protection program for vital records maintained by a business, government agency, or other organization, senior management should issue a written directive that:

- Acknowledges the value of recorded information as an organizational asset essential to mission-critical operations.

---

[9]   In re Eastern Transportation Co. (The T.J. Hooper), 60 F.2d 737 (2d Cir. 1932).

- Emphasizes the importance of protecting vital records as an integral component of the organization's security policies and contingency planning initiatives.
- Establishes a program for systematic, comprehensive, and economical protection of vital records.
- Identifies records management as the business function responsible for implementing the program.
- Solicits the cooperation of personnel in all program units where vital records are maintained.

As with other records management activities discussed in this book, the development and implementation of a successful vital records program depends upon the knowledge and active participation of program unit personnel who are familiar with the nature and use of recorded information in specific work environments. An advisory committee of program unit representatives can provide a formal structure for such participation. Such a committee can support the records management unit in planning, implementing, and operating a program to protect vital records.

Identifying Vital Records

To be considered vital, a record must be essential to a mission-critical activity, its unavailability must have a significant adverse impact on that activity, and its contents must not be fully duplicated in other records from which essential information can be recovered or reconstructed.

Protection of these essential information assets is an indispensable component of emergency preparedness, business continuity, and disaster recovery initiatives.

Vital records are typically identified by surveying individual program units to determine which mission-critical operations they perform and which records, if any, are essential to those operations. Some mission-critical operations are easily identified and widely encountered. All organizations, for example, must pay their employees, withhold payroll taxes for periodic submission to government agencies, account for pensions and other benefits, collect receivables, and maintain office buildings, factories, warehouses, or other facilities that they own or occupy. Other mission-critical operations are associated with particular types of organizations or industries. A municipal government, for example, must maintain public safety, assess and collect taxes, issue building permits, enforce building codes, and process zoning applications. A healthcare facility must provide patient care. A charitable institution or social services agency must process applications for aid, dispense payments, and otherwise assist those in need. A manufacturer must develop, test, make, sell, and support its products. A law or accounting firm must represent its clients. An insurance company must sell policies and process claims. A bank must process deposits, withdrawals, and other transactions; make loans and collect payments; and safeguard and transfer funds.

The following data elements should be included for each records series determined to be vital:

1. The series title

2. A brief description of the purpose, scope, and operational and physical characteristics of the records

3. The mission-critical operation(s) that the records support

4. The adverse consequences to the organization if the records were lost, destroyed, or otherwise unavailable

5. The name of the program unit responsible for protecting the vital records series

6. The method of protection to be implemented

With the assistance of knowledgeable persons in individual program units, records managers can identify essential information for successful performance of these and other mission-critical operations. The end product of this process is a descriptive list of vital records series.

When determining that a given records series is vital, a records manager must be able to clearly and convincingly identify the mission-critical operations that will be prevented by the loss, destruction, or other unavailability of the indicated records series. The inability to perform mission-critical operations is the ultimate test of a vital record.

Vital Records vs. Important Records

By definition, vital records are associated with mission-critical operations. Nonvital records may play a role in those operations as well. When asked to identify vital records, program unit personnel often include most, if not all, records that they routinely utilize, which is understandable. Employees place a high value on useful information and would not want to lose any of it, but the contents of a particular records series may be helpful yet not truly essential to mission-critical operations. Records managers must help program unit employees distinguish vital records from important ones.

Important records support a program unit's business operations and help it fulfill its assigned responsibilities. The loss of such records may cause delays or confusion that impede a program unit's work, but such loss will not bring mission-critical business operations to a halt. In the event of a disaster, vital records will have the highest priority for recovery, repair, or reconstruction. Important records will be repaired or reconstructed as time and resources permit.

Some important records are replaceable; their contents may be reconstructed from other records, although this process may involve considerable time, inconvenience, and expense. In some computer applications, for example, operations supported by important electronic records may be performed—though, admittedly, less quickly or efficiently—by reversion to manual procedures. Truly vital records, by contrast, are essential and irreplaceable. Their contents cannot be reconstructed from alternative sources, and the business operations they support cannot be performed without them.

As a complicating factor, a records manager must differentiate records that are vital to a company, government agency, or other organization as a whole from those that are vital to a specific program unit within that organization. Records series in the former category support operations that are truly mission-critical, while those in the latter group support valuable but not essential activities. In many organizations, certain program units perform useful functions that are not critical to the organization's mission. Loss or destruction of recorded information may cause a temporary or permanent disruption of business operations in such program units, but the organization's mission will not be imperiled. Such records cannot be considered vital, because the activities they support are not essential to the organization as a whole. As an example, a bank's community relations department may maintain records about local charitable institutions, housing preservation associations, cultural organizations, or other groups with which it interacts. If those records are lost, the department's work will be impeded or possibly discontinued, but the bank's mission-critical business operations, such as processing cash transactions or making loans, will not be curtailed.

Vital Records Survey

As noted in Chapter 2, a vital records survey can be integrated with inventories conducted for purposes of preparing retention schedules. That approach is recommended where practical. A combined records inventory/vital records survey will minimize duplication of effort. Vital record status can be discussed with knowledgeable employees and evaluated as each series is identified during the inventory. Vital records protection can also be coordinated with retention-oriented management actions such as offsite storage, scanning, or microfilming of specific records series.

Where a separate vital records survey must be conducted, the procedures are similar to those employed in a retention-oriented records inventory. Based on interviews with program unit personnel, a records manager prepares a tentative list of vital records for consideration and comment by interested parties, both within and outside the program unit that maintains the records. A series of meetings or other consultations will resolve concerns and disagreements, leading eventually to a final approved list of vital records. Several drafts may be required before a final version is obtained, however. A sample vital records index worksheet used for listing and describing vital records is shown in Figure 6-1.

As with retention scheduling, the records manager coordinates the meetings, directs the discussion, redrafts the vital records lists, and provides a broad perspective on information management issues that transcend the responsibilities and requirements of specific program units. Vital records surveys prepared for individual program units may be combined to form a master list of vital records maintained by an entire organization or by a specific administrative component such as a division or subsidiary. A sample vital records master list form is shown in Figure 6-2.

Although many records series are undeniably useful, vital record status should not be conferred indiscriminately. In most organizations, a small percentage of nonelectronic records are properly considered vital. A somewhat greater, but not necessarily large, percentage of an organization's electronic records may be essential to mission-critical operations. In companies, government agencies, and other organizations, the most important business operations have historically been priority

Figure 6-1

**Sample Vital
Records Index
Worksheet**

Vital Records Index		
	Organization Unit With Original	No.

Records Name

Schedule No.

Classification
☐ Vital
☐ Important

Physical Description

Distribution of Copies

Unit	No.	Location	Media

Purpose of Record

Impact if Destroyed

Suggested Method of Protection
☐ Duplication   ☐ Dispersal
☐ Extra Copies   ☐ Protected Storage
☐ Fast Copies   ☐ Remote Storage
☐ Microfilm   ☐ Reduction Ratio
(____ mm   ____ : ____)

Explain Method

Other Protection Details

Method of Recovery

Comments

Requested By	Date	☐ Approved ☐ Not Approved	Corp. Records Mgmt.	Date

(*Source:* Sample Forms for Archival & Records Management Programs, *published by ARMA International and the Society of American Archivists*)

Figure 6-2

Sample Vital Records Master List Form

Vital Records Master List		
Records Title	**Responsible Department**	**Method of Protection**

Example:

Records Title	**Responsible Department**	**Method of Protection**
Accounts Receivable Invoices	Accounts Receivable	COM – Original stored offsite
Corporate Documents	Legal	Microfilm – Original stored offsite
Inspection Reports	Quality Assurance	Dispersal
Journal Entries and Register	Controller	Microfilm – Original stored offsite
Payroll Reports	Payroll	Microfilm – Original stored offsite
Personnel File – Terminated	Human Resources	Microfilm one year after termination & shred paper
Standard Operating Procedures	Compliance	Dispersal

(*Source:* Sample Forms for Archival & Records Management Programs, *published by ARMA International and the Society of American Archivists*)

candidates for computerization. Certain mission-critical operations, such as accounts receivable and payroll processing, are encountered in a broad range of work environments. Information that supports those activities has been computerized for decades. Other widely computerized records are associated with mission-critical operations in specific types of organizations or industries. Examples include:

- Policy and claim files in an insurance company

- Customer account records in a bank or other financial institution

- Inventory control data in a retail organization

- Customer files and order fulfillment records in a catalog sales company

- Records related to development and testing of drugs in a pharmaceutical company

- Product specifications in a manufacturing company

- Patient records in a hospital

- Student transcripts in an academic institution

Lists of vital records prepared for individual program units may be combined to form a master list of vital records maintained by an entire organization or by a specific administrative entity such as a division, subsidiary, or field office.

If exactly the same information exists in multiple records series or multiple formats, one records series or format should be selected for vital records protection. If purposeful duplication and offsite storage will be used, it will typically prove faster and more economical to protect electronic records than paper or photographic records that contain the same information. Compared to their nonelectronic counterparts, electronic records are more compact and easier to duplicate.

Risk Analysis

The process of evaluating the exposure of vital records to specific risk is known as risk analysis.

The following discussion is based on the common business definition of operational risk as a danger of damage or loss to an organization resulting from inadequate internal processes, including inadequate information management practices, or from external events. This definition, which was originally developed for the banking industry, has since been widely applied to other types of organizations. The definition encompasses legal risks resulting from failure to comply with laws, regulations, or contractual obligations.

Operational risk is a function of three variables:

1. Threats or hazards that may harm an organization.

2. Vulnerabilities that render an organization susceptible to threats.

3. Consequences or negative impacts associated with specific threats.

The next section surveys threats and vulnerabilities that an organization must consider when developing a program to protect vital records. Adverse consequences associated with the loss of vital records were discussed earlier in this chapter.

Threats and Vulnerabilities

Various calamitous events can damage or destroy mission-critical information resources. For example:

- *Malicious destruction of recorded information may result from warfare or warfare-related activities such as terrorist attacks and civil insurrections.* Vital records are also subject to purposeful sabotage or seemingly aimless vandalism by current or former employees, contractors, intruders, or others. An organization's vulnerability to these threats depends on various factors, including the nature of the organization's business, the local socio-political environment, proximity to sites that are subject to terrorist attack or armed conflict, and security provisions in place.

- *Potentially catastrophic agents of accidental destruction or natural disasters.* Natural disasters may include violent weather, floods, earthquakes, landslides, and volcanic eruptions, as well as fires, explosions, building collapses, and other events may result from carelessness, negligence, or lack of knowledge about the consequences of specific actions. An organization's vulnerability to these disastrous events depends on geographical, geological, and meteorological factors that may be unpredictable and unpreventable. Vulnerability is obviously increased by close proximity to factories or laboratories that manufacture or utilize flammable materials, airports, military bases, power plants, refineries, storage facilities for oil or natural gas, and major highways and railway lines that are used for transport of hazardous materials. Vital records can also be damaged or destroyed by fire. Vulnerability is increased in rural locations that are remote from firefighting services. Water is a potential threat to records in many locations. Water damage can result from weather-related events, such as clogged sewers or other drainage problems during heavy rainfall, or from building-related problems such as leaking or broken pipes, malfunctioning HVAC equipment, open or leaking windows, and accidental activation of fire sprinklers.

- *More likely causes of accidental record destruction are less dramatic and more localized but no less catastrophic in their consequences for mission-critical operations.* Records in all formats can be damaged by careless handling. Paper documents, for example, are easily torn, damaged by spilled fluids, or otherwise mutilated. Microforms, x-rays, and other photographic films can be scratched. With very active records, the potential for such damage is intensified by use. In many work environments, for example, valuable engineering drawings subject to frequent retrieval are characteristically frayed and dog-eared. Paper records stored in basements or humid areas can be damaged by mold, mildew, insects, rodents, and other biological organisms. Information recorded onto magnetic media and certain optical disks can be erased by exposure to strong magnetic fields.

Careless work procedures, such as mounting tapes or disks without write protection, can expose vital records to accidental erasure by overwriting. Mislabeled media may be inadvertently marked for reuse, their contents being inappropriately replaced by new information. The implementation of systematic procedures for media storage, care, and handling can reduce an organization's vulnerability to these threats.

- *Records in all formats can be misplaced.* Like many business tasks, filing of paper records is subject to errors. Documents can be placed into wrong folders, and folders can be placed into wrong drawers or cabinets. Various sources claim misfile rates ranging from one-half of one percent to more than five percent for documents in office files. However, such claims are typically substantiated by anecdotal reports rather than scientific studies that present detailed statistical data about filing activity in specific work environments. Nonetheless, even a very low misfiling rate can pose significant problems in large filing installations. In a central filing area with 25 four-drawer cabinets totaling 200,000 to 250,000, for example, a misfiling rate of just one-half of one percent means that over 1,000 pages are filed incorrectly. Of course, even a single misfiled document can have serious consequences if it contains information needed for an important business purpose. In digital document management implementations that use computer-based indexing, data entry errors are the counterparts of misfiles. While effective methods, such as double-keying of information, are available for error detection and correction, they are not incorporated into all data entry operations.

- *Like any valued asset, recorded information can be stolen for financial gain or other motives by intelligence operatives or by disgruntled, compromised, or coerced employees.* Traditionally, espionage-related concerns have been most closely associated with government and military records, but they apply to other work environments as well. Commercial information brokers, for example, are interested in names, addresses, telephone numbers, social security numbers, and other information about an organization's employees, a company's customers, a hospital's patients, an academic institution's students, and a professional association's members. Trade secrets, product specifications, manufacturing methods, marketing plans, pricing strategies, and customer information are of great interest to a company's competitors. Burglars, confidence artists, and other criminals are interested in financial and asset information contained in donor and patron records maintained by charitable and cultural institutions. A museum's records, for example, indicate the owners and locations of valuable art works. A university development office's files contain addresses and possibly financial data about prospective benefactors. The use of compact, easily concealed storage media—such as high-density magnetic tapes, solid-state memory devices, optical disks, and microforms—facilitates theft, while the high capacity of such media increases the amount of information affected by a single incident of theft. In fact, the inherent and continuously improving compactness and high storage density of electronic storage media, when compared to paper documents, exposes more information to loss-related incidents. An organization's vulnerability to theft of vital records is further increased by the widespread storage of compact media in users' work areas where systematic handling procedures are seldom implemented and security provisions may be weak or absent.

- *Computer hardware and software failures can damage valuable information.* Head crashes or other hardware malfunctions, while much less common than in the past, can destroy valuable information recorded on hard drives. Improperly adjusted equipment, such as misaligned tape guides, can cause scratches or other media damage. An organization can minimize its vulnerability to these problems by keeping its computer hardware in good working order and replacing aging equipment, but hardware malfunctions cannot be eliminated completely. Software failures are more difficult to control. When a computer program locks up or terminates abnormally, information may not be properly recorded. Similarly, computer records may be accidentally deleted during database reorganizations or by utility programs that consolidate space on hard drives. Viruses and other malicious software are much publicized causes of corruption of computer-stored records. Software that detects malicious software is constantly improving, but it is not completely effective.

- *Tampering is a leading cause of corruption of recorded information, but not all record formats are equally vulnerable.* With microforms, tampering is difficult and detectable. The contents of individual microimages cannot be altered, and insertion or removal of images requires splicing of film, which is readily apparent. By contrast, information in paper documents can be added to, obliterated, or changed, although such modifications can often be detected by skilled forensic examiners. The potential for unauthorized tampering with electronic records has been widely discussed in publications and at professional meetings. Records stored on rewritable media—such as magnetic disks, magnetic tapes, and certain optical disks—are subject to modification by unauthorized persons in a manner that can prove very difficult to detect. Such unauthorized modification may involve the deletion, editing, or replacement of information. Password protection, encryption, and other countermeasures can reduce but not entirely eliminate an organization's vulnerability to such data tampering.

- *Whether accidental or intentional, improper disclosure of recorded information has been the subject of considerable discussion by a variety of interested parties, including records managers, computer specialists, lawyers, public policy analysts, and civil rights advocates.* While such discussions have typically warned against the unauthorized disclosure of sensitive personal information protected by privacy legislation, an organization's records may also store business plans, pricing information, trade secrets, or other proprietary technical, strategic, or financial information of interest to competitors. Certain government agencies store records with national security implications. Improper disclosure of vital records may result from espionage-related activities such as unauthorized access to computer systems, electronic eavesdropping, or bribery of employees who have access to desired information. Computer networks are vulnerable to intrusion by hackers. Accidental disclosure is also possible when computer output is routed to the wrong device in a local or wide area network, when correspondence of email messages are incorrectly addressed or distributed, or when incompletely erased computer media are distributed for reuse.

Qualitative Risk Assessment

Regardless of the specific threats involved, risk assessment may be based on intuitive, relatively informal qualitative approaches or more structured, formalized quantitative methods. Qualitative approaches rely principally on group discussions that identify and categorize risks. They are particularly useful for physical security problems and other vulnerabilities. A risk assessment team or committee, possibly led by a records manager, evaluates the dangers to specific vital records series from catastrophic events, theft, and other threats enumerated previously. The team typically produces a prioritized list of vital records judged to be at risk and for which protective measures are recommended.

A qualitative risk assessment is usually based on a physical survey of locations where vital records are stored, combined with an examination of reference activity and patterns that may increase vulnerability and a review of security procedures already in place. Geophysical and political factors, such as the likelihood of destructive weather or the possibility of warfare or civil unrest, are also considered. In the case of paper or photographic records stored in centralized or decentralized filing areas or electronic records stored on hard drives in centralized or decentralized computing installations, the team may examine the following factors:

- Access card systems, supervised entrances, and other physical security arrangements in areas where vital records are stored and used

- The number and types of employees who have access to those areas

- Network security arrangements and password controls for vital electronic records

- Availability of fire control apparatus and proximity to fire department services

- Implementation of backup procedures and offsite storage arrangements for recorded information

- Frequency of hardware or software malfunctions that can damage electronic records

- Proximity of records storage and work areas to flammable materials, leaky pipes, or other hazards

- History of destructive weather or other adverse conditions in locations where vital records are stored and used

A qualitative risk assessment does not estimate the statistical probabilities associated with destructive events or the financial impact of the resulting losses. The intent is to develop an understanding of the interplay of threats, vulnerabilities, and consequences as they relate to specific vital records and the mission-critical

Threats to vital records may be categorized as unlikely, likely, or very likely to occur, while vulnerabilities may be categorized as limited, acceptable, or high. The adverse impact associated with a particular combination of threat and consequences may be similarly described as low (little or no disruption of mission-critical activities), medium (some disruption but mission-critical activities will continue, although possibly at a lower level of effectiveness), or high (mission-critical activities will terminate or be severely disrupted).

activities that they support. Typically, the likelihood of a given threat and the extent of an organization's vulnerability are evaluated in general terms, although the nature and frequency of adverse historical events, such as destructive weather, power outages, network security breaches, infiltration of computer systems by malicious software, or reported theft of records, are considered.

In the project team's report, evaluative designations should be accompanied by definitions or clarifying narrative. The greatest concern is for vital records with high vulnerability to threats that have a high likelihood of occurrence with sudden, unpredictable onset—laboratory notebooks or other vital research information stored in areas where flammable materials are used in scientific experiments, for example, or confidential product specifications and pricing information stored on desktop computers in unsecured areas.

Quantitative Risk Assessment

Quantitative risk assessment is based on concepts and methods that were originally developed for product safety analysis and subsequently adapted for computer security applications. Like its qualitative counterpart, quantitative risk assessment relies on site visits, discussions, and other systems analysis methods to identify vulnerabilities, but it uses numeric calculations to measure the likelihood and impact of losses associated with specific vital records series. The calculations are expressed as dollar amounts, which can be related to the cost of proposed protection methods. If the calculated cost of a given loss exceeds the cost of protective measures, those measures should be implemented. As an additional advantage, quantitative risk assessments provide a useful framework for comparing exposures for different vital records series and prioritizing them for protection.

While various quantitative assessment techniques have been proposed by risk analysts and others, all are based on the following general formula:

$$R = P \times C$$

where:

$R =$ the risk, sometimes called the *Annualized Loss Expectancy (ALE)*, associated with the loss of a specific vital records series due to a catastrophic event or other threat;

$P =$ the probability that such a threat will occur in any given year; and

$C =$ the cost of the loss if the threat occurs.

This formula measures risk as the probable annual dollar loss associated with a specific vital electronic records series. The total annual expected loss to an organization is the sum of the annualized losses calculated for each vital electronic records series.

Quantitative risk assessment begins with the determination of probabilities associated with adverse events and the calculation of annualized loss multipliers based on those probabilities. Information systems specialists, program unit personnel, or others familiar with a given electronic records series are asked to estimate the likelihood of occurrence for specific threats. Whenever possible, their estimates should be based on the historical incidence of adverse events. Reliable probability estimates are easiest and most conveniently obtained for events such as burglaries, fires, power outages, equipment malfunctions, software failures, network security breaches, and virus attacks for which security reports, maintenance statistics, or other documentation exists. Statistical data about potentially destructive weather events, such as hurricanes or floods, is available in books, scholarly journals, newspapers, and other reference sources, including a rapidly increasing number of websites. At its website, for example, the Federal Emergency Management Agency (FEMA) provides online access to flood hazard maps for any U.S. location. Various websites provide information about the frequency of hurricanes, tornadoes, earthquakes, landslides, volcanic eruptions, and tsunamis worldwide. Similarly, accident data is available for specific airports.

In the absence of written evidence or experience, probability estimates must be based on informed speculation by persons familiar with the broad information management environment within which a given vital records series is maintained and used. In this respect, quantitative risk analysis resembles the qualitative approach. Often, the records manager must ask a series of probing questions, followed by lengthy discussion, to obtain usable probability estimates. As an example, the records manager may ask a file room supervisor whether lost documents are likely to be reported once a year. If the answer is yes, the records manager should ask whether such an event is likely to occur once every half year, once a quarter, once a month, and so on. This procedure can be repeated until a satisfactorily specific response is obtained.

Once probabilities are estimated, annual loss multipliers can be calculated in any of several ways. Using one method, a calamitous threat to vital records with a given probability of occurrence is assigned a probability value of 1. Other threats are assigned higher or lower values, based on their relative probability of occurrence. As an example, a threat estimated to occur once a year is assigned a probability value of 1, which serves as a baseline for other probability estimates. An event estimated to occur once every three months (four times a year) is assigned a probability value of 4, while an event with an estimated frequency of once every four years is assigned the probability value of 0.25.

Applying the risk assessment formula, the probability value is multiplied by the estimated cost of the loss if the event occurs. Factors that might be considered when determining costs associated with the loss of vital records include, but are by no means limited to, the following:

- The cost of file reconstruction, assuming that source documents or other input materials remain available.

- The value of canceled customer orders, unbillable accounts, or other losses resulting from the inability to perform specific business operations because needed electronic records are unavailable.

- Labor costs associated with reversion to manual operations, assuming that such reversion is possible.

- The cost of defending against or otherwise settling legal actions associated with the loss of vital records.

Quantitative risk assessment is an aid to judgment not a substitute for it. The risk assessment formula presented previously is an analytical tool that can help records managers clarify their thinking and define protection priorities for vital electronic records. As an example, assume that a hospital administrator, based on previous experience, estimates that one patient folder essential to mission-critical medical care is lost each year through misfiling, a clinician's failure to return the folder to the medical records area following treatment, or for some other reason. A probability (P) of 1 is assigned to the risk that a patient folder will be lost in this manner. If the estimated cost (C) is $1,500 to reconstruct medical records contained in the lost folder by obtaining copies of records from physicians' offices, re-examining the patient, repeating medical tests, or other means, the risk (annualized loss expectancy) is 1 times $1,500.

Again based on experience, the hospital administrator estimates one chance in 10 years that as many as 50 patient folders will be destroyed by flood, fire, or destructive weather. A probability (P) of 0.1 is assigned to that risk, indicating that it is one-tenth as likely to occur as the loss of one patient folder a year for reasons previously described, but the risk affects many more folders. If the cost (C) to reconstruct lost patient records is $1,500 per folder, the damage will total $75,000. The risk (annualized loss expectancy) is 0.1 times $150,000, or $7,500.

These calculations indicate that destruction of patient records by a catastrophic event, while having a much lower probability of occurrence, poses a more significant risk than loss of patient records by misfiling or other reasons. Consequently, greater attention should be given to protecting records against fire, flood, or destructive weather than to implementing procedures that will prevent misfiling of patient folders, but a lower probability estimate for catastrophic events will support a different conclusion. If the hospital administrator estimates one chance in 100 years that a catastrophic event will destroy 50 patient folders at a cost of $75,000, the probability assigned to that risk will be 0.01 and the annualized loss expectance will be 0.01 times $75,000, or $750. Based on these assumptions, misfiling poses a more significant risk than destruction of patient records by a catastrophic event.

Risk Management

Risk management consists of coordinated policies, plans, processes, resources, and activities that direct and control the risks to which an organization is exposed.

As defined in ISO/Guide 73, *Risk Management—Vocabulary*, risk management is a component of an organization's overall strategic and operational policies and practices. **Risk analysis** is the process of identifying and evaluating risks. As an important part of vital records planning, records managers must identify and evaluate the risks to which specific records series are subject. This process provides the basis for protection planning and other records management decisions. Standards and published guidelines that deal with risk management and analysis include ISO 31000, *Risk Management—Principles and Guidelines*; ISO/TR 31004, *Risk Management—Guidance for the Implementation of ISO 31000*; IEC 31010, *Risk Management—Risk Assessment Techniques*; ISO/TR 18128, *Information and Documentation—Risk Assessment for Records Processes and Systems*; ISO/IEC 27005, *Information Technology—Security Techniques—Information Security Risk Management*; *A Risk Management Standard*, issued by the European Federation of Risk Management Associations; and *Enterprise Risk Management—Integrated Framework*, issued by the Committee of Sponsoring Organizations (COSO).

Risk management is an important component of any vital records program. Where vital records protection is part of a broader business continuity and disaster recovery plan, risk control measures may also safeguard facilities, computer hardware and software, laboratory equipment, and other resources. Regardless of scope, risk management encompasses preventive and protective measures.

Some recorded information may be reconstructable in the event of a disaster, but the high cost of such reconstruction makes it a last-resort component of risk management. Prevention is the first line of defense against risk. Preventive measures are designed to minimize the likelihood of damage to vital records from one or more of the threats enumerated in the preceding discussion. Preventive measures apply to both working copies and security copies of vital records. By contrast, protective measures are typically limited to security copies, sometimes described as *backup copies*, of vital records. Protective measures permit the reconstruction of essential information and the restoration of business operations if vital records are destroyed, damaged, or lost.

Whether prevention or protection is involved, risk management begins with heightened security awareness formalized in organizational policy and procedures, which must be communicated to every employee who works with vital records. Security of recorded information is the responsibility of every employee. A directive from senior management to line managers or other key personnel in individual program units should acknowledge the mission-critical importance of vital records and emphasize the need to safeguard them. Risk management guidelines should be conspicuously posted in areas where vital records are stored or used. One person in each program unit should be assigned specific responsibility for the implementation of risk management guidelines; ideally, that person will also serve as the program unit's records management liaison. Program unit managers should be instructed to review risk management policies and procedures at staff meetings. The records manager should be available as a resource person to address such meetings and clarify risk management policies and procedures. To publicize the vital records initiative, the records manager can prepare articles on vital records and the importance of risk management for employee newsletters, intranet web pages, or other in-house publications.

Preventive Measures

Risk prevention emphasizes precautionary measures that address the physical environment where vital records are stored and used. To the greatest extent possible, storage facilities for vital records should be located in areas where floods and destructive weather are unlikely. Locations near chemical factories, utility plants, airport landing patterns, and other potential hazards should also be avoided. Vital records repositories should be situated away from high traffic locations, preferably in buildings or portions of buildings without windows. Often, records managers have little control over the geographic locations where working copies of vital records are maintained, but they can specify storage locations for backup copies. Storage areas for vital records must be properly constructed and include appropriate smoke detection and fire extinguishing equipment, as discussed in Chapter 4.

Certain preventive risk control measures promote the physical security of vital records against malicious destruction or unauthorized access:

- *One storage location is easier to secure than many.* In this respect, centralized records repositories are preferable to decentralized ones. Where vital records are maintained in user areas, security is difficult to enforce and easily compromised. Records storage areas should be situated away from high traffic locations, preferably in rooms without windows.

- *Vital records should be stored in areas that are structurally sound and have no history of flooding, leakage, or other water-related problems.* Storage areas must have adequate floor drainage. Records should not be stored under or near windows or water pipes. Records storage areas should be checked for flooding during and immediately after periods of heavy or continuous rainfall.

- *Fire alarms and fire extinguishers should be clearly marked on floor plans for areas where vital records are stored.* At least one portable fire extinguisher with a minimum rating of A4 as specified in UL711, *Rating and Fire Testing of Fire Extinguishers*, should be readily accessible in the records storage area. Vital records should not be stored near kitchens, boiler rooms, rooms that contain electrical equipment, areas that house cleaning fluids or other flammable materials, or other parts of a building that may represent a fire hazard.

- *Areas that store vital records should be cleaned regularly and fumigated for pest control where indicated.*

- *Access to vital records storage areas should be limited to a single supervised entrance.* Other doors should be configured as emergency exits with strike bars and audible alarms. Records storage areas should be subject to regular, but not necessarily constant, observation and periodic inspection for water on the floor, leaking pipes, and dampness. Records storage areas should be locked when unattended.

- *Access to vital records storage areas should be restricted to authorized persons who have specific business reasons for entering such areas.* Badges should identify authorized individuals. Employees should be instructed to challenge and report suspect persons who enter vital records repositories.

- *All containers should be examined.* This examination may occur upon entry into or removal from a vital records repository.

- *Janitorial services must not be permitted in the vital records repository alone.* Authorized employees must be in the vital records repository when janitorial services are working in the area.

- *Areas where vital records are stored should never be included in building tours to impress visitors.*

- *Vital records should be stored in secure locations.* They should be filed in locked drawers, cabinets, or other metal containers until needed and returned to their filing locations immediately after use.

- *A "clean desk" policy is recommended.* Vital records must never be left unattended on work surfaces, and all vital records must be put away at the end of the workday.

- *Confidential personal data, trade secrets, or other sensitive information should not be stored in mobile computing devices, which are easily stolen.* If this situation is unavoidable, the devices must never be left unattended.

- *Circulation control records should be kept for every medium removed from a vital records storage location.* For each transaction, the circulation control records should identify the records removed, the authorized borrower, the time and date that the records were removed, the location to which the records were taken, and the time and date when the records are to be returned.

- *Vital electronic records stored on networked computers can be accessed, and possibly damaged, by remote users.* Physical security measures must consequently be supplemented by safeguards against electronic intrusion.

- *Access to vital electronic records and their associated software should be controlled.* Passwords or personal identification numbers should be used to prevent unauthorized access.

- *Access to computer workstations must be restricted to authorized employees, and such workstations should be turned off—and locked, if possible—when not in use.* They should never be left unattended while operational. System software should automatically terminate a computer session after a predetermined period of inactivity.

- *Mission-critical applications and vital electronic records should be isolated from publicly accessible computer resources.* For organizations connected to the Internet, this practice is especially important.

Protective Measures

Protective measures permit the recovery or reconstruction of vital records to support the resumption of mission-critical operations following a disaster. Such measures have historically relied on specially designed storage enclosures and purposeful duplication of vital records for offsite storage. These measures are most effective when combined.

UL 687, *Standard for Burglary-Resistant Safes*, issued by Underwriters' Laboratories, rates file cabinets, safes, and other containers for their resistance to break-in by prying, drilling, chiseling, hammering, sawing, or other means. A container with a TL-30 rating, for example, will resist attack against the door and front face by high-speed drills, saws, pry bars, grinders, or other mechanical or electrical penetrating tools for 30 minutes. A container with a TRTL-30 or TRTL-60 rating will resist attack against the door and front face by cutting or welding torches and mechanical or electrical tools for 30 or 60 minutes, respectively. A container with a TXTL-60 rating will resist attack against the door and front face by torch, mechanical or electrical tools, and explosives for 60 minutes. Other Underwriters' Laboratories ratings measure resistance to an attack against all surfaces. As discussed in Chapter 4, Underwriters' Laboratories also rates insulated storage containers, which offer some protection against fire by limiting the records' exposure to potentially destructive heat for a defined time period.

Specially designed filing cabinets, vaults, and other storage enclosures provide onsite protection of vital records against certain threats previously enumerated. Vital records can be protected against theft, for example, by storing them in locked file cabinets, safes, or other containers, although simple key locks offer little resistance to a skilled intruder. Containers with high security key locks or combination locks are preferable.

While tamperproof and fire-resistant storage containers can prove useful in certain situations, the most effective approach to continuity of information-dependent business operations involves the purposeful preparation of backup copies for storage at a secure offsite location. Scanning and microfilming are usually the best practices for production of backup copies of vital paper records. Compared to full-size photocopies, digital images and microfilm copies are usually faster and cheaper to produce. They also require less storage space at the offsite location, which is an important consideration where backup copies will be housed in a commercial records center that charges by the amount of space consumed. A cubic-foot container can store over ninety 215-foot rolls of 16mm microfilm, which can contain almost half a million letter-size pages reduced 24x. By contrast, a cubic-foot container can store about 1,200 letter-size photocopies. When records are scanned or microfilmed for retention purposes, additional backup copies can be produced at a small incremental cost.

The creation of backup copies of essential electronic records at predetermined intervals is routine operating procedure in most centralized computer installations, but back-up operations may be performed sporadically, if at all, in desktop computer installations where procedures are typically less routinized and users may be unaware of the need for backup copies. For effective vital records protection, backup responsibilities must be clearly delineated. Backup schedules must be established and rigidly enforced.

Offsite storage repositories for vital records may be established and operated by a business, government agency, or other organization on its own behalf. Alternatively, a commercial records center or data vault may be utilized for offsite storage of physical records of offline electronic storage media. In either case, the offsite facility must be secure. Some vital records repositories are located underground in salt, limestone, or iron mines. The best facilities combine natural restrictions on accessibility with armed guards and electronic surveillance apparatus for stringent perimeter security.

The typical vital records repository has suitable storage facilities for paper documents, microforms, and electronic media, although some data vaults exclude paper records to minimize the danger of fire. Environmental specifications appropriate to the type of media being stored and the retention period for recorded information must be observed. Backup electrical generators should be available to maintain environmental controls in the event of power outages.

Backup copies of vital records must be stored at a sufficient distance from the working copies as to be unaffected by the same natural disasters or destructive events. The storage facility must be close enough, however, for convenient delivery of vital records as well as timely retrieval of backup copies to support disaster recovery. For pickup and delivery of records, some in-house and commercial storage facilities offer courier services equipped with environmentally controlled trucks or vans. Some facilities also support electronic vaulting in which backup copies of vital electronic records are transmitted to offsite storage over high-speed telecommunications facilities.

Implementation and Compliance

Implementation of preventive and protective measures for designated vital records series is typically the responsibility of the records management coordinator or another designated employee in the program unit that maintains the records. Periodic audits should be performed to confirm compliance. Such audits may be conducted by records management staff or delegated to another organizational unit, such as an internal audit department, that has other compliance-oriented responsibilities. In such cases, auditing for vital records compliance can be coordinated with financial or other auditing activities, thereby simplifying the scheduling of audits as well as saving both time and labor. Internal auditors can report the results of vital records compliance audits to the records manager for follow-up and corrective action where indicated. To gain the attention of top management, the internal audit reports should also be distributed to organizational officials who receive reports of important financial audits.

In the event of a disaster that damages or destroys vital records, the responsible program unit will determine which records should be recovered or reconstructed and in what sequence. Mission-critical information will be recovered from backup copies where such copies are available. The records management coordinator or another designated program unit employee will identify the locations of backup copies and arrange for additional working copies to be made. The records management coordinator will evaluate the need to repair or reconstruct records for which no backup copy exists. Factors to be considered should include the value of the records for mission-critical operations and their remaining retention periods. As warranted, document restoration companies, fumigation services, or other external suppliers should be contacted to determine options and costs for repair or reconstruction of damaged records.

When disaster-related issues have been resolved to the greatest extent possible, the records management coordinator should prepare an incident report that summarizes the disaster, the types and quantity of records involved, the extent of damage to the records, and the effectiveness of disaster recovery initiatives. The report should also identify steps to be taken to prevent or mitigate the effect of a future disaster.

Summary of Major Points

☑ Vital records contain information that is essential to an organization's mission-critical operations. If vital records are lost, damaged, destroyed, or otherwise rendered unavailable or unusable, mission-critical operations will be curtailed or discontinued, with a resulting adverse impact on the organization.

☑ For many organizations, information contained in vital records is their most important asset. Often, the loss of recorded information can have more devastating consequences for continuation of an organization's operations than the loss of physical plant or inventory, which may be replaceable and insured.

☑ A vital records program is a set of policies and procedures for the systematic, comprehensive, and economical control of adverse consequences attributable to the loss of mission-critical information. A vital records program will help an organization withstand and limit the impact of adverse events, enabling it to continue information-dependent business operations—though possibly at a reduced level—following a disaster.

☑ When determining that a given records series is vital, a records manager must be able to clearly and convincingly state which mission-critical operations will be impeded by the loss, destruction, or other unavailability of the indicated records series. In most organizations, a small percentage of nonelectronic records are properly considered vital. A somewhat greater, but not necessarily large, percentage of an organization's electronic records may be essential to mission-critical operations.

☑ A vital records survey can be integrated with inventories conducted for purposes of preparing retention schedules. That approach will minimize duplication of effort. Vital records status can be discussed with knowledgeable employees and evaluated as each series is identified during the inventory. Vital records protection can also be coordinated with retention-oriented management actions such as offsite storage or microfilming of specific records series.

☑ Protection of essential information against malicious or accidental destruction is a well-established component of vital records planning. Malicious destruction of recorded information may result from warfare or warfare-related activities such as terrorist attacks, civil insurrections, purposeful sabotage, or seemingly aimless vandalism. Potentially catastrophic agents of accidental destruction include natural disasters and human-induced accidents such as fire or explosions that result from carelessness, negligence, or lack of knowledge about the consequences of specific actions. More likely causes of accidental records destruction are less dramatic and more localized but no less catastrophic in their consequences for mission-critical operations. Records in all formats, for example, can be damaged by careless handling.

☑ Risk assessment may be based on intuitive, relatively informal qualitative approaches or on more structured or formalized quantitative methods. Qualitative risk assessment is particularly useful for identifying and categorizing physical security problems and other vulnerabilities. A risk assessment team or committee, preferably led by a records manager, identifies and evaluates the dangers to specific vital records series. Quantitative risk assessment relies on site visits, discussions, and other systems analysis methodologies to identify risks, but it uses numeric calculations to estimate the likelihood and impact of losses associated with specific vital records series. The losses are expressed as dollar amounts, which can be related to the cost of proposed protection methods.

☑ The most effective approach to vital records protection involves the purposeful preparation of backup copies for storage at a secure offsite location. Vital paper records can be scanned or microfilmed for that purpose. The production of backup copies of essential electronic records at predetermined intervals is routine operating procedure in most centralized computer installations.

☑ The implementation of preventive and protective measures for designated records series will usually be the responsibility of the program unit that maintains the record. Periodic audits should be performed to confirm compliance.

Chapter 7

Managing Active Paper Records

Systematic management of inactive records emphasizes timely destruction of obsolete records and cost-effective storage of recorded information that must be retained for specific periods of time. Systematic management of vital records emphasizes protection and recoverability of mission-critical information assets. Systematic management of active records is principally concerned with the organization of recorded information for convenient, timely retrieval when needed. By definition, active records are likely to be consulted until the matters to which they pertain are resolved.

Active records can be organized for retrieval in two ways: by filing them or by indexing them. Filing identifies related records—those records that deal with the same person, case, project, or other matter, for example—and places them in close physical proximity to one another in a folder or other enclosure. Related folders are arranged in a predetermined sequence within a drawer, filing cabinet, or other containers. Indexing, by contrast, uses descriptive words or phrases to define relationships among specific records without regard to their physical arrangement. While filing concepts were originally developed for paper-based recordkeeping, the subject of this chapter, they are also applicable to photographic records, such as film negatives and microforms, and to digital documents, which are discussed in Chapter 8. Computer operating systems use filing models and terminology to organize electronic records. Word processing files, e-mail messages, spreadsheets, presentation aids, digital images, computer-aided design files, and other digital documents are commonly grouped in electronic folders, which are labeled to identify the matters to which they relate. Directories and subdirectories, which contain electronic folders, are the computer-based counterparts of filing cabinets.

As the name implies, a **filing system** provides a coherent, methodical approach to the organization of records in a specific application or situation. To be truly systematic, a filing system for paper records must encompass all components related to the organization of records. Those components include, but are not necessarily limited to:

- Written policies, procedures, manuals, and other documentation that specifies how filing is to be performed for a particular collection of documents.

- Administrative and supervisory personnel involved in filing activities.
- Filing equipment, including cabinets, shelving units, and accessories.
- Folders, labels, and other filing supplies.
- Office space or other facilities where filing activities are performed or where filed documents are stored.

Among their responsibilities, records managers plan, implement, advise about, and, in some cases, operate or supervise filing installations for specific document collections. Such initiatives involve, but are not necessarily limited to, preparing policies and procedures that define a filing system's purpose, scope, and operating characteristics; developing filing arrangements and rules that facilitate the retrieval of documents when needed; selecting or advising about the selection of appropriate filing equipment and supplies; training employees who will do filing; and managing or monitoring file room operations.

This chapter examines records management principles and practices that guide the development and implementation of filing systems for paper records. The chapter begins with a discussion of centralized filing, followed by surveys of file arrangements, equipment, and supplies. The chapter is written from an analytical and managerial rather than operational and administrative perspective. The discussion emphasizes essential concepts; it does not explain how to file or provide filing practice. The section on alphabetic filing, for example, examines important characteristics and considerations that affect the implementation and performance of alphabetic arrangements. It does not provide a detailed explanation of alphabetic filing rules, which are well covered in other publications.

The principles and methods discussed in this chapter are well established. Most of them have been widely implemented for more than half a century. They are no longer subject to procedural refinements or technological innovation. Rather than improving their paper-based filing installations, many organizations want to replace them with digital document management systems. As previously noted, however, those systems often utilize filing concepts that were developed for paper records. Filing principles and methods are not obsolete. They are likely to remain important aspects of records management practice.

Central Files

In many companies, government agencies, and other organizations, documents associated with specific business processes, operations, or activities are consolidated for filing in a single location where authorized persons can access them—a **central file**.

Widely encountered examples include student transcripts in an academic institution; patient records in a hospital or medical clinic; deeds and mortgages in a county clerk's office; client files in a social services agency; incident reports in a police department; claims processing records in an insurance company;

litigation files in a law firm; customer account records in a financial services company; laboratory notebooks in a pharmaceutical company; and project-related drawings in a construction company. Such consolidated collections of records are often characterized as central files, but that phrase encompasses a variety of filing configurations. Recordkeeping can be centralized at any level in an organization; a central file may serve an entire enterprise, one or more divisions or departments, a workgroup or project team, or any subset or combination thereof. Central filing concepts are applicable to paper, photographic, and electronic records. In computer installations, word processing documents, spreadsheets, or other digital documents may be centralized on network file servers at the workgroup, departmental, or enterprise level.

Information sharing is a major motive for centralized filing. Where recorded information must be available to more than one worker, consolidated document repositories are usually preferable to decentralized filing arrangements in which records relating to a particular business process, operation, or activity are scattered in multiple locations. Often such decentralized files are kept in the work areas of individual employees. In a law firm, for example, members of a litigation team may each keep their own records relating to those aspects of a case for which they are responsible. Each team member possesses a subset of case information. Individual files may be organized differently, even idiosyncratically. If a team member is absent from work, reassigned, or otherwise unavailable, locating documents needed by others can be difficult or impossible. By contrast, a well-organized central file of case documents can address this problem by providing a single, authoritative, presumably complete repository of recorded information about all aspects of a case. Such a repository increases the likelihood that litigation team members will have full access to information about a case's purpose, scope, and activities, including accomplishments and problems outside their areas of direct responsibility. The repository might be centralized in the litigation team's work area or combined with other case files at the department, division, or enterprise level.

Other advantages of centralized filing are based on a straightforward principle: *Recorded information is easier to manage in one location than in many locations.* In particular:

1. **Less floor space, equipment, and supplies needed.** Centralized file rooms can be configured for economical high-density storage. When compared to decentralized filing of an equivalent quantity of records in cabinets scattered throughout office areas, consolidated files typically require less floor space, equipment, and supplies.

2. **Filing is the top priority.** Centralized filing permits more efficient and effective use of administrative support personnel when compared to decentralized arrangements. Where files are scattered throughout an organization, office workers may perform filing in addition to word processing, answering the telephone, making photocopies, arranging meetings, and other tasks, which have high visibility and often must be performed immediately. In such situations, filing

may be treated as a low-priority activity that can be deferred until other work is completed. In a centralized installation, by contrast, filing is the top priority. Central file room employees have narrowly focused duties, which simplifies training, facilitates work scheduling, encourages accuracy and reliability as experience is gained with a particular collection of records, promotes accountability, and increases the likelihood that filing tasks will be completed in a timely manner.

3. **Consistent recordkeeping procedures.** Keeping records in a single location and servicing them exclusively by designated employees, centralized filing facilitates the implementation of uniform file arrangements and consistent recordkeeping procedures, including timely purging of obsolete records with elapsed retention periods.

4. **Minimal duplicate recordkeeping.** By making a single, complete repository of recorded information available to authorized persons, a central file can minimize duplicate recordkeeping.

5. **Better security.** Compared to decentralized filing arrangements, central files provide better security for records with confidential content such as personally-identifiable information, protected health information, trade secrets business plans, and financial information about an organization, its customers, and business associates. Central file rooms are typically supervised during normal business hours. They can be equipped with locks, alarms, and other anti-intrusion mechanisms to restrict access at other times. Central file room employees can log all retrieval requests, ensure that access to specific records is limited to authorized persons, and keep track of records removed from the file room.

The advantages of centralized filing generally outweigh the most widely cited disadvantage: a central file area may not be located in convenient proximity to all authorized users. As a result, employees often withhold records that they consult frequently, thereby compromising the completeness of a central file. To address this problem, employees may be allowed to keep convenience copies of records submitted to a central file. Limiting the quantity of such convenience copies is usually advisable, and they should be discarded when no longer needed. The problem of proximity does not apply to centralized filing of electronic records. The digital document management systems discussed in Chapter 8 employ central filing concepts, but they nullify proximity concerns by providing online access to records when needed.

To realize these advantages, a central file must have a written policy that defines its purpose and scope. The policy must identify the operations or activities that the central file will serve, the types of records to be included in the central file, and, where applicable, the types of records that are excluded. The policy must be supported by clear written procedures that specify who is responsible for submitting records to the central file, and when and how they are to be submitted. Generally, employees who create or receive documents or other records that come within the scope of a central file should be instructed to submit one copy of such records as soon as possible after the records are created or received. To ensure file completeness, all relevant records must be submitted. Where doubt exists about the appropriateness of submitting a specific record to the central file, it should be sent. The central file staff will reject inappropriate records and return them to the submitter.

File Arrangements

A file arrangement places logically related records in a predetermined sequence for retrieval when needed.

Records may be arranged by the name of a person or organization to which they pertain; by a numeric identifier for a case, project, or transaction; by the date that a record was created; by a code that represents the way that a name is pronounced; by a geographical unit; or by subject categories. Requirements for filing arrangements are discussed in ARMA Guideline, *Establishing Alphabetic, Numeric, and Subject Filing Systems.* The following sections describe these file arrangements, emphasizing their most important characteristics and the type of records management applications and retrieval requirements for which they are best suited.

Alphabetic Filing

An often-cited records management aphorism advises filing system planners to select an arrangement that corresponds to the way in which records are requested. While that advice is necessarily oversimplified, it frequently applies to alphabetic arrangements, which are well suited to records that are requested by the name of a person or organization. Examples include personnel files, student records, patient records, and customer files. Alphabetic arrangements are also widely, but less successfully, used for topical subject files. As discussed later in this chapter, hierarchical subject arrangements are often preferable for that purpose.

Basic alphabetic filing concepts are straightforward and familiar. Letters are ranked in alphabetic sequence from A to Z. File arrangement is determined by the spelling of filing units, which are words, phrases, abbreviations, acronyms, or other information elements that identify a document for filing purposes. Commonly encountered examples of filing units for alphabetic arrangements include personal names; the names of companies, government agencies, or other organizations; geographic place names; and topical headings that represent the contents of folders, documents, index cards, microfiche, or other objects. In most cases, the filing unit is contained within or inscribed upon the object to be filed. Tabs of file folders, for example, are labeled with names or other words that identify the filing unit for documents contained therein. Alphabetization is performed word by word and, within words, letter by letter. If the first words on two folder tabs are identical, alphabetization is based on the second words; if the second words are identical, alphabetization is based on the third words; and so on. If the first letters of two words are identical, alphabetization is based on the second letter; if the second letters are identical, alphabetization is based on the third letter; and so on. An example of alphabetic filing is shown in Figure 7-1.

Some alphabetic filing practices are so widely observed that they require little comment. Personal names, for example, are customarily inverted so that the initial

Figure 7-1

Alphabetic Filing

(Courtesy: Smead)

filing unit is the surname. Rules are necessary to ensure consistent filing practices and facilitate retrieval in special situations. Common examples include but are not limited to:

- Hyphenated surnames such as "David Lloyd-George"
- Surnames that begin with a prefix, such as "Van" or "Von," followed by a space
- Personal names preceded by titles such as "Dr." or "Senator"
- Personal names with suffixes—such as "Jr.," "CPA," or "M.D."—that represent seniority or professional designations
- Acronyms and abbreviations, including abbreviated personal names such as "Wm." or "Jos."
- Company names that begin with "The"
- Government names that begin with common expressions such as "Department of" and "City of"
- Corporate and government names with embedded prepositions such as "Bureau of Consumer Affairs"

- Personal or company names that include numbers, punctuation marks, or other nonalphabetic characters such as "James O'Hara," "3M Company," and "Amazon.com"

While library publications, such as *ALA Filing Rules*, published by the American Library Association, and *Library of Congress Filing Rules*, provide comprehensive alphabetization guidelines, they are principally intended for catalog entries and other bibliographic records that describe books or other publications.[10] Bibliographic filing rules are also covered by ISO 7154, *Documentation—Bibliographic Filing Principles*. The previously cited ARMA guideline, *Establishing Alphabetic, Numeric, and Subject Filing Systems*, is a more useful authority for business records. It provides specific recommendations with clear examples for alphabetization of personal and corporate names and for preparation of cross-references for abbreviations and acronyms. Records managers responsible for planning and supervising alphabetic filing operations can accept the ARMA guidelines in their entirety or adapt them for their own purposes. In either case, written alphabetization procedures and staff training sessions, repeated periodically, are essential for successful implementation of an alphabetic file arrangement.

Alphabetic file arrangements are compatible with both drawer- and shelf-type filing equipment discussed later in this chapter. Guides or other dividers, marked with single- or double-letter alphabetic designations, can separate groups of individual folders and draw the user's eye to the desired alphabetic section of a drawer or shelf. Alphabetic file arrangements can also employ color-coding for misfile detection. **Color-coding** employs the use of color to identify file folders or records with specific attributes.

Numeric Filing

Numeric arrangements are widely used for case files, customer order files, financial records, insurance policy and claim files, and other records that are numbered and that, when needed, are requested by an identifying number. Numeric arrangements are also used for name files or other alphabetic files where alphabetic filing units are converted to numeric codes for filing purposes. Advocates of this approach contend that numeric coding increases privacy and decreases training requirements and filing labor. Compared to alphabetic arrangements, numeric filing requires fewer rules to cover special situations, although a name-to-file-number index must be created in most cases.

Sequential numeric filing is the simplest and most widely encountered type of numeric arrangement. As its name indicates, a sequential numeric filing system features a consecutive arrangement of numbered folders with higher numbered folders placed after lower numbered ones. Thus, the folder for case number 403581

---

[10] Some library filing practices may be confusing or unacceptable for business use. For example, *ALA Filing Rules* equates names that begin with "Mc" and "Mac" so that "McDougal" and "MacDougal" are treated as identical spellings. Both names are filed after names that begin with "Mab" and before names that begin with "Mad."

comes after the folder for case number 403580 and before the folder for case number 403582. Like alphabetic arrangements, sequential numeric systems are compatible with drawer- and shelf-type filing cabinets. Preprinted or customized guides can be used to subdivide drawers or shelves into readily identifiable segments. Numeric identifiers can be color coded to simplify misfile detection.

Sequential numeric filing systems are easily learned and implemented, but several significant disadvantages can limit their usefulness:

1. **Filing areas often congested.** In many filing installations, numeric identifiers are sequentially assigned to newly created folders as cases are opened, orders are received, financial transactions are processed, insurance policies are written, or claims are submitted. Records are consulted most frequently when they are newest, and the matters to which they pertain are unresolved. Where file numbers are sequentially assigned, the highest numbered and presumably most active folders will be clustered together in drawers or on shelves. In busy filing installations, those areas can become congested. Workers may have to stand in line to retrieve folders from drawers or shelves and to replace them when they are returned to the filing area. By contrast, accessing filing cabinets that contain lower numbered folders, which are older and less active, will be much easier.

2. **Specific storage unit staff assignments prohibited.** As a related limitation for large filing installations, this unbalanced distribution of retrieval and refiling activity prohibits the assignment of particular cabinets, drawers, or shelves to designated employees, a technique that promotes accountability for accurate filing procedures.

3. **Folder backshifting often required.** Sequential numeric filing systems usually require the time-consuming movement or "backshifting" of folders to make room for newly created records as older records are purged from drawers or shelves.

The terminal digit filing method was developed to address these limitations in large records repositories such as a medical records room in a hospital, a central policy file in an insurance company, or a cumulative student record file in a university registrar's office. A terminal digit filing installation is divided into 100 primary sections, each of which is subdivided into 100 secondary sections. Primary sections may be file cabinets, drawers, or sections of shelving units. They are identified by the digits 00 through 99. Within each primary section, the secondary sections are identified by file guides, which are labeled with the digits from 00 through 99. The terminal digital method is based on the sequential numeric arrangement. Case numbers, account numbers, claim numbers, or other numeric folder identifiers are transposed for filing in specific primary and secondary sections. The transposition is based on the following procedure:

1. The folder identifier is divided into three sets of digits. Terminal digit filing works best with six-digit numeric identifiers that can be divided into three pairs of digits. Thus, the case number 403581 would be divided for filing and retrieval

purposes into 40-35-81. The third pair (81)—the terminal digits—is considered the primary filing unit, the middle pair (35) is considered the secondary filing unit, and the first pair (40) is considered the tertiary filing unit. The terminal digit method is intended for large filing installations. Six-digit numeric identifiers can accommodate up to one million folders. Terminal digital filing with shorter or longer numeric identifiers is possible but not optimal. Shorter numeric identifiers must be padded with zeros, in front or back, to reach the six-digit length. Longer identifiers, such as social security numbers, can be truncated to six digits, but that approach may yield duplicate folder numbers. Alternatively, the secondary or tertiary filing units can have more than two digits.

2. The numeric identifier is read backwards in primary, secondary, and tertiary unit sequence. Thus, the folder for case number 40-35-81 will be filed as if it read 81-35-40. Note that the case number, claim number, or other numeric identifier on the folder tab is not actually changed. The number is transposed for filing and retrieval purposes only.

3. The folder is placed into the appropriate primary section behind the appropriate secondary file guides. For case number 403581, the folder will be filed in primary section 81 behind secondary guide 35 where it will be the fortieth folder, surrounded by folders for case numbers 393581 and 413581.

As their defining characteristic, terminal digital transpositions radically alter the sequence of folders within cabinet drawers or on shelves. In a sequential numeric arrangement, the folder for case number 403581 would be filed in primary section 40 behind secondary guide 35 where it would be the eighty-first folder, surrounded by folders for case numbers 403580 and 403582. (See Figure 7-2.)

Where numeric identifiers are sequentially assigned to newly created folders, the terminal digit method evenly distributes the newest and presumably most active records throughout a filing installation, thereby eliminating contention and congestion resulting from clustering of active records within a few drawers or shelves—the principal advantage of terminal digit filing. In a large, active file room, workers can be assigned to specific groups of cabinets with reasonable assurance that filing, retrieval, and refiling workloads will be equitably distributed. Because records are evenly distributed within primary sections and behind secondary file guides, backshifting of folders following purging of older records is not necessary. Identifying older records that are eligible for destruction or transfer to offsite storage can be difficult because these records will be scattered throughout the terminal digit arrangement.

Middle digit filing is a variant form of nonsequential numeric arrangement. Like the terminal digit method, it divides a six-digit folder identifier into three pairs of digits, but the middle pair is considered the primary filing unit,

> Terminal digit filing procedures may seem initially confusing, but they are soon mastered with practice. Proponents of the terminal digit system argue that it is easier to use, faster, and more accurate than sequential numeric filing. As with sequential numeric filing, terminal digit systems are compatible with drawer- and shelf-type file cabinets. Numeric identifiers can be color-coded to simplify misfile detection.

Figure 7-2

**Sequential
Numeric vs.
Terminal Digit
Filing**

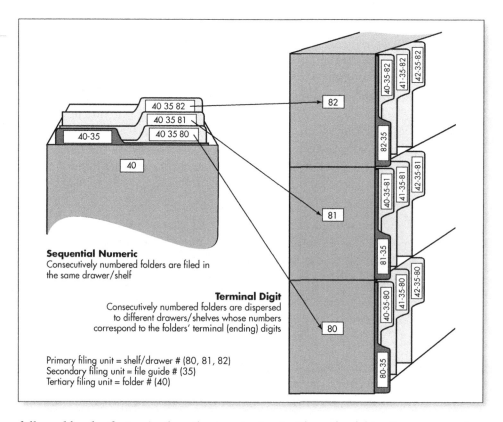

Sequential Numeric
Consecutively numbered folders are filed in
the same drawer/shelf

Terminal Digit
Consecutively numbered folders are dispersed
to different drawers/shelves whose numbers
correspond to the folders' terminal (ending) digits

Primary filing unit = shelf/drawer # (80, 81, 82)
Secondary filing unit = file guide # (35)
Tertiary filing unit = folder # (40)

followed by the first pair, then the terminal pair. Thus, the folder for case number 403581 would be read as 35-40-81 for filing or retrieval. The folder would be filed into primary section 35 behind file guide 40 where it would be the eighty-first folder. Middle digit filing offers the same advantages as terminal digital filing. Compared to sequential numeric filing, newly created folders and employee workloads are more evenly distributed throughout a filing installation, and back-shifting folders when older records are purged is not needed. Because they are scattered through a middle digit filing installation, however, identifying older records that are eligible for destruction or transfer to offsite storage can be difficult.

Alphanumeric filing systems, in which folder identifiers combine alphabetic characters and numeric digits, are sometimes categorized as *numeric filing methods*, but they have more in common with alphabetic arrangements. Depending on the filing rules, numeric digits may be sorted before or after alphabetic characters. This topic is covered by NISO TR03, *Guidelines for Alphabetical Arrangement of Letters & Sorting of Numerals & Other Symbols*, published by the National Information Standards Organization.

Chronological Filing

Chronological filing, a variant form of numeric filing, arranges records by date. Early filing systems consisted of simple chronological log books that listed all records created or received by an organization. Typically, the records themselves were also filed in chronological order. While some organizations continue to log all or selected documents chronologically, that approach typically supplements other filing methodologies. As their principal limitation, chronological logs are not compatible with demanding retrieval requirements. To identify a given document, large portions of a log must be examined.

In some organizations, chronological filing is used for storing copies of outgoing correspondence. Sometimes described as "reader" files, chronological correspondence files were originally developed to keep selected employees advised about important developments, as reflected in outgoing correspondence. They also provide an alternative method of identifying correspondence that cannot be located in a subject file. At one time, reader files were widely implemented, especially for executive correspondence, in businesses, government agencies, and not-for-profit organizations; but as email has replaced conventional correspondence, these entities have less need for reader files.

Chronological filing can be used for transaction files, including so-called tickler or suspense systems in which records are filed by the date on which they must be consulted or acted upon. Chronological files may contain correspondence, reminder notes, invoices, notifications to be sent, travel documents, or other information about other matters that require attention on a particular date. Chronological files are organized by month with subdivisions, if necessary, for each day within the month.

Phonetic Filing

Phonetic filing was developed for large name files where surnames may sound alike but are subject to spelling variations or frequent misspellings. Names are filed by the way they are pronounced in English rather than by the way they are spelled. In a primitive form of phonetic filing, one of the possible spellings of a given surname is selected for use and all variant spellings of that surname are filed under that form. Cross-references are placed into the file to direct the user from variations to the accepted spelling.

The Soundex method offers the most effective approach to phonetic filing. Sometimes described as the *Russell Soundex method*, it was initially developed by Robert Russell, who received a patent for an alphanumeric coding scheme for phonetic filing of personal names in 1918. In 1936, Remington Rand proposed a refined version of the Russell Soundex method for a name index to microfilmed records of the 1900 U.S. Census. It was subsequently used to index records of the 1880 and 1920 Censuses, in indexing projects involving twentieth-century immigration records, and to index other records created and maintained by federal and state government agencies. Over the years, computer scientists and others have developed Soundex variants with improved capabilities or special features. The Daitch-Mokotoff Soundex system, for example, is particularly useful for Germanic or Slavic surnames. Soundex systems have been applied to medical records, birth and death records, prison inmate records, bank customer records, insurance policy holder files, and other records that might otherwise be arranged alphabetically by name.

Remington Rand's version of Soundex filing is the most widely encountered form of this file arrangement. Described as the American Soundex method, it converts surnames to a four-character alphanumeric code that generally results in the identical filing of similar sounding names of different spellings. In Soundex coding, the first letter of the surname becomes the first alphanumeric code character. All vowels and the consonants h, w, and y are ignored, and the first three remaining characters are converted to numeric digits using the following table:

Letters	Code Number
B, F, P, V	1
C, G, J, K, W, S, X, Z	2
D, T	3
L	4
M, N	5
R	6

Thus, the surname "Johnson" would be coded as J525, as would "Jonson" and "Jahnsen." If a name lacks a sufficient number of consonants, the code is completed with zeros. Thus, "Smith" is coded as S530 as is "Smythe." Double letters are treated as a single character, as are adjacent characters with an equivalent numeric value in the Soundex table. American Soundex coding can yield confusing results. "Mailer," "Miller," "Mueller," and "Mahler" are each coded as M460 despite noticeable differences in pronunciation. "Peterson" and "Petersen" are each coded as P362, but so are "Peters" and "Petrosian." On the other hand, phonetically identical names may be coded differently. Examples include "Kohn" (K500) and "Cohn" (C500) and "Moskowitz" (M232) and "Moskovitz" (M213).

Soundex codes are filed according to rules for alphanumeric arrangements. In large filing installations, many folders will have the same Soundex code. The file folder tab is consequently inscribed with both the Soundex code and the person's name. In addition to its use for paper files, Soundex coding is supported by some database applications. Other phonetic algorithms, such as Metaphone, have been used by spell-checking software and other applications.

Geographic Files

Geographic arrangements are recommended where records are requested by location. In a geographic arrangement, documents may be filed by street addresses, counties, municipalities, states or provinces, countries, postal codes, tax map subdivisions, or combinations of these geographic designations. While less common than alphabetic and numeric arrangements, geographic filing is well suited to a variety of records. For example:

- Political, topological, weather, and road maps produced by cartographers, geologists, meteorologists, petroleum exploration and mining companies, urban planners, and property surveyors are obvious candidates for geographic arrangement, but some business documents are filed geographically as well.

- Municipal building departments, for example, typically maintain property folders that are arranged by section-block-lot designations or by street address. Individual folders may contain ownership information, property descriptions, building permit applications, code enforcement complaints, and other records for a given property.

- A social services agency that serves a large geographic area may group case files by the counties or municipalities in which clients live.

- An operator of fast food restaurants may file records relating its store locations by country, then by state or province, then by the name of the franchisee.

- In an insurance agency or office equipment dealer, customer files may be grouped by predetermined sales territories, which may be based on ZIP codes, municipal boundaries, or other geographic parameters.

Although place names are typically sequenced alphabetically, geographic arrangements sometimes combine alphabetic and numeric filing rules. Street names, for example, are arranged alphabetically, and individual addresses for a given street are sequenced numerically. Geographic arrangements are easily expanded, but large geographic files can have complicated multilevel subdivisions.

Subject Files

Many corporations, government agencies, and other organizations have a need to file documents that relate to specific organizations, events, activities, initiatives, products, or other topics. The contents of such subject files are as varied as the organizations that maintain them and the business operations they support. Subject files may include, but are by no means limited to, the following types of documents:

- Correspondence and reports
- Budgets and financial information
- Policies and procedures
- Agendas, minutes, handouts, or other materials distributed at meetings
- Planning documents
- Information about contractors and suppliers
- Competitive intelligence
- Information about government agencies, community groups, or other organizations product specifications and brochures
- Press releases
- Copies of articles or other publications

The purpose and value of subject files likewise vary. They may provide indispensable support for highly focused business operations, or they may contain general reference or background information that is seldom consulted.

Alphabetic arrangements are compatible with subject filing. In such filing installations, folders labeled with topical headings are arranged, dictionary fashion, in alphabetic order. As an example of this approach, consider a hypothetical subject file of technical and competitive intelligence information in a company that sells magnetic and optical storage media for computer, video, and audio applications. This subject file includes specification sheets, product literature and reviews, copies of publications, and other documents pertaining to specific storage technologies and products. A typical alphabetic section of such a file might include folders with these topical headings:

AIT	Magneto-optical disks
Blu-ray	Maxell audiotapes
CD-R	Mini-DV tapes
CD-RW	Optical disks
DAT	QIC formats
DLT	Recordable CDs
DVD-R	Removable hard disks
DVD-RAM	Super DLT
DVD-RW	Travan tapes
DVD+R	Verbatim tapes
DVD+RW	VHS cassettes
Floppy disks	VXA tape cartridges
Imation media	8mm data tapes
LTO Ultrium tapes	8mm video tapes

This approach to subject filing has several significant shortcomings. The folder list comingles general headings, such as "Recordable CDs," and more specific headings, such as "CD-RW," in a single alphabetic sequence. Information about related subjects, such as the various types of magnetic tapes, is scattered throughout alphabetic sections of the file. None of the general headings are subdivided to reflect specialized facets of a given topic, and, other than expansion within a given alphabetic section, no framework is available for creating new headings. In practice, some folders will likely contain many documents while others will have only a few pages.

Hierarchical subject filing systems, sometimes called *classification systems*, are designed to address these problems. Rather than arranging topical headings in alphabetic sequence, hierarchical systems create a tree-like structure of logically related categories that represent general and specific facets of a given subject or activity. Hierarchical filing systems are conceptually similar to library classifications systems such as the Dewey Decimal System and the Library of Congress classification system that organize published information about a wide range of subjects. Like their library counterparts, hierarchical filing systems for records management group related documents and provide a flexible framework for the incorporation of new subjects at various levels in the filing hierarchy. Some hierarchical filing systems—such as the Modern Army Recordkeeping System and its predecessors, the Army Functional Filing System and the War Department Decimal System—are ambitious enterprise-wide solutions to the problem of organizing paper documents. Most hierarchical filing systems, however, have a narrower scope. They are designed to organize documents associated with a specific business activity.

Hierarchical filing systems for records management are typically custom-developed for specific collections of documents. In most cases, a hierarchical filing system replaces an ineffective alphabetic subject arrangement. As a first step, the existing topical headings are studied and divided into top-level categories. For the hypothetical file of magnetic and optical storage media cited previously, a hierarchical subject file might include three top-level categories:

Computer media

Video media

Audio media

Each of these top-level categories would be subdivided into second-level categories. For example:

Computer media
    Magnetic disks
    Magnetic tapes
    Optical disks

Video media
    Videocassettes
    Optical disks

Audio media
    Audio cassettes
    Optical disks

These second-level categories may be further subdivided into third-level categories. For example:

Computer media
    Magnetic disks
        Floppy disks
        Removable hard disk cartridges
    Magnetic tapes
        Digital linear tape (DLT)
        Digital audio tape (DAT)
        8mm data tapes
        QIC tapes

Optical disks
    Compact discs
    DVDs
    Blue-ray
    Magneto-optical disks
    Ultra density optical

Third-level categories may require additional subdivisions. For example:

Computer media
    Magnetic disks
        Floppy disks
            Standard formats
            Proprietary formats
        Removable hard disk cartridges
    Magnetic tapes
        Digital linear tape (DLT)
            Conventional DLT
            Super DLT
        Digital audio tape (DAT)
        LTO Ultrium
        8mm data tapes
            Conventional 8mm cartridges
            Advanced intelligent tape (AIT)
        QIC tapes
            Older QIC formats
            Travan formats
    Optical disks
        Compact discs
            CD-R
            CD-RW
        DVD media
            DVD-R
            DVD-RAM
            DVD-RW
            DVD+R
            DVD+RW
        Blue-ray
            BD-R
            BD-RE
        Magneto-optical disks
        Ultra density optical

If warranted by the quantity and characteristics of documents to be filed, some fourth-level categories may be subdivided. For example:

Magnetic tapes
   Digital linear tape (DLT)
      Conventional DLT
      Super DLT
   Digital audio tape (DAT)
   LTO Ultrium
   8mm data tapes
      Conventional 8mm cartridges
      VXA cartridges
      Advanced intelligent tape (AIT)
         AIT-1
         AIT-2
         AIT-3
         Super AIT
   QIC tapes
      Older QIC formats
      Travan formats
         TR-1
         TR-2
         TR-3
         TR-4
         TR-5
         TR-7

Following library models, some hierarchical filing systems assign numeric or alphanumeric designations to categories. Decimal subdivisions are sometimes used to represent the hierarchical interrelationship of categories. For example:

1 Computer media
   1.1 Magnetic disks
      1.1.1 Floppy disks
         1.1.1.1 Standard formats
         1.1.1.2 Proprietary formats
      1.1.2 Removable hard disk cartridges
   1.2 Magnetic tapes
      1.2.1 Digital linear tape (DLT)
         1.2.1.1 Conventional DLT
         1.2.1.2 Super DLT
      1.2.2 Digital audio tape (DAT)
      1.2.3 LTO Ultrium

1.2.4 8mm data tapes
    1.2.4.1 Conventional 8mm cartridges
    1.2.4.2 Advanced intelligent tape (AIT)
        1.2.4.2.1 AIT-1
        1.2.4.2.2 AIT-2
        1.2.4.2.3 AIT-3
        1.2.4.2.4 Super AIT
1.2.5 QIC tapes
    1.2.5.1 Older QIC formats
    1.2.5.2 Travan formats
        1.2.5.2.1 TR-1
        1.2.5.2.2 TR-2
        1.2.5.2.3 TR-3
        1.2.5.2.4 TR-4
        1.2.5.2.5 TR-5
        1.2.5.2.6 TR-7
1.3 Optical disks
    1.3.1 Compact discs
        1.3.1.1 CD-R
        1.3.1.2 CD-RW
    1.3.2 DVD media
        1.3.2.1 DVD-R
        1.3.2.2 DVD-RAM
        1.3.2.3 DVD-RW
        1.3.2.4 DVD+R
        1.3.2.5 DVD+RW
    1.3.3 Blue-ray disks
        1.3.3.1 BD-R
        1.3.3.2 BD-RE
        1.3.4 Magneto-optical disks
    1.3.5 Ultra density optical

As its principal feature and most attractive characteristic, the hierarchical approach to subject filing is truly systematic. Encompassing all facets of a given application, the logical organization and subordination of subject categories mirrors the application's scope and provides a place for every document—the more general the document, the higher its place in the hierarchy; the more specific the document, the lower its place in the hierarchy. In the previous example, technical specification sheets, brochures, copies of publications, or other documents about DVD-R media will be filed in the 1.3.2.1 category. Documents that deal with several different DVD formats—the catalog of a vendor that sells both DVD-R and DVD-RW formats, for example—will be filed one level up in the 1.3.2 category.

Documents that deal with DVD and compact disc media will be filed in the 1.3 category, which encompasses all optical disks. File categories are selected from a master list that must be updated periodically as categories are added, revised, or deleted.

Hierarchical filing systems provide useful retrieval functionality. In particular, hierarchical filing systems facilitate browsing of related documents, which are physically grouped within categories. In alphabetic subject arrangements, by contrast, related documents may be scattered in multiple folders, each labeled with a different topical heading. Hierarchical subject arrangements also permit the retrieval of documents at varying levels of specificity. In the previous example, all information about magnetic tapes can be obtained by examining the entire 1.2 category with its various subdivisions, while documents relating to specific magnetic tape formats can be retrieved by consulting the appropriate third- or fourth-level categories.

Hierarchical subject filing systems are readily expandable. New categories can be introduced at any level in the hierarchy without affecting other categories, and existing categories can be subdivided as necessary. In the previous example, fourth-level categories can be added if new DVD formats are introduced, and existing DVD categories can be subdivided, if desired, to differentiate specific products or vendors. Such subdivisions may be needed to manage large quantities of documents in a given category.

As their principal disadvantage, hierarchical subject filing systems are time-consuming and difficult to construct. They typically require a comprehensive understanding of the subject area with which the documents to be filed are associated. Thus, to develop a hierarchical subject filing system for a company that sells magnetic and optical storage media, a records manager must be familiar with the storage media industry and with information storage requirements for computer, video, and audio applications. As a further limitation, hierarchical arrangements provide only one place for filing a given document. They are consequently best suited to correspondence, reports, or other documents that deal with a single subject. If a document deals with multiple subjects, it is typically filed in the category for the principal subject. This limitation can be addressed by copying documents for filing in multiple categories, a common approach that greatly increases the size of a file, or by making cross-references among related categories, a procedure that must be followed faithfully to be effective. A simple method of cross-referencing involves copying the first page of a long document for filing in multiple categories. An annotation on the first page indicates the location of the complete document.

Filing Equipment and Supplies

To be readily retrievable when needed, records must be properly organized, but an effective filing installation also requires appropriate equipment and supplies.

Properly selected, filing equipment and supplies can clarify file arrangements, enhance productivity in filing and refiling operations, simplify the identification and retrieval of records when needed, protect records from damage, and prevent unauthorized access to recorded information. The following sections describe the most common types of filing cabinets, file folders, and accessories. The discussion emphasizes features and functions that affect the utility of these filing system components in specific records management applications.

Vertical Filing Cabinets

Vertical-style drawer-type filing cabinets, simply known as *vertical files*, were introduced in the late nineteenth century as alternatives to cabinets that stored folded documents in small compartments. Wooden cabinets, the original configuration, were ultimately supplanted by metal construction. Often preferred in installations where functionality is more important than aesthetics or where wall space is limited, vertical files are the most widely encountered storage containers for office records. They are available in models that measure 15 inches wide for letter-size pages and 18 inches wide for legal-size documents. Letter-size cabinets are preferable to legal-size models, which cost more, require more expensive filing supplies, and occupy more floor space. Special vertical filing cabinets are available for small records, such as index cards and microforms, or for large records such as computer printouts.

Figure 7-3

Vertical Filing Cabinet with Folder Tabs Aligned on the Right

(Source: Smead)

A typical letter- or legal-size vertical file cabinet measures 27 or 28 inches deep and provides about 25 linear inches of filing space per drawer, although slightly more compact cabinets measure about 25 inches deep and provide less filing space per drawer. Within each drawer, documents are filed from front to back. (See Figure 7-3.) A follower block mechanism keeps folders upright when a drawer is partially full. Cabinet capacity depends on several factors, including the number of drawers, document characteristics, and the ratio of pages to file folders. A reasonably full vertical file drawer can hold 2,000 to 2,500 pages, allowing space for folders and file guides. Very full drawers may contain more than 3,000 pages. Each cabinet has from two to five drawers. The four-drawer vertical file is the most common configuration. Five-drawer cabinets offer greater storage capacity without an increase in floor space consumption, but the top drawer can be hard to reach and, when fully extended, may tip the cabinet forward. Two- and three-drawer vertical files are typically employed in desk-side or under-desk installations.

ANSI/BIFMA X5.3, *American National Standard for Office Furnishings—Vertical Files*, presents technical specifications developed by the Business and Institutional

Furniture Manufacturer's Association. It is incorporated into Commercial Item Description A-A-3186A, *File Cabinets, Vertical, Steel,* which specifies physical characteristics and performance requirements for vertical filing cabinets to be purchased by U.S. government agencies. Other standards include Australian Standard AS 5079.2, *Filing Cabinets: Part 2—Vertical Filing Cabinets,* which is a modified adaptation of the BIFMA standard; British Standard BS 4438, *Specification for Filing Cabinets and Suspended Filing Pockets;* and British Standard BS EN 14073-2, *Office Furniture—Storage Furniture—Safety Requirements.*

Desirable features include heavy-gauge construction (wooden cabinets remain available to meet special décor requirements), drawers that open and close easily, counterweights or other mechanisms that prevent tipping when multiple drawers are open at the same time, and full-height drawers that keep documents in place and permit the use of hanging file folders. While most vertical filing cabinets are lockable, some models are equipped with combination locks or pick-resistant key locks for extra protection. Federal Specification FF-L-2740B presents requirements for combination locks for secure file cabinets. Some vertical file cabinets have Class 5 and Class 6 GSA security ratings that satisfy the requirements of Federal Specification AA-F-358J for file cabinets that store classified documents maintained by federal government agencies. Class 5 cabinets are rated for resistance to forced entry. Class 6 cabinets are not.

Insulated vertical files provide fire protection, but they are up to 10 times more expensive than conventional models. Like the fire-resistant safes discussed in Chapter 4, insulated file cabinets for paper records are rated by Underwriters Laboratories for the period of time, in hours or fractions thereof, that interior drawer temperatures will remain below 350 degrees Fahrenheit (175 degrees Celsius) when exposed to fire temperatures up to 1,700 degrees Fahrenheit (920 degrees Celsius). Cabinets that pass the test are described as *Class 350 products.* Thus, a Class 350-1 hour cabinet will maintain interior drawer temperatures below 350 degrees Fahrenheit for one hour. Underwriters Laboratories imposes more stringent fire resistance requirements for file cabinets that store electronic media. Described as *Class 125 products,* such cabinets must maintain an interior temperature below 125 degrees Fahrenheit (53 degrees Celsius) with a relative humidity below 85 percent for a specified period of time. File cabinets that combine fire- and impact-resistance are recommended for installations above ground level. Cabinets that pass Underwriters Laboratories' impact test will remain intact when exposed to high temperatures for 30 minutes then dropped onto concrete rubble from a height of 30 feet.

Lateral Filing Cabinets

With vertical filing cabinets, depth exceeds width. With lateral drawer-type cabinets, simply known as *lateral files,* width exceeds depth. Most lateral files measure 18 inches deep. The most popular cabinet widths are 30 and 36 inches. Some manufacturers also offer lateral cabinets that measure 42 inches wide. While vertical files are available in letter- and legal-size models, lateral file drawers can accommodate both letter- and legal-size pages. Documents are usually filed from side to side within each drawer. Alternatively, a drawer can be divided into sections for front-to-back filing.

Lateral file capacity depends on several factors, including the number and width of drawers, document characteristics, and the ratio of pages to file folders. A 36-inch lateral cabinet drawer provides about 33 linear inches of side-to-side filing space.

Figure 7-4

Lateral Filing Cabinet

(Courtesy: TAB Products)

A reasonably full drawer can hold 2,600 to 3,300 pages, allowing space for folders and guides. A very full drawer may contain more than 4,000 pages. A 30-inch lateral cabinet drawer provides about 27 inches of side-to-side filing space. A reasonably full drawer can hold 2,500 to 3,000 pages, allowing space for folders and guides. A very full drawer may contain more than 3,600 pages. As with vertical files, cabinets may have from two to five drawers. Two- and three-drawer models may be installed under desks or, when fitted with a countertop, used as credenzas. Four- and five-drawer models are the popular configurations. With five-drawer models, the top drawer is usually a rollout shelf. (See Figure 7-4.)

Lateral files are often preferred over vertical files for aesthetics, particularly in open plan offices where filing cabinets will be used as room dividers. Some vendors claim that lateral files make more efficient use of floor space than vertical cabinets, but that claim is not correct for letter-size pages. A four-drawer 36-inch lateral file occupies 4.5 feet of floor space and provides 132 linear inches of filing space, or about 30 filing inches per square foot. A four-drawer 30-inch lateral file occupies 3.75 feet of floor space and provides 108 linear inches of filing space or 28.8 filing inches per square foot. By comparison, a four-drawer letter-size vertical file occupies three square feet of floor space and provides 100 linear inches of filing space or about 33 filing inches per square foot. Lateral files are slightly more efficient for storing legal-size pages. Floor space requirements and cabinet capacities cited above apply equally to letter- or legal-size pages. By contrast, legal-size vertical filing cabinets require more floor space than letter-size models. A four-drawer legal-size vertical file occupies 3.5 square feet of floor space and provides 100 linear inches of filing space or about 28.5 filing inches per square foot.

Technical specifications for lateral files are presented in ANSI/BIFMA X5.9, *American National Standard for Office Furnishings—Storage Units.* Other relevant documents include Australian Standard AS 5079.1, *Part 1: Lateral Filing Cabinets,* and Commercial Item Description A-A-3187A, *File Cabinets, Lateral and Shelf Files, Steel,* which specifies physical characteristics and performance requirements for lateral files to be used by U.S. government agencies. Like vertical files, lateral files are available in secure and fire-resistant configurations, although the selection of these products is not as great as it is for vertical cabinets. Lateral files are usually more expensive than vertical files of comparable capacity and construction.

Shelf Files

Whether vertical or lateral in design, drawer-type files are poorly suited to large active filing installations. Vertical and lateral cabinets require wide aisles to accommodate extended drawers. The total floor space requirement is three times the cabinet's base dimensions. As explained in Chapter 1, a letter-size vertical file occupies three square feet of space on its base, but the total floor space commitment is about nine square feet when space is reserved for extended drawers and room for users to stand while accessing open drawers. Further, filing and retrieval productivity are degraded by the time and effort required to pull out and close drawers. As an added complication, only one person can conveniently access a given cabinet at a time; to prevent tipping, some vertical and lateral cabinets have safety mechanisms that prohibit simultaneous opening of multiple drawers.

Shelf files, sometimes described as *open-shelf filing cabinets*, address these problems. Typically the filing equipment of choice in large, active centralized file rooms, shelf files are bookcase-like units in which folders are filed from side to side on steel shelves. Multiple units may be joined together, back to back and/or side to side. Movable dividers help keep folders upright on shelves, which may measure 30, 36, or 42 inches wide. Side-tab folders, which face outward, are preferred for visibility. Shelves may be fixed or adjustable; the latter type is useful where shelf files will store paper records along with microforms, magnetic tapes, or other nonpaper media. With some products, the shelves slide forward for easier access. Some units feature receding front panels that can close over shelves for improved confidentiality and/or appearance. Such configurations resemble lateral drawer-type files, with which they are sometimes confused. (Some lateral cabinets, as previously noted, are fitted with one roll-out shelf in place of the top drawer.) The front panels may be equipped with key locks. Front panels can also protect records from dust.

Compared to vertical and lateral drawer-type files, shelf files offer greater storage density and more effective use of available floor space. Shelf files are taller than drawer-type cabinets—six-shelf, seven-shelf, or even eight-shelf configurations, which exceed seven feet in height, are available. By contrast, the height of drawer-type cabinets rarely exceeds five feet. Shelf files for office records are available in 15-inch and 18-inch depths for letter- and legal-size folders, respectively. A letter-size unit with six 36-inch shelves occupies 3.75 square feet of floor space and provides 210 filing inches, or about 56 filing inches per square foot—twice as much as lateral or vertical files that occupy the same amount of floor space. A legal-size unit with eight 30-inch shelves occupies 4.5 square feet of floor space and provides 280 filing inches or about 62 filing inches per square foot—again, twice as much as lateral or vertical files that occupy the same amount of floor space. More significantly, shelf cabinets do not require wide aisles to accommodate extended drawers. Compared to vertical or lateral files, more cabinets can be installed and many more

Figure 7-5

**Shelf Filing
Installation**

(Source: Iron Mountain)

records stored in a given area. Because paper records are heavy—about 2.5 pounds per filing inch for letter-size pages—a structural engineering inspection is typically necessary to confirm that the weight of shelving units and records is within floor loading limits. (See Figure 7-5.)

Figure 7-6

**Mobile Shelving
System**

(Courtesy: TAB Products)

Mobile shelving systems increase storage density by drastically reducing aisle space. In a typical installation, a single aisle is allocated to a bank of double-sided shelving units. The end units in the bank are typically anchored in place. The other units are mounted on tracks. To access a given shelving unit, the adjacent units are moved aside manually or through motorized controls to create an opening as shown in Figure 7-6. Safety mechanisms restrict the movement of shelving units when someone enters the opening. In a variant form of mobile shelving, single-sided shelving units are installed two or three rows deep on tracks. Shelving units in the front rows slide from side to side to provide access to the units behind them.

As their principal advantage, mobile shelving systems can increase the records storage capacity of a given area by as much as 50 percent when compared to stationary shelf files and by more than 100 percent when compared to vertical or lateral drawer-type files. While stationary shelf files are usually less expensive than vertical or lateral drawer-type cabinets on a cost-per-filing inch basis, mobile shelving is considerably more expensive to acquire and install than stationary filing equipment of any type. Mobile shelving should consequently be reserved for filing installations where large quantities of paper records must be stored in a relatively small amount of space. The filing area must be able to bear the weight of the shelving and records. A structural engineering evaluation is mandatory, and floor reinforcement or other costly building modifications may be necessary before mobile shelving can be installed.

Shelf files, whether stationary or mobile, are compatible with alphabetic and numeric file arrangements. They are the only type of cabinets suitable for terminal digit filing and for color-coding for misfile detection. Stationary and mobile shelf filing installations are expandable within the confines of available space. Compared to drawer-type filing equipment, however, shelf files are more difficult to move. Often, they must be fully or partially disassembled for transport then reassembled at the new destination—obviously the case with mobile shelving. They are not practical where file room relocations are likely. Further, shelf files may not be acceptable for confidential records. Shelving units can be fitted with lockable doors, but such locking mechanisms cannot satisfy stringent security requirements. Unlike vertical or lateral drawer-type cabinets, shelf files are not available in fire-resistant models.

Motorized Files

With vertical, lateral, and shelf files, users must go to a specific cabinet and open a drawer or consult a shelf to retrieve desired records. As their name implies, motorized files utilize mechanical and/or electronic components to deliver records to users. Motorized files were popular during the 1960s and 1970s when computerized document storage and retrieval systems were largely experimental and very expensive. While they are no longer widely installed, motorized filing devices remain available. When properly selected and implemented, motorized files offer fast retrieval, effective security for confidential information, and good storage density for paper records.

The *vertical motorized file*, the most widely encountered example, dates from the early 1960s. It consists of shelves mounted onto a revolving transport mechanism inside a large cabinet. Cabinet heights and shelf widths vary. Shelves may store letter-size folders or documents, legal-size folders or documents, or computer printouts. Special models are available for index cards, microforms, checks, fingerprint cards, and other small records. To retrieve or replace a folder or document, the operator consults an index to determine its shelf location. The index may be manually prepared or computerized. In either case, the operator enters the shelf number at a calculator-style keypad. The transport mechanism revolves to position the indicated shelf at an opening, allowing the operator to remove or replace the desired folder or document. Vertical motorized files are compatible with accessibility guidelines for buildings and facilities under the Americans with Disability Act as specified in 28 CFR Part 36.

The vertical motorized file exhibits the advantages and limitations of mechanized filing equipment. Given a suitable index, folders or documents can be located quickly. The newest models can operate under computer control; following an index search, a computer program initiates shelf movement, eliminating the need to key-enter shelf numbers. To protect confidential information, the opening where records are retrieved or replaced can be covered by a locked door when the vertical motorized file is not in use. A vertical motorized file can store a given quantity of records in about one-third the floor space occupied by vertical or lateral drawer-type cabinets, but vertical motorized files cost substantially more to purchase and maintain than manual files of comparable capacity. Further, high-density storage of large quantities of paper records has structural implications. Floor reinforcement or other expensive site preparation may be required prior to installation of vertical motorized files. Like mobile shelving, vertical motorized files are difficult to move, which makes them a poor choice for departments that change locations frequently. While vertical motorized files are reliable, downtime is always possible and, over a period of years, inevitable. An equipment malfunction can render records completely inaccessible. As a final, often overlooked limitation, a vertical motorized file works best with a trained equipment operator who will handle all document retrieval requests.

Special Filing Equipment

Most drawer- and shelf-type cabinets are intended for office records, especially letter- or legal-size pages. Special filing equipment is available for smaller and larger records. Vertical files are available for index cards, checks, microforms, tabulating cards, and other small documents. A vertical drawer-type filing cabinet that measures 15 inches wide by 52 inches high by 27 inches deep can store up to 15,000 microfiche or 4-inch by 6-inch index cards. Some shelf files are specifically designed for x-ray films, which are larger and heavier than office documents.

Flat files are drawer-type cabinets for flat storage of unfolded engineering drawings, architectural plans, maps, prints, circuit diagrams, and other large documents measuring up to 36 inches by 48 inches (E-size). Flat file cabinets are typically configured with 5 to 10 drawers, each measuring 1.5 inches to 3 inches deep. A flat file drawer that measures two inches deep can hold about 100 drawings when reasonably full. Flat file cabinets with shallow drawers, which store fewer drawings, are more expensive but easier to access. Drawer dividers allow flat files to be used for smaller documents. *Hanging files* are useful for drawings and large documents that are consulted frequently. The drawings are suspended from rails or clamps. As their name indicates, roll files store rolled drawings or other large documents. While flat files are preferable for preservation of drawings, roll files are often the only practical storage equipment for drawings that are larger than 36 by 48 inches.

Shelf files have been used for decades in centralized magnetic tape libraries associated with mainframe and mid-range computer installations. Depending on cabinet design, magnetic tape reels may rest on shelves separated by wire racks that maintain the reels in an upright position; alternatively, tape reels may be suspended from clips inserted into a specially designed hanger bar. A 50-inch shelf can hold about 50 reels of magnetic tape wrapped in tape-seal belts and suspended from clips. Shelf capacities are reduced when wire racks are used. A typical cabinet contains five or six shelves, the latter configuration approaching a height of seven feet. Similar high-capacity shelf files are available for half-inch data cartridges, which have replaced magnetic tape reels in mainframe and mid-range computer installations.

For maximum versatility, several manufacturers offer *mixed-media storage units* that use interchangeable shelves and racks to accommodate different sizes and types of electronic media within the same cabinet. Such a cabinet might, for example, contain one or more hanging bars for magnetic tape reels, several racks for half-inch data cartridges, and additional shelves for hard disk cartridges or optical disks. If desired, shelves and hanging frames can be included for binders, computer printouts, file folders, microfilm, and microfiche trays, thereby permitting storage of electronic media and related human-readable documentation in the same cabinet.

Drawer-type vertical and lateral filing cabinets are poorly suited to magnetic tape reels, but they are available for smaller media, including data cartridges, video cassettes, audio cassettes, hard disk cartridges, diskettes, and optical disks. As an example, a nine-drawer unit measures approximately 42 inches wide by 18 inches deep by 64 inches high. It can be configured to store up to 790 computer tape cartridges or 2,140 compact discs or DVDs. *Tub files* house frequently referenced records in an open cabinet that is accessed from the top. Often mounted on casters, tub files can store paper documents, microforms, or electronic media. A *tub desk*, as its name suggests, combines a tub file with a work surface. *Carousel files* consist of storage racks or bins mounted on turntables that can be manually rotated. They are available for microforms, magnetic tape cartridges, audio cassettes, videocassettes, diskettes, optical disks, and other media.

File Folders

File folders keep logically related documents together. **Filing** is the process of organizing information by placing logically related records in close physical proximity to one another. Manila folders are the most common filing supplies. Manufactured from paperboard and characteristically light tan in color, they are available in letter, legal, metric, and special sizes that, when folded along a designated score line, are slightly larger than the documents they will contain. A letter-size manila folder, for example, measures approximately 11.75 inches wide by 9 inches high, excluding the tab, which typically bears a label or other identifying markings and adds about one-half inch to the folder's height or width. Folders with top tabs are intended for drawer-type vertical or lateral files. Folders with side tabs, also known as end tabs, are intended for shelf files. Legal-size manila folders measure 9 inches by 14.75 inches, excluding the top or side tab. Folder characteristics are described in several national standards, including BS 1467, *Specification for Folders and Files*, issued by the British Standards Institution, and DIN 821-1, *Files and Folders—Dimensions*, and DIN 821-3, *Files and Folders—Concepts*, both published by the Deutsches Institut fuer Normung.

File folders must be able to withstand repeated handling without tearing or other damage. Durability is determined, in large part, by folder thickness, which is measured in points, where one point equals 0.001 inch. An 11-point manila folder is suitable for many office records, but thicker 14-point or 18-point folders offer greater durability for files that will be consulted frequently over long periods of time. Where greater thickness is required, 20-point or 25-point folders are manufactured from pressboard, which is heavier and more durable than paperboard. Most pressboard folders feature expanding box-like bottoms that can accommodate many pages. Some products, described as *classification folders*, have interior dividers or pockets to separate documents into predefined groups. As might be expected, thick folders are more expensive than thin ones. Some vendors offer economical lightweight manila folders that are less than 11 points thick, but such products are rarely suitable for records management applications. As with other types of papers, the life expectancy of file folders is determined by their acidic content. Acid-free file folders are available for valuable documents with long-retention periods.

Suspended folders hang from rails that are built into or installed in file drawers. The top edges of suspended folders are equipped with metal rods that have hook-shaped ends for that purpose. Suspended folders slide along the rails, facilitating the insertion or removal of records. Suspended folders may be constructed of paperboard, recycled paper products, or plastic. The top edges have slots for the insertion of plastic tabs. Suspended folders are available in a variety of sizes and configurations, including folders with box-shaped bottoms, internal dividers, and internal pockets. Documents can be inserted directly into suspended folders or enclosed in manila folders, which are inserted into suspended folders. As a potentially significant limitation, suspended folders take up more space than conventional folders. They can decrease drawer capacity by 10 to 25 percent, depending on application characteristics.

Color-coding

Identifying information can be written or typed directly onto a folder tab. More often, the information is written, typed, or computer-printed on a pressure-sensitive, adhesive label, which is then affixed to the tab. Some labels feature color strips, which can be used to signify specific folder attributes such as destruction dates or access restrictions that are not reflected in the file arrangement. In a terminal digit filing installation, where records with different retention periods are characteristically scattered rather than clustered together, different colors can identify the years when specific folders are to be purged. Similarly, colors can identify folders that contain confidential records or folders that cannot be removed from a designated area. Colored folders can be purchased for such purposes, or colored stickers can be affixed to manila, pressboard, or suspended folders.

A more complex form of color-coding is used to minimize misfiling and simplify misfile detection in large alphabetic and numeric filing installations. This form of color-coding is intended for shelf files with side-tab folders. Colors are assigned to specific numeric digits or letters of the alphabet. Folder tabs display color bands that represent alphabetic or numeric identifiers. In numeric filing installations, color-coding is typically limited to the first three numbers in a folder identifier. Thus, for a folder tab labeled with the identifying number 362415 only the digits 3, 6, and 2 will be color-coded. In alphabetic name files, color-coding is usually applied to the first two or three letters of the surname and, if needed, the person's first initial. When folders are properly filed, their tabs present uninterrupted bands of color. Misfiled folders, which interrupt the continuous color bands, are readily detectable, provided that the misfiling involves the color-coded digits or letters. Undetectable misfiles are limited to the remaining digits or letters, which narrows the area of the file that must be searched.

Several vendors offer preprinted adhesive color strips that can be affixed to side-tab folders to implement color-coding. Alternatively, software is available for custom-printing of color-coded labels from computer-generated lists of numeric or alphabetic file identifiers. In either case, numeric filing installations require a maximum of 10 different colors. In alphabetic filing installations, which require more colors, the same color may be assigned to two different letters.

Filing Accessories

File guides enhance the appearance and usability of filing installations. They divide drawers or shelves into readily identifiable segments, which makes locating the segment where a given document will be filed or retrieved easier. File guides are available in letter- and legal-size for drawer- and shelf-type cabinets. They are usually constructed of 25-point pressboard with three or five tab positions along the top edge. Some products feature metal reinforced tabs. File guides can be purchased with preprinted alphabetic characters, numeric digits, or days of the week for alphabetic arrangements, numeric arrangements, and tickler files, respectively. In hierarchical subject filing systems, file guides can identify and demarcate topical categories and subcategories. Guides with tabs in the leftmost position can identify primary categories, those with tabs with positions to the right identify secondary categories, and so on.

Out guides, also known as *charge-out cards,* are pressboard cards in the shape of a file folder with the word "OUT" printed on the tab, usually in red letters or in white letters on a red background. When a folder is removed from a drawer or shelf, the out guide is put into its place. The body of the out guide is a printed form with spaces for recording the date a folder was removed, the name of the person who removed it, and other information. A variant version, usually made of red vinyl, features a pocket for temporary filing of records to be added to the removed folder when it is returned.

Out guides are most effective in supervised centralized filing installations where staff members will ensure that they are completed each time a folder is removed.

Even then, out guides are merely placeholders. A manual charge-out system provides little information about how many records have been removed from a filing installation and which folders have not been returned as expected. Where greater control over records is required, computer software can charge out folders or individual documents, keep a record of charge-out transactions, and check items in when they are returned. Such software is modeled after library circulation control systems, which have been widely computerized for over three decades. When a charge-out transaction occurs, the folder's barcode number, a borrower's identifier, and the date are entered into a computer database. To simplify data entry, barcode labels can be affixed to folders and, if item removal is permitted, individual documents. Among its useful capabilities, charge-out software can define access privileges and restrictions for specific types of records and employees, limit the number of records that an employee can remove at one time, impose time limits on charge-out periods for specific types of records, generate lists of items that are not returned by a specified time, print overdue notices, block charge-out transactions for employees who have not returned records, and produce statistical summaries of charge-out activity for specific time periods, folders, or borrowers.

Some Filing Guidelines

The concepts, equipment, and supplies described in preceding sections are a filing system's building blocks, but, to be effective, they must be appropriately applied. The following discussion presents widely cited advice to support filing installations. While they are typically associated with paper-based recordkeeping, some of the guidelines presented here can be adapted for the digital document implementations discussed in the next chapter:

- *Prepare a detailed written description for each filing installation.* The description should define the purpose and scope of the installation. It should indicate the layout of the filing area and the arrangement of records within cabinets and specify how filing and retrieval will be performed for particular types of records.

- *Label all drawers, shelves, file guides, and folders clearly to indicate their contents.* Drawer and shelf labels should indicate the span of folders contained therein. At a minimum, folder labels should include a name, an identifying number, a subject heading, or another descriptor, along with a date where meaningful.

- *Make filing a high priority activity.* Records should be filed as soon as possible after they are created or received. Records are filed so that they can be located quickly and reliably when needed. Filing backlogs impede access to important information resources.

- *Sort records into the correct sequence prior to filing them.* Where large quantities of records will be added to existing folders, the records should be sorted into the same sequence as the file arrangement before interfiling them. Where customer records are arranged alphabetically by the customer's name, for example, newly received documents should be sorted into alphabetic order before filing. Sorting racks are available for that purpose.

- *Avoid overcrowding filing cabinets.* Allow several inches of working space within drawers or shelves. Remove inactive records from filing cabinets as specified in retention schedules. This process will make active records easier to identify when needed.

- *Avoid storing multiple copies.* Do not file multiple copies of documents unless there is a demonstrable need for them.

- *File the most active records in middle cabinet drawers or shelves where practical.* Those drawers and shelves are easy to reach. Reserve top and bottom drawers or shelves for older records that are less likely to be retrieved.

- *Use file guides where necessary.* As previously discussed, file guides demarcate a file into readily identifiable subdivisions. Do not create subdivisions or prepare file guides until they are needed. File subdivision requirements depend on the quantity of records. Subdivisions may need to be added over time as the quantity of records increases. The number of file guides per drawer or shelf depends on the file arrangement and the level of retrieval activity; the more active the records, the more file guides needed.

- *Replace damaged folders as soon as possible.* Prevent filing errors when a folder label is missing, and filers are unable to determine quickly where the folder should be filed, for example.

- *File related documents together.* As previously described, file folders keep related documents together. Place the most recent documents into the front of the folder. Select folders with prongs where documents must be kept in order or to prevent removal of individual pages.

- *Subdivide folders where necessary.* Conventional manila folders can hold about three-quarters of an inch of paper. Subdivide folders by date or topic when they approach capacity. Include the folder sequence number on the folder label. To keep them together, several related manila folders can be placed into one suspended folder. Use box-bottom folders if subdivision of records within conventional folders is impractical or undesirable. Box-bottom folders are also useful for multipage documents, such as bound reports, that cannot be subdivided.

- *Use color-coding to reduce misfiles.* Some misfiling of records is inevitable. Color-coding can simplify detection of misplaced folders within alphabetic and numeric file arrangements, but color-coding cannot prevent filing documents in the wrong folders. When documents cannot be located in a given folder, check folders surrounding it and the bottom of the file drawer or shelf.

- *Use binders for some records.* Consider using binders rather than folders for small quantities of related records that are consulted frequently and that must be conveniently and quickly available when needed. For accessibility, binders should be stored on shelves rather than in drawer-type cabinets. Like folders, binders must be clearly labeled to indicate their contents.

- *Advise employees about safety precautions when using filing equipment.* Repair cabinets with sharp or rough edges. Make sure cabinets and shelves are level to avoid accidental opening of drawers and to keep records from sliding off shelves. Fully close filing cabinet drawers after use. Never leave an open drawer unattended. To prevent tipping, avoid overloading the top drawers of a cabinet, particularly if the bottom drawers are partially full or empty. To reduce the effort required to open them, avoid filling drawers to capacity. Open only one drawer of a given filing cabinet at a time. (As noted previously, some cabinets have anti-tipping mechanisms to prevent simultaneous opening of multiple drawers.) Use a stepstool, if necessary, to access high shelves or the top drawers of a cabinet. Never climb onto shelves or onto open cabinet drawers. Empty filing cabinets before moving them. Do not stack filing cabinets on top of one another.

Summary of Major Points

☑ Filing organizes information by identifying related records and placing them in close physical proximity to one another—in the same folder, in the same drawer, in the same cabinet, and so on. Broadly defined, a file is a collection of related records that are stored and used together.

☑ A filing system encompasses all components related to the organization of records. Those components include, but are not necessarily limited to, written policies and procedures, administrative and supervisory personnel, filing equipment, filing supplies, and office space or other facilities where filing activities will be performed or where filed documents will be stored.

☑ Where recorded information must be available to more than one worker, centralized files are usually preferable to decentralized filing arrangements in which records relating to a particular business process, operation, or activity are scattered in multiple locations. The advantages of centralized filing generally outweigh the most widely cited disadvantage: a central file area may not be located in convenient proximity to all authorized users.

☑ A central file must have a written policy that defines the purpose and scope of the file. The policy must identify the business applications that the central file will serve, the types of records to be included in the central file and, where applicable, the types of records that are excluded. The policy must be supported by clear written procedures that specify who is responsible for submitting records to the central file, and when and how they are to be submitted.

☑ A file arrangement places logically related records in a predetermined sequence for retrieval when needed. Depending on the application, records may be arranged by the name of a person or organization to which they pertain, by a numeric identifier, by date, by a code that represents the way a name is pronounced, by a geographic unit, or by subject categories.

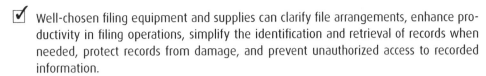 Well-chosen filing equipment and supplies can clarify file arrangements, enhance productivity in filing operations, simplify the identification and retrieval of records when needed, protect records from damage, and prevent unauthorized access to recorded information.

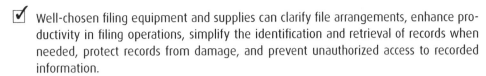 Vertical files are the most widely encountered storage containers for office records. Lateral files are often preferred over vertical files for aesthetics, particularly in open plan offices where filing cabinets will be used as room dividers.

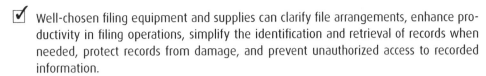 Shelf files are bookcase-like units in which folders are filed from side to side on steel shelves. They are the filing equipment of choice for large, active centralized file rooms. Compared to vertical and lateral drawer-type files, shelf files offer greater storage density through more effective use of available floor space. Shelf files are taller than drawer-type cabinets, and they do not require wide aisles to accommodate extended drawers. Compared to vertical or lateral files, more cabinets can be installed and many more records stored in a given area. Mobile shelving systems increase storage density by drastically reducing aisle space, but they are more expensive than stationary shelving.

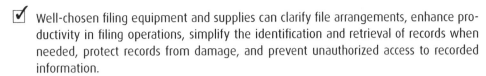 Special filing equipment is available for smaller and larger records. Drawer-type cabinets are available for index cards, checks, microforms, tabulating cards, and other small documents. Flat and hanging files can store unfolded engineering drawings, architectural plans, maps, prints, circuit diagrams, and other large documents.

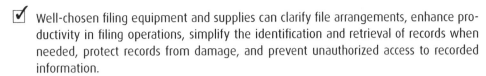 File folders are available in many types and sizes. Color-coding can minimize misfiling and simplify misfile detection in large alphabetic and numeric filing installations.

[This page intentionally left blank]

Chapter 8

Digital Documents

Paper-based recordkeeping presents significant challenges. Voluminous filing installations can occupy large amounts of office space. While inactive records can be sent to offsite storage, active records must be kept on hand for retrieval when needed. File arrangements can be difficult to develop and implement, particularly where records are retrieved by subject. Written procedures must clearly delineate filing responsibilities and methods; even seemingly obvious alphabetic and numeric file arrangements require rules for special situations. Centralized filing is often recommended for efficiency and effectiveness, but some users may be poorly served by centralized filing installations, which are not practical in every work environment. Filing equipment and supplies must be compatible with file arrangements, retrieval activity, and installation constraints. Keeping track of documents that have been removed from filing installations can be difficult. Misfiling is inevitable, but misplaced folders and documents can be difficult to detect, even when color-coded folders are used.

Other office operations, such as typing, faced comparable difficulties that were successfully addressed by computerization. Yet, among commonly encountered office tasks, filing is the least likely to be automated, even in organizations that make extensive use of information processing technology for other purposes. While documents are routinely created by word processing software and distributed as email messages and attachments, some percentage of them continue to be filed and retrieved manually. Typewriters, where present in the workplace at all, are relegated to the occasional preparation of forms and business envelopes, but filing cabinets and folders remain well-established fixtures in modern offices.

Nonetheless, effective computerized alternatives to paper-based recordkeeping have been available for many years. These computer applications support the organization, storage, retrieval, and retention of digital documents in image and character-coded text formats. Digitized images, as defined in Chapter 5, reproduce the appearance of textual information within the source documents from which the images were made. With character-coded digital documents, by contrast, each letter of the alphabet, numeric digit, punctuation mark, or other textual symbol is represented by a predetermined sequence of bits. As textual information is typed at a computer keyboard or processed from digitized images by optical character recognition software, bit sequences that represent specific characters are automatically generated. These bit sequences are defined by standardized coding schemes, such as the Universal Coded Character Set, which is defined by ISO/IEC 10646, *Information Technology—Universal Coded Character Set (UCS)*, or the American Standard Code for Information Interchange (ASCII), which is defined by ISO/IEC 8859-1, *Information Technology—8-bit Single-Byte Coded Graphic Character Sets—Part 1: Latin Alphabet No. 1*.

For purposes of this discussion, a digital document is defined as a computer-processible record created for purposes that would otherwise be served by a paper document or photographic record. Examples include word processing files, spreadsheets, and presentations created by office productivity applications; page-formatted, computer-generated reports that are stored electronically instead of being printed for distribution; email messages, which are the digital counterparts of correspondence and memoranda; digital images produced by document scanners and digital cameras; computer-aided design (CAD) files, which are digital versions of architectural plans, engineering drawings, surveys, and other schematics; and radiological images generated by CT scanners, MRI devices, and other medical systems as alternatives to conventional photographic x-rays. If a digital document did not exist, the same information could be created in nondigital form. Digital documents can be printed to produce paper or photographic documents of comparable content, appearance, and functionality. These characteristics apply to documents that are "born digital" as well as to those created from paper or microfilm records.

Digital document technologies can simplify records management operations and facilitate the execution and completion of information-dependent business processes, transactions, and tasks. Compared to paper filing systems, digital documents offer significant advantages that address the principal concerns of active records management. In particular:

1. *Digital document technologies permit convenient, fast retrieval of records needed for specific purposes, thereby expediting business processes and improving employee productivity for information-dependent tasks.* Digital document technologies employ indexing as an alternative or complement to filing methods. Rather than grouping related documents in folders, an index database keeps track of digital documents that relate to a given person, account, case, claim, subject, or other matter. Assuming that an appropriate indexing plan is in place, digital documents with specific characteristics can be quickly identified and retrieved.

2. *By providing online access to document collections and their associated metadata,*[11] *digital document technologies address a significant limitation of paper filing installations—the requirement that users be in the same location as the documents*

---

[11] In this context, metadata is defined as descriptive or indexing information pertaining to specific digital documents. Metadata is covered by many standards. Examples include ISO 23081-1, *Information and Documentation—Records Management Processes—Metadata for Records, Part 1: Principles*; ISO 23081-2, *Information and Documentation—Records Management Processes—Managing Metadata for Records, Part 2: Conceptual and Implementation Issues*; ISO/TR 23081-3, *Information and Documentation—Records Management Processes—Managing Metadata for Records, Part 3: Self-Assessment Method*; IEC 82045-1, *Document Management—Part 1: Principles and Methods*; and IEC 82045-2, *Document Management—Part 2: Metadata Elements and Information Reference Model*.

in order to retrieve them. Assuming that appropriate computing and networking arrangements are in place, digital documents can be accessed by authorized persons at any time from any location, including international locations. Such remote access facilitates the creation and maintenance of central files as comprehensive, authoritative repositories of documents relating to specific business processes, projects, products, clients, or other matters. Centralized repositories of digital documents can be accessed from branch offices and field locations, thereby eliminating the need for satellite files at those sites. Because users do not take exclusive physical possession of digital documents when they retrieve them, the same documents can be accessed simultaneously by multiple persons in multiple locations.

3. *Because digital documents are accessible online, document distribution is simplified.* Organizations need not produce multiple copies of documents for manual distribution to employees or others. Instead, digital documents can be routed automatically to designated recipients as email attachments. Alternatively, digital documents intended for a specific audience can be stored in shared folders or posted on Internet or intranet websites for viewing or downloading, with password protection if controlled access is desired. If documents are accessible online, photocopying requirements and costs will be reduced. Faxing of documents will likewise be minimized or simplified.

4. *Assuming that they are properly indexed and barring accidental destruction by hardware or software malfunctions, digital documents cannot be misfiled or lost in circulation.* Because digital documents are not physically removed from files for reference or distribution, file completeness is maintained and document tracking requirements are eliminated, as is re-filing of previously removed documents with its attendant potential for misfiling.

5. *Digital document technologies can provide effective version control for policies, standard operating procedures, reports, engineering drawings, technical specifications, and other documents that are subject to revision.* Successive revisions can be tracked upon entry into a digital repository. Software can conclusively identify and limit retrieval to the latest version of a digital document. Document revision histories can be displayed during the retrieval process. Superseded, withdrawn, or otherwise obsolete documents are clearly identified. They can be rendered inaccessible or, where appropriate, deleted. Authorized users can be notified when new versions of documents are released.

6. *Compared to paper filing systems, digital document technology can provide more effective security for confidential or proprietary records, including documents that contain personally identifiable information, protected health information, trade secrets, financial information, and business plans.* Access to digital documents can be restricted to specific employees or other authorized persons on a need-to-know basis. Retrieval can be strictly controlled by password privileges or other computer-based security measures. When employees rely on digital documents for reference or other purposes, the number of paper records maintained in

office areas will be reduced, thereby minimizing exposure of confidential or proprietary information to unauthorized employees or visitors. If desired, printing of specific digital documents can be prohibited or limited to designated users. Downloading of digital documents for local storage, which poses significant risks of unauthorized disclosure, can likewise be prohibited.

7. *Compared to paper files, digital documents can reduce or eliminate requirements and costs for office space, records storage equipment, and filing supplies.* As discussed in Chapter 5, digital images occupy much less space than an equivalent quantity of paper documents, and character-coded textual documents, such as word processing files and email messages, can be stored even more compactly. A terabyte of hard disk space can store word processing files and email messages equivalent to more than 300 million pages, which would fill 20,000 four-drawer filing cabinets and require 160,000 square feet of office space for storage and access. Unlike the cost of office space, records storage equipment, and filing supplies, the cost of computer storage has declined steadily and significantly over the last decade and is likely to continue to do so.

8. *Because they are not physically handled by users, digital documents are not subject to wear and tear through frequent use.* Digital document technology also provides a convenient method for creating backup copies of essential documents through duplication and storage at remote locations. Where digital documents are stored on network servers, backup copies are produced as a routine aspect of computer operations.

This chapter begins with an overview of basic document indexing and retrieval concepts, which provide the essential foundation for successful implementation of digital document technologies. Later sections describe and discuss three types of software products that create and manage repositories of digital documents: **document management systems**, records management application (RMA) software, and email archiving software. The discussion summarizes the most important characteristics of each of these products, emphasizing their advantages for records management.

Document Organization and Retrieval

The successful implementation and distinctive capabilities of digital document technologies depend on the characteristics and effectiveness of organization and indexing concepts and procedures applied to specific document collections.

If documents are not organized logically and indexed accurately, they cannot be retrieved reliably. Research studies spanning four decades confirm that indexing errors, particularly the omission or inappropriate use of subject terms, are a leading cause of retrieval failures in computer-based information systems. If a document is not properly indexed, it is, in effect, lost.

While collections of digital documents are often described as databases, systems that store and retrieve digital documents actually employ two interrelated databases: a document collection and an index to it. The index, which is searched first, contains pointers to digital documents with specific attributes. The following discussion summarizes document organization and indexing concepts and procedures, emphasizing factors that affect the identification of indexing parameters and selection of indexing values for digital document implementations.

File Plans for Digital Documents

In some implementations, digital documents are saved in labeled folders according to a predefined file plan. Sometimes described as a *file taxonomy,* a *file plan* is a systematic categorization scheme that groups documents pertaining to a given matter. A file plan defines topical or other categories into which documents will be grouped. A labeled electronic folder is established for each category. Within a given folder, digital documents are stored as individually labeled computer files. Where large numbers of documents are involved, a folder may be divided into subfolders.

This approach, which emulates conventional filing practices for paper documents, is suitable for medical records, legal cases, student records, personnel records, and other straightforward applications where multiple related documents are retrieved as a group without differentiation by document type or other parameters. In a school, for example, digital documents for a given student can simply be grouped in an electronic folder labeled with the student's name. Individual digital documents are identified by file labels, which may include a date, document type, or other information. Employing a more complex organization, folders may be nested within folders. A master folder may be created for each student with subfolders for specific types of documents such as report cards, correspondence, health records, disciplinary actions, and so on. Subfolders may be subdivided to further organize digital documents. The subfolder for health records, for example, may contain nested subfolders for immunization records, physicians' notes related to absences for medical reasons, physical examinations for participation in athletic programs, reports of treatment given by a school nurse, and so on.

File plan concepts are straightforward and logical. However, the development of a suitable file plan for a specific collection of digital documents is a significant effort that involves investigative, prototype, and test phases:

- *In the investigative phase, the file plan developer must identify the digital documents to be filed, as well as issues and concerns to be addressed.* For contract documents, for example, the investigative phase will require a detailed examination of active and/or terminated contracts. The developer must also interview persons who are knowledgeable about the organization's contract filing practices and retrieval requirements. Where available, the developer will obtain and study file plans developed by government agencies and other organizations for comparable document collections.

- *In the prototype phase, the developer will prepare a draft file plan, accompanied by instructions and appropriate supporting procedures.* The draft file plan will specify folder and subfolder structures for the digital document collection. It will also include procedures that define responsibilities for filing specific types of digital documents. The draft file plan will be circulated among knowledgeable persons for review and suggestions. One or more meetings may be needed to clarify the reviewers' comments and criticisms, which will be incorporated into a revised draft to be recirculated for further review and comment. Additional revisions may be required to produce an acceptable prototype file plan.

- *The prototype file plan will be tested in a pilot implementation using a subset of the documents for which the file plan is intended.* The developer will monitor the pilot implementation, discuss the prototype file plan with users and other interested parties, and make further revisions to the file plan in order to ultimately produce an operational version, which will be reviewed periodically and modified as necessary to address changing requirements.

With its orderly arrangement of categories and subcategories, a well-designed file plan embodies an appealing principle: there is a place for everything and everything is in its place. As a cautionary note, however, file plans are best applied to highly structured business activities with well-defined recordkeeping characteristics. Even then, as discussed in Chapter 7, some documents deal with multiple topics and might reasonably be filed in more than one folder. At retrieval time, time-consuming browsing through folder contents is often necessary to identify pertinent documents within a folder or subfolder. When a folder is opened, a list of files (documents) is displayed for operator perusal. Depending on the circumstances, this list may contain many entries. Descriptive labels, which are necessarily brief, may not conclusively identify the documents needed for a given purpose. In such situations, digital documents must be individually opened for examination, either by launching their originating applications or by using a viewer program that can display documents in various formats.

Indexing Parameters

As an alternative or complement to the file plan approach, indexing provides greater flexibility in categorizing digital documents. Index characteristics, indexing methods, and metadata concepts are treated in various international standards and related publications, including ISO 5963, *Documentation—Methods for Examining Documents, Determining Their Subjects, and Selecting Indexing Terms*; ISO 999, *Information and Documentation—Guidelines for the Content, Organization and Presentation of Indexes*; NISO TR02, *Guidelines for Indexes and Related Information Retrieval Devices*; and AIIM TR40, *Information and Image Management—Suggested Index Fields for Documents in EIM Environments*.

An **indexing parameter** is a category of information by which documents will be indexed for retrieval. The file plan approach is essentially indexing with a single parameter, which may be a personal name, subject heading, project number, case file number, or other identifier. When a digital document is filed in a given folder, it is indexed under the category that the folder represents. Each document is typically filed in a single folder. Indexing, by contrast, allows documents to be categorized by multiple parameters, which is equivalent to making copies for filing in multiple folders. Compared to the file plan approach, multiparameter indexing is suitable for a broader range of digital documents, and it gives searchers more retrieval options to locate a desired document.

The identification of appropriate indexing parameters is an essential first step in planning a digital document implementation. If a document is not indexed by a given parameter, it cannot be retrieved by that parameter. A digital document implementation creates and maintains a computer database that serves as an **index** to individual items in a document collection. The index database contains one record for each digital document included in a given collection. Index records contain pointers to the digital documents to which they pertain. A computer file that contains a list of words with pointers to the digital documents in which they appear is an **inverted index**. Multipage documents are typically treated as a unit for indexing purposes.

Records in the index database consist of fields that correspond to indexing parameters selected for the corresponding document collection. These fields are customarily divided into two types: key fields and nonkey fields. Key fields, the most important type in digital document implementations, correspond to the retrieval requirements identified for a particular application. Nonkey fields, by contrast, contain descriptive information that is important but will not be used for retrieval. The information contained in nonkey fields is displayed when index records are retrieved through searches involving key fields.

To illustrate these concepts, the following list presents possible key and nonkey fields for indexing correspondence, reports, and other commonly encountered office documents that might be included in a hierarchical subject filing system of the type described in the preceding chapter:

☐ Document date	key field
☐ Indexing date	nonkey field
☐ Document type	key field
☐ Author	key field
☐ Author affiliation	key field
☐ Recipient	key field
☐ Recipient affiliation	key field
☐ Subject(s)	key field
☐ Notes	nonkey field

The examples of key and nonkey fields presented above are similar to those delineated in ISO 15836, *Information and Documentation—The Dublin Core Metadata Element Set*. All suggested fields are key fields except the notes and the date that the document was indexed. Depending on the circumstances, documents may be requested by the author, the author's affiliation, the recipient, the recipient's affiliation, the date, the subject, or some combination thereof. A folder-oriented file taxonomy cannot effectively address these varied retrieval requirements. The "notes" field may contain a document summary, evaluative comments, instructions for further action, or other descriptive information. The "date" field, which is a key field, stores the date on which a given document was written, assuming that the document is dated, or the date that it was received, for documents that are date-stamped upon receipt. Date information is frequently used to narrow retrieval operations to specific time frames. The "document type" field identifies particular types of office records such as correspondence, memoranda, budgets, or reports. Retrieval can consequently be limited to a particular type of document.

The "author" and "recipient" fields, which contain personal names, may not be applicable to all documents. The "recipient" field is typically associated with correspondence, memoranda, and other documents received from external sources. While personal names are important, authors and recipients may be more meaningfully identified by the internal departments or external organizations with which they are affiliated. The manager of an engineering project, for example, may need to retrieve all correspondence to or from a given contractor or supplier, regardless of the specific author or recipient of the correspondence. The "subject(s)" field contains words or phrases that represent the subject content of a document, one of the most important retrieval parameters for office records. The subject field is typically a multivalue field, because many documents cover multiple topics. In theory, documents can be indexed with dozens of subject terms at varying levels of specificity, but such exhaustive indexing is seldom required.

Index Values

Indexing is based on the premise that the subject content or other characteristics of documents can be adequately represented by descriptive labels that serve as document surrogates. Indexing involves an analysis of document characteristics and the determination of appropriate labels for designated indexing parameters. For purposes of this discussion, the descriptive labels associated with specific indexing parameters are termed *index values*. Indexing parameters are defined for an application as a whole; index values describe specific documents in a manner determined by those parameters.

Often, the values appropriate to specific indexing parameters can be identified by a cursory examination of documents; for example, with dates, authors' names, and recipients' names used to index email messages, which include labeled heading areas for dates and names. Similarly, purchase orders and other standardized business forms contain labeled sections for dates, purchase order numbers, vendor names, and other information. The date, author(s), title, and originating department usually appear on the cover of a technical report. The title block of an engineering drawing typically contains the drawing number, date, project identifier, creator, and revision number in labeled boxes. The drawing's size, material, and number of pages can usually be determined by physical examination.

In such straightforward situations, appropriate index values can be quickly and easily extracted from documents by administrative or data entry personnel who have limited knowledge about the document collection and the business operation with which it is associated. Subject indexing, however, is more difficult. Documents must be read to determine what they are about, and that determination must be expressed in words or phrases that are variously called *subject terms, subject headings, subject descriptors, subject identifiers,* or *subject keywords.* Because subject indexing is an intellectually demanding and potentially time-consuming task, simpler indexing parameters—such as names, dates, and numeric identifiers—are preferable, but subject indexing is often required. Examples include correspondence, reports, policy statements, standard operating procedures, proposals, and technical specifications.

In some applications, subject terms are selected from a predefined list of authorized words or phrases. Such an indexing aid is variously called a *thesaurus* (plural form: *thesauri*) or a *subject authority list.* Applicable standards include ISO 25964-1, *Information and Documentation—Thesauri and Interoperability with Other Vocabularies—Part 1: Thesauri for Information Retrieval,* and ISO 25964-2, *Information and Documentation—Thesauri and Interoperability with Other Vocabularies—Part 2: Interoperability with Other Vocabularies.* An effectively designed thesaurus presents a structured view of a particular activity or field of knowledge as reflected in subject words or phrases. In addition to providing a codified, standardized list of authorized index terms, a thesaurus typically includes cross-references from unauthorized synonyms to approved terms and from authorized terms to broader, narrower, or otherwise related terms. Thesauri have been developed for published reference books and online databases that index scholarly articles and other publications in specialized subject areas such as aeronautics, medicine, petroleum engineering, education, or pharmaceuticals. Typically, however, the time and cost associated with thesauri creation and maintenance preclude their use in business-oriented records management applications.

A *name authority list* is a variant form of thesaurus. It establishes approved forms for personal and corporate names to be used as index values. It also provides cross-references from unauthorized forms, such as abbreviations and acronyms, to approved forms. Compared to thesauri, name authority lists are easier to construct and maintain. Employee names and departmental names can be taken from organizational directories. Published reference sources, such as business and government directories, can establish authorized forms for names of external organizations. Indexing rules can specify whether full corporate names or acronyms are to be used, as well as procedures for cross-references.

Index Data Entry

After names, subject terms, or other index values are selected, they must be converted to computer-processable form for inclusion in the index database. As in other computer applications, key-entry of index values is the most prevalent data entry methodology. Typically, a data entry workstation displays a formatted screen with field names and adjacent blank spaces for entering index values. The data entry operator fills in the blanks, using the tab key or another designated key

Key-entry rates are affected by operator skill, data entry procedures, source document characteristics, and other factors. Entered data must be checked for incorrectly typed characters and any errors corrected. Errors can be detected by proofreading displayed or printed data or by double-keying, in which index data is typed twice and the operator is alerted to discrepancies in the first and second typing. Double-keying is more accurate but takes longer than proofreading. It is often reserved for selected information, such as numeric values, that is difficult to proofread or for indexing critical documents where data entry errors are intolerable.

to advance from field to field. In some installations, names, subject terms, or other index values can be selected from preformulated lists, eliminating the need to type them. With certain types of digital documents, such as email messages and digital images of business forms, specific index values may be automatically extracted from labeled headings or designated areas within the document.

Full-text Indexing

The foregoing discussion is based on the assumption that manual selection and entry of index values are employed for specific fields associated with a collection of digital documents. As an automated alternative, **full-text indexing** is a computerized indexing method for word processing files, email messages, and other character-coded digital documents. The subject of much research over the past four decades, full-text indexing identifies the words that digital documents contain and extracts them for inclusion in a computer file that lists words with pointers to the digital documents in which they appear. While a full-text index can include an entry for every word in a digital document, some words are typically excluded. These words include prepositions, conjunctions, interjections, adverbs, and certain adjectives that rarely convey subject content, as well as single-letter words, such as "I" and "a," and possibly two-letter words such as "an" and "if." Compared to **field-based indexing**, full-text indexing provides great **indexing depth**, which is defined as the number of index terms per document. Field-based indexing is necessarily limited to significant names and major subject concepts. With full-text indexing, by contrast, most nouns and verbs become searchable index terms.

Full-text indexing is limited to character-coded digital documents. It is not applicable to CAD files, audio files, video files, or other nontextual information. Full-text indexing can be applied to digital document images if optical character recognition (OCR) is used to generate a character-coded version of the images. OCR is a computer input method that combines scanning technology with image analysis to identify or "read" characters contained in typewritten or printed documents. An OCR program processes document images to recognize the alphabetic characters, numeric digits, punctuation marks, or other textual symbols they contain. The recognized characters are converted to machine-readable, character-coded form, just as if they had been typed.

Compared to key-entry of index values, OCR is faster and requires less labor, but satisfactory accuracy is not attainable in every case. While OCR technology has improved steadily and significantly since its introduction in the 1960s, its ability to recognize characters depends on a source document's physical, typographic, and formatting attributes. OCR programs work best with original documents that contain black characters on a white background. These documents are likely to produce clear, high-contrast images. Recognition accuracy is degraded by faded characters, photocopies with toner flecks or other blemishes, skewed images, text printed in small sizes, pages with tables or other complex formatting. Recognition errors, which are inevitable, must be detected and corrected by proofreading and overtyping.

Automatic Categorization

Automatic categorization is a form of automatic indexing in which software analyzes digital documents and assigns them to categories in a predefined file plan or indexing scheme. As with full-text indexing, the documents to be categorized must be character-coded. Depending on its content, a given digital document may be assigned to one or more index categories.

Categorization software products, sometimes described as *categorization engines*, employ synonym lists, pattern matching algorithms, word clustering, word frequencies, word proximities, and other lexical and statistical concepts and tools to analyze a document's content and identify key words or phrases for indexing purposes. Unlike full-text indexing programs, which create index entries for all words except those on a stop list, categorization software analyzes rather than extracts words.

Automatic categorization may involve dozens of choices. Documents may be categorized by the projects to which they pertain in an engineering firm, by courses or curricula to which they pertain in an educational institution, by the products to which they pertain in a manufacturing company, by the clients to whom they pertain in a social services agency, by the events to which they pertain in a meeting planning company, or by the medical procedures to which they pertain in a hospital. Documents might also be categorized by type—a contract, a complaint, an order, an invoice, a resumé, a financial document, or a privileged attorney-client communication, for example. Some categorization engines can identify documents that contain personally identifiable information and account numbers.

Some categorization engines employ rule-based approaches in which certain words or phrases are associated with specific file plan categories. The categorization rules must be developed by persons familiar with the document collection served by the file plan. Other categorization engines use an example-based approach in which documents are compared to a training set of documents that have been manually categorized and assigned to topical folders by a knowledgeable person. To be effective, this example-based approach may require manual categorization of dozens or even hundreds of documents per folder. An automatic categorization engine compares new documents to previously categorized documents and assigns them to topical folders.

The subject of several decades of information science research, automatic categorization is an evolving technology. It is most effective for documents associated with managed activities and formalized business processes. The ability to accurately categorize documents depends on several factors, including document content and the nature and complexity of the topical categories to which documents must be assigned. Documents that deal with less-structured business operations or that comingle information about multiple topics are difficult to categorize. With most programs, automatic categorization can be supplemented by human intervention if the analysis of document content falls below a predetermined confidence threshold.

Retrieval Functionality

Folder-oriented filing is suitable for well-organized collections of digital documents with straightforward retrieval requirements; but, apart from providing convenient online access to documents, it offers no performance advantages over paper recordkeeping systems. Time-consuming browsing may be required to locate a desired document within an electronic folder. Faster, more accurate retrieval, an anticipated source of enhanced productivity and improved operating efficiency, depends on indexing rather than filing methodologies. An index search can quickly identify and display digital documents with specific characteristics. In addition, document indexing permits complex retrieval operations that cannot be conveniently performed, and may not even be possible, with folder-oriented filing methodologies. In particular, documents can be retrieved by multiple index categories, which can be combined to precisely identify documents needed for a specific purpose.

Document retrieval operations are based on users' information requirements, which may vary in scope, specificity, complexity, and clarity of expression. In some cases, a retrieval operation involves specific documents that are known to contain required information. Correspondence, for example, may be conclusively identified by the author, recipient, and date. A purchase order or invoice may be conclusively identified by an order number or customer name. An engineering drawing may be conclusively identified by a project number and the object depicted. With very little training, novice users can easily initiate and successfully execute such retrieval operations. More complex information requirements involve searches for documents pertaining to particular subjects, events, or other matters, which may be described in vague terms or otherwise poorly articulated. Such ambiguous information requirements must be analyzed and clarified to develop an appropriate retrieval strategy. This process may require assistance from someone knowledgeable about information retrieval concepts and experienced with a particular implementation's indexing methodologies.

Ultimately, an information requirement must be expressed as a search specification, or query, to be executed by the database management software that indexes digital documents. Some information retrieval software can accept "natural language" queries expressed as questions or instructions, which are entered in a sentence format without regard to formal syntax: "Find the floor plans for the municipal building," for example, or "Locate all correspondence between Thomas Smith and Mary Jones from 2007 to the present." With more or less success, the software parses such queries to identify search terms and determine the specific retrieval operations to be performed.

More often, however, search specifications must be entered in a structured format. With field-based indexing, a typical query includes a field name, a field value, and a relational expression. Searchable fields, previously defined as key fields, are determined by the indexing plan developed for a particular collection of digital documents. Field values may be words, phrases, numbers, dates, or other index information to be matched. With some systems, they may be selected from a scrollable list of previously entered or permissible field values. Relational expressions, sometimes described as *relational operators*, specify the type of match desired. Relational expressions include:

Equal to

Not equal to

Greater than

Greater than or equal to

Less than

Less than or equal to

In an application involving technical reports, for example, a search specification of the form:

author = smith

will initiate a search for index records that contain the character string "smith" in the author field. The equals sign, or an abbreviation such as EQ, is the most meaningful relational expression for index searches involving names, subjects, or other textual field values. It can also be applied to quantitative values, telephone numbers, social security numbers, and other numeric field entries. In most cases, the equals sign specifies an exact match of a designated field value, but it can be combined with other search capabilities to obtain different results. The "not equal to" operation is its opposite, but it is rarely used in document retrieval operations. The other relational expressions may be represented by symbols, such as > or <, or by abbreviations such as GT for greater than or LT for less than. They are obviously useful for numeric or date information. When combined with Boolean operators, relational expressions permit range searches that identify field values between an upper and lower numeric limit.

Depending on the retrieval software and user interface, a search specification, including a field name, field value, and relational expression, may be entered in a prescribed syntax at a command prompt or typed into a dialog box. More commonly, retrieval software may display a search form with labeled fields accompanied by blank areas for entry of search terms preceded by relational expressions. That approach is well suited to novice or occasional searchers, but both methods require some training for effective use. Both approaches are subject to considerable variation, and some systems combine them, supporting command-oriented retrieval operations for experienced searchers and form-based searches for novice users.

As an initial response, most retrieval software displays a count of the number of index records and, by implication, the number of digital documents that satisfy the search specification. Depending on this response, which is sometimes termed "hit prediction," the searcher may reconsider the retrieval strategy and modify the search specification, broadening it if too few index records are identified or narrowing it if the number of retrieved index records is excessive. The Boolean operators are useful for that purpose. They are used to combine two or more search specifications in a single retrieval operation.

The most common Boolean operators are AND, OR, and NOT. Of these, the AND operator is the best known and most widely implemented. Virtually indispensable for effective retrieval operations in digital document implementations, it limits the scope of a given retrieval operation by combining two or more search specifications, both of which must be satisfied. For retrieval of digital versions of technical reports in a research laboratory, for example, a search specification of the form:

author = smith AND date > 2014

will limit retrieval to index records that contain the value "smith" in the author field and any value greater than "2014" in the date field. The Boolean OR operator, by contrast, broadens an index search by specifying two retrieval requirements, either of which must be satisfied. Thus, a search specification of the form:

author = smith OR author = jones

will retrieve index records that contain either or both of the two indicated values in the author field; that is, reports written by either Smith or Jones or both. The Boolean OR operator is particularly useful for subject searches based on synonymous or otherwise related terms. In a pharmaceutical company, for example, a search specification of the form:

subject = prilosec OR subject = omeprazole

will retrieve index records that contain either the brand name, "Prilosec," or its generic equivalent, "omeprazole," in the subject field. Although convenient and useful, the Boolean OR operator is not indispensable. The same results can be obtained, albeit in a more cumbersome way, by conducting separate retrieval operations for each search term.

The Boolean NOT operator, which may be implicitly or explicitly combined with the AND operator, will narrow a database search by excluding records that contain specified values in designated fields. In the case of technical reports, a search specification of the form:

author = smith NOT date < 2014

will limit retrieval to documents written by Smith in 2014 or later. Depending on software capabilities, several Boolean operators may be combined in a given search specification, thereby permitting very complex retrieval operations involving multiple field matches.

Some digital document implementations support additional search capabilities to enhance retrieval flexibility. In addition to retrieving database records that match exact field values specified in search statements, some systems can identify field values that begin with, contain, or end with specified character strings. In particular, searches for field values that begin with a specified character string are particularly useful for retrieving subject terms, personal names, or corporate names with common roots, as well as singular and plural forms of field values. Some retrieval software supports "fuzzy" search capabilities, which will match field values that are similar to, but do not exactly satisfy, a given search specification. Fuzzy searches are particularly useful for subject terms with variant spellings, "color" and "colour," for example. They can also be used to retrieve misspelled field values or personal names of uncertain spelling.

Where full-text indexing is employed, authorized users can search for digital documents that contain specific words. Such full-text searches may employ relational expressions, Boolean operators, or other retrieval features. Certain additional capabilities are unique to full-text searching. Phrase searching, a form of proximity searching, will retrieve documents that contain two adjacent words in a specified sequence, "document scanner," for example. With some software, proximity commands allow a searcher to specify the number of permissible intervening words between two search terms and/or the sequence in which the two terms appear. With some proximity commands, a searcher can specify that two terms appear in the same line, sentence, paragraph, or page within a digital document. This capability is sometimes described as *context searching*. Some software products offer unusual full-text retrieval capabilities. Examples include index browsing to facilitate term selection, case-sensitive searches, automatic searches for synonymous or related terms based on an online thesaurus, and conflation operators, which automatically match different verb tenses or related forms of nouns.

Managing Digital Documents

The indexing and retrieval concepts discussed in preceding sections are supported by software products that manage digital documents for specific purposes.

Such products include document management systems, records management application software, and email archiving software. All three of these product groups are well established and widely implemented by companies, government agencies, and other organizations. As a group, they are designed to organize, index, store, retrieve, track, provide controlled access to, and otherwise manage digital documents, but they support records management operations at different phases in the information life cycle.

Document management systems are principally intended for active records. They create managed repositories for digital documents that will be consulted regularly and frequently to support specific business operations. Records management application software and email archiving software create managed repositories for

International standards for digital document management include ISO 10244, *Document Management—Business Process Baselining and Analysis*; ISO 12651-1, *Electronic Document Management—Vocabulary—Part 1: Electronic Document Imaging*; ISO 12651-2, *Electronic Document Management—Vocabulary—Part 2: Workflow Management*; ISO/TR 14105, *Document Management—Change Management for Successful Electronic Document Management System (EDMS) Implementation*; ISO/TR 15801, *Document Management—Information Stored Electronically—Recommendations for Trustworthiness and Reliability*; ISO 16175-1, *Information and Documentation—Principles and Functional Requirements for Records in Electronic Office Environments—Part 1: Overview and Statement of Principles*; ISO 16175-1, *Information and Documentation—Principles and Functional Requirements for Records in Electronic Office Environments—Part 2: Guidelines and Functional Requirements for Digital Records Management*; ISO 16175-1, *Information and Documentation—Principles and Functional Requirements for Records in Electronic Office Environments—Part 3: Guidelines and Functional Requirements for Records in Business Systems*; ISO/TR 22957, *Document Management—Analysis, Selection and Implementation of Electronic Document Management Systems (EDMS)*; ISO 22938, *Document Management—Electronic Content/Document Management (CDM) Data Interchange Format*; and ISO 26122, *Information and Documentation—Work Process Analysis for Records*.

retention of digital documents, although they also provide effective indexing functionality to support retrieval of stored documents when needed. Given their different purposes, these products complement rather than compete with one another. Organizations that implement document management systems for actively referenced digital documents may also utilize records management application software or email archiving software to ensure retention in compliance with established policies and procedures.

Document Management Systems

A **document management system**, also known as an *electronic document management system (EDMS)*, is a computer application that creates and maintains organized, searchable repositories of digital documents in text and image formats. Examples include word processing files, spreadsheets, email messages, digital images generated by document scanners or digital cameras, presentation aids, HTML or XML files (web pages), computer-aided design files, graphic arts files, and PDF files created from these or other sources.

The characteristics and capabilities of document management products evolved out of computerized document storage and retrieval systems introduced in the 1980s. Characterized as optical imaging or optical filing systems, these products were developed specifically and exclusively for digital images, which were stored on optical disks. They attracted considerable records management attention as an alternative to paper-based filing methodologies and computer-assisted microfilm indexing systems, which the earliest implementations closely resembled. Successive versions of these products incorporated improved indexing and retrieval capabilities to address customer requirements. By the early 1990s, their scope had broadened to accommodate word processing files and other digital documents in character-coded formats. Since that time, these more versatile document management products have completely supplanted their image-only predecessors, and their functionality has expanded steadily and significantly.

Since the late 1990s, document management products have been reconceptualized and enhanced to accommodate a wider variety of digital content, including web pages, video clips, audio clips, and other computer files that are outside the scope of digital documents as defined earlier in this chapter. These broader configurations are collectively described as *electronic content management (ECM) software*. Among their other capabilities, full-featured ECM products support conversion of digital documents and other content from one file format to another; incorporation of digital content into web pages on the public Internet and organizational intranets; version control for website content; preparation of presentation aids with media content; and managing rights and permissions for video presentations, conference call recordings, artworks, and audio-visual media.

Document management systems create and maintain organized, searchable repositories of digital documents. Document management repositories may be stored on network drives or, much less commonly, on local hard drives or optical disks. Digital documents in different formats from a variety of sources can be comingled within a given repository, and multiple repositories can be established for specific organizational units, document collections, or business processes. Within a repository, document management software supports folder-oriented document organization as well as indexing methodologies. Authorized users can define hierarchically structured file plans (taxonomies) with labeled folders and subfolders nested to multiple levels. As a starting point, some software developers offer pre-built taxonomies for specific industries, such as banking or insurance, or for widely encountered business functions such as human resources, sales and marketing, or project management. These pre-built taxonomies can be customized for specific situations. Some products support automatic categorization as an optional feature. For indexing and descriptive purposes, document management software supports customer-defined metadata with a combination of key and nonkey fields at the folder, subfolder, and document level. Full-text indexing can be applied to all or selected documents within a repository. Full-text indexing is limited to character-coded documents.

Digital documents can be imported into designated repositories by dragging and dropping them into specified folders or subfolders, by batch transfers from directories or subdirectories on network servers, or by saving them within their native (originating) applications. A word processing document or presentation can be saved to a designated repository when it is created, for example. Some metadata, such as the date a folder or document was created, can be derived automatically. Other information must be key-entered when a folder, subfolder, or document enters a repository. Some document management products incorporate a digital imaging component for scanning of paper records, with the resulting images being saved to a designated repository. Alternatively, documents can be scanned by a different application, and the resulting digital images imported into a document management repository.

When properly selected and implemented, document management systems can expedite information-dependent business processes by providing convenient online access to digital documents:

- Digital documents can be retrieved quickly by authorized persons at any time from any location with appropriate network connections.

- Digital documents needed for a given purpose can be identified by browsing through folders and subfolders; by searching metadata associated with specific folders, subfolders, and documents; or by words or phrases contained in documents, assuming that full-text indexing is utilized. Retrieval functionality includes exact matches of specified field values, relational expressions, Boolean operators, and phrase searching (where full-text indexing is utilized).

- Some document management products allow multiple repositories to be searched simultaneously. This capability, sometimes characterized as *federated searching*, may be limited to repositories maintained by the document management system or extended to other information sources such as online databases, websites, SharePoint sites, shared files on network servers, or digital documents stored on local hard drives. A retrieval command submitted to document management software by an authorized user is automatically reformatted for simultaneous submission to other sources. Results obtained from the various sources are merged and presented to the searcher in a consistent format.

Retrieved documents are typically displayed in their native applications if the applications are installed on the retrieval workstation. When a word processing document is retrieved, for example, the document management software will automatically launch the application that created it; when a PDF file is retrieved, the document management software will automatically launch Acrobat Reader®; when an HTML file is retrieved, the document management software will automatically launch a compatible web browser; and so on. Where the native application or a compatible equivalent is not available, the document management software provides a multiformat viewer application for display of retrieved documents. Such viewers typically support a broad range of document formats, including formats associated with discontinued applications. Once retrieved, a digital document can be printed, faxed, or attached to an email message.

Document management software's storage and retrieval capabilities are typically integrated with authoring tools. When a digital document is retrieved, it can be reviewed and edited by authorized persons within its originating application. To avoid confusion, check-out capabilities can limit or prohibit access to digital documents while they are being edited. Among their other features, document management products allow authorized users to append comments, instructions, or free-form annotations to folders, subfolders, or documents, and they will track changes and conclusively identify the latest versions of documents that are subject to multiple revisions. These capabilities are particularly useful for legal briefs, contracts and agreements, engineering specifications, regulatory submissions, standard operating procedures, and other documents that are subject to multiple revisions and a prescribed approval process.

Document management software products provide well-developed security controls to limit access to digital documents on a need-to-know basis and prevent unauthorized retrieval of documents with personally identifiable information, protected health information, or other confidential or sensitive content. An organization can define access privileges at the repository, folder, subfolder, and document levels. Access privileges determine which users or groups of users, such as members of a specific department or project team, are authorized to search for, view, print, add, delete, move, edit, or replace documents in a given folder or subfolder. Search results are limited to documents that a user is authorized to see, and searchers are not aware of the existence of unauthorized documents. Some document management systems provide a secure collaboration space where digital documents can be saved for controlled access by approved external parties— litigation-related documents that an organization's legal department wants to share with outside counsel, for example, or technical drawings that an organization wants to share with engineering consultants.

> Document management software maintains an audit trail of document-related activity. It tracks all input, editing, deletion, retrieval requests, display, printing, or other actions performed by a specific user with a given digital document, including failed access attempts by unauthorized persons.

In addition to flexible indexing and retrieval capabilities, some document management products support workflow functionality for business processes that involve routing of documents among authorized persons in a prescribed sequence in order to complete transactions or other operations. In a bank, for example, mortgage applications and supporting documents, such as credit reports and property appraisals, are typically routed from loan officers to underwriters and others for review, approval, and preparation of customer notifications and loan agreements. Documents requiring special attention may be referred to supervisors or fraud prevention personnel, accompanied by the loan officer's questions or comments. Similar document routing requirements are encountered in insurance claims processing, customer order fulfillment, loan payment processing, accounts payable, enrollment processing, and other transaction-based activities that require review of documents by multiple persons.

Performed manually, these document routing procedures are subject to errors and delays. Documents may be referred to the wrong parties or lost in transit. Recipients may fail to act on received documents in a timely manner, thereby delaying the completion of transactions or tasks. Supervisors are often unaware of delays until customers complain about them. As a document management component, workflow functionality routes digital documents among designated recipients according to user-defined rules and relationships. Rules for document routing are defined by special programs called *workflow scripts*, which are custom-developed for specific situations. Document management systems provide tools for that purpose. Depending on the circumstances, workflow routing rules may be based on document types, on the tasks to be performed, or on external events such as elapsed time or the arrival of new documents. Workflow programs monitor the progress of document routing to detect and report delays.

Workflow programming is not an integral component of all document management implementations. It is best suited to highly structured transaction-processing or production-oriented operations that are governed by clearly defined procedures for document review and approval. Workflow capabilities are often implemented in the context of business process re-engineering, which involves the analysis and improvement of existing methods of accomplishing specific operational objectives.

Records Management Application Software

Document management systems are principally intended for actively referenced digital documents. Records management application (RMA) software provides a reliable repository for retention of digital documents that are in the inactive phase of the information life cycle. As such, RMA software is designed to complement rather than compete with document management systems. To provide a complete life cycle solution for recorded information, some developers of document management systems offer RMA software for integration with their products. When reference activity diminishes, digital documents can be transferred from a document management repository to an RMA repository, which functions as a back-end retention component. RMA software provides retention functionality that is absent from document management products. In particular, RMA software can identify digital documents that are eligible for destruction in conformity with an organization's retention policies. While RMA products can also track the retention status of paper and photographic records stored in file rooms or offsite locations, they are more closely associated with electronic records.

Baseline functionality and desirable characteristics of RMA software are delineated in DoD 5015.2-STD, *Electronic Records Management Software Applications Design Criteria Standard,* which was first issued by the U.S. Department of Defense in 1997 and subsequently revised several times. The Defense Information Systems Agency's Joint Interoperability Test Command tests RMA products to verify compliance with requirements specified in DoD 5015.2-STD. The U.S. National Archives and Records Administration has endorsed DoD 5015.2-STD for use by U.S. government agencies when selecting RMA software to store electronic records as official copies and to facilitate the transfer of permanent electronic records to the National Archives. Other organizations, including companies, not-for-profit institutions, academic institutions, and state and local government agencies, have found DoD 5015.2-STD useful in establishing criteria for evaluation and selection of RMA products.

The Model Requirements for the Management of Electronic Records (MoReq) provides specifications that can be used to evaluate and prepare requests for proposals or other procurement solicitations for RMA products. The first version of MoREQ was issued in 2001 by the DLM Forum, a not-for-profit membership community of public archives, and the European Commission. MoReq2 was issued in 2008. MoReq 2010, the latest version available at the time of this writing, was issued in 2011. The DLM Forum accredits test centers that evaluate and certify RMA products for compliance with functional requirements specified in MoReq 2010.

The Victorian Electronic Records Strategy (VERS) was developed by the Public Record Office Victoria, the archival agency for the State Government of Victoria. VERS has been adopted by other Australian states to complement their own electronic recordkeeping initiatives. The VERS Standard PROS 99/007, *Management of Electronic Records*, specifies system, format, and metadata requirements for long-term preservation and accessibility of electronic records. The Public Record Office Victoria tests and certifies RMA products for VERS compliance.

RMA software is compatible with many types of digital content, including database records, audio files, and video files, but the RMA concept is best suited to digital documents as defined in this chapter. RMA software creates an organized repository for digital documents, which may be transferred to the repository from office productivity software, email systems, CAD programs, imaging software, workgroup collaboration software, or other originating applications. Digital documents may also be transferred from a document management system. An RMA repository is organized into folders that correspond to categories in a user-defined file plan, which is based on a hierarchical folder/subfolder model. As an example, a file plan for contract records might provide a master folder for each contract with subfolders for proposals, signed contracts, amendments, invoices, payment authorizations, and other types of contract-related documents. Similarly, a file plan for archived loan files might provide a master folder for each borrower with subfolders for the loan application, income verification documents, estimates and disclosures, the signed loan agreement, and other documentation. As yet another possibility, an RMA repository may be organized into folders and subfolders that correspond to a records series in an organization's retention schedule. If the organization has a departmental retention schedule, the RMA repository can have a top-level folder for each program unit with subfolders for each records series listed in the departmental schedule. If the organization has a functional retention schedule, the RMA repository can have a top-level folder for each records series with subfolders for program units that transfer such records to the repository. To facilitate retention actions, subfolders can contain nested subfolders for the years in which the records were created.

RMA repositories can import electronic records in a variety of file formats. As with document management systems, records may be transferred into a repository in batches, or files may be individually dragged and dropped into appropriate subfolders from their originating applications. The latter approach is suitable for small quantities of electronic records or where an entire folder from an originating application can be dragged and dropped into one of the repository's subfolders. Depending on the method employed, an RMA repository may contain the actual records, or it may store links to word processing files, PDF files, email messages, spreadsheets, or other records that are located elsewhere—on a network file server, for example.

Regardless of format and storage location, an RMA repository must be implemented as a managed resource. It must not be a dumping ground for digital documents that have been purged from other storage locations. No digital documents should be accepted unless they are covered by retention guidance. Use of and access to the repository should be controlled by an organization's records management program. Digital documents transferred to an RMA repository will be considered the official copies for reference and retention purposes. Duplicate copies, drafts, and other digital documents of transitory value will be excluded. As discussed in Chapter 3, such documents should be discarded when no longer needed. When digital documents enter an RMA repository, they are "locked down"; that is, they cannot be edited, deleted, or replaced until their designated retention periods elapse. If revised documents are added to closed files, they are treated as unique records rather than as replacements for older versions.

As determined by an application planner, authorized persons have read-only access to specific records. Access privileges can be defined for individuals or groups at the folder, subfolder, or document level. Electronic records can be retrieved by browsing through subfolders, as is the case in paper filing installations. Alternatively, RMA software allows folders, subfolders, and files to be indexed by user-defined fields. As an example, master contract folders may be labeled with project names and indexed by contract number, the name of the contractor, and other parameters. Similarly, a subfolder label may identify the contents as "addenda," with individual files being indexed by the date, the type of addendum, or other descriptors. Some RMA programs also support full-text indexing of word processing files, email messages, and other character-coded documents. RMA software also provides a conclusive method of identifying successive versions of electronic records that are subject to revision.

> Retention functionality is RMA software's distinctive characteristic. Authorized users can specify retention periods for electronic records in conformity with an organization's approved retention policies and schedules. Retention periods may be specified at the folder, subfolder, or individual file level. Retention periods may be based on elapsed time or events. In the former case, electronic records are eligible for destruction after a fixed period of time. In the latter case, electronic records are eligible for destruction after a designated event, such as termination of a contract or completion of a project, plus a specified number of years. To address evidentiary requirements, RMA software allows authorized users to suspend destruction of or extend retention periods for specific electronic records or groups of records that are relevant for litigation, government investigations, audits, or other purposes.

Retrieved records are displayed by launching their originating applications. If original applications are not available, viewing modules that can display electronic records in a variety of file formats may be downloaded. Depending on user privileges, retrieved records may be printed, copied, annotated, attached to email messages, or transferred to other applications. RMA software provides an audit trail for importing, retrieving, printing, exporting, copying, and other activity involving specific electronic records, including unsuccessful retrieval attempts as well as completed operations. The audit trail indicates the date that the activity occurred, the type of activity, and the identity of the user who initiated the activity.

Destruction of electronic records is not automatic: RMA software generates lists of electronic records that are eligible for destruction on a specified date. The list is submitted to designated persons for approval before destruction is executed. RMA software provides safeguards against the unauthorized destruction of electronic records by issuing a warning to the user when such destruction is attempted. RMA software can print lists, certificates of destruction, or other documentation for electronic records that were destroyed in conformity with an organization's retention policies and schedules.

A related category of digital preservation software is intended for electronic records of historical value. Implemented by archival agencies, libraries, and other scholarly repositories in government, universities, cultural institutions, and other organizations, these products comply with ISO 14721, *Space Data and Information Transfer Systems—Open Archival Information System (OAIS—Reference Model)*, which provides a framework and functional model for long-term preservation and accessibility of electronic records. Because they focus exclusively on permanent electronic records, digital preservation software products are not intended for electronic records with defined destruction dates. While they are intended for records management not archives management, some RMA software products are compatible with the OAIS reference model for digital preservation. As required by ISO 14721, RMA software products can ingest archival content submitted by various producers. They support mechanisms to prevent deletion or modification of archival content. They allow implementing agencies to define policies and privileges for accessibility and usability of archival content by a designated user community.

Email Archiving Systems

While RMA software supports retention of email messages among other types of electronic records, email archiving software is designed specifically for that purpose. As its name indicates, email archiving software creates and maintains repositories for retention of messages and their associated attachments apart from an organization's email system. When combined with comprehensive policy guidance, an email archiving solution will ensure that messages and attachments are retained for the periods of time required to satisfy all legal, operational, and scholarly requirements to which the messages and attachments are subject. Archived messages and attachments cannot be deleted until their retention periods elapse. From a technical perspective, transfer of messages and attachments to an email archiving product will improve the performance of an organization's email system without sacrificing convenient access to information. To simplify legal discovery and compliance with freedom of information laws, email archiving software aggregates messages and attachments in organized, searchable repositories, eliminating the need to search all network and local drives for messages that come within the scope of a subpoena or freedom of information request.

Specific characteristics and capabilities vary, but most email archiving solutions support some combination of the following features and functions:

- *An email repository creates and maintains an archive mailbox for each active mailbox that exists on designated email servers.* The owner of the active mailbox is the owner of its archive counterpart. Any folders and subfolders established in an active mailbox will be replicated in the archive mailbox.

- *Messages are retained in mailboxes on email servers for a specified period of time— six months, for example.* After being stored for the specified amount of them, they are transferred to the corresponding archive mailboxes in the repository where they will be stored until their retention periods elapse, or they are otherwise deleted as permitted by an organization's retention guidelines.

- *Message archiving is performed automatically at specified intervals.* Transfer of messages from email servers to archive mailboxes may be based on the age of a message or on the amount of free space in a given mailbox. Alternatively, mailbox owners may be permitted to archive messages manually. The archiving process can omit messages marked as deleted by mailbox owners but not permanently removed from mailboxes.

- *Archived messages and attachments remain accessible online by mailbox owners or other authorized persons.* Access privileges are typically synchronized with the mailbox from which the messages and attachments were archived. With most email archiving software, shortcuts for archived messages are placed into the mailboxes from which the messages were transferred. These shortcuts, which are displayed as distinctive icons, facilitate retrieval of archived messages by mailbox owners. Using email client software, a mailbox owner can browse through folders and subfolders to locate messages in an archive mailbox.

- *Email archiving software supports various levels of indexing, ranging from predefined index fields to full-text indexing of messages and attachments.* Depending on the product, archived messages may be retrievable by the sender's name or other identifier, the mailbox from which the message was archived, a date or range of dates, the message size, a file extension (for attachments), or specific words or phrases in the subject line. For full-text indexing, email archiving software supports Boolean operators, root-word searching, wildcard symbols in search terms, and other retrieval functions previously described. Full-text indexing is especially useful when searching for messages that come within the scope of a subpoena or a freedom of information law request. In such cases, email software permits cross-mailbox searching by authorized persons.

- *Archived messages can be read, forwarded, replied to, printed, or otherwise handled like any other messages.* An archived message can be restored to an active mailbox if, for example, a closed project or other discontinued matter is reactivated.

- *Retention periods can be based on the date that a message was sent or received or the date that it was transferred to the repository site.* A message and its attachments will be deleted when its retention period elapses unless it is identified as relevant for litigation, government investigations, or other legal matters. To ensure that they are preserved, copies of such messages can be transferred to a separate repository for preservation until the matters to which they pertain are fully resolved.

- *Email archiving software imposes no significant limits on the size of email messages or attachments to be stored in an archive mailbox.* To reduce total storage requirements, however, some products combine data compression with single-instance storage when archiving duplicate copies of messages. Removal of duplicate messages prior to archiving is consequently unnecessary.

- *Email archiving software can generate reports and graphs about email activity in aggregate or for individual mailboxes.*

The retention functionality of email archiving software is intended specifically for messages. Other digital documents are accommodated as attachments. As such, email archiving software is not a replacement for RMA software, which can accommodate a broader range of digital documents, including word processing files, spreadsheets, digital images, and other digital documents that were not sent or received as email attachments. An email archiving implementation does not preclude the subsequent transfer of selected messages or attachments to an RMA repository for long-term retention with other digital documents related to a specific business operation or initiative. For a manufacturing or construction project, for example, an RMA repository can integrate email messages along with engineering drawings saved as CAD files, technical specifications saved as word processing files, digital images of signed contracts saved as PDF files, and so on.

From a retention perspective, most email archiving software lacks some capabilities supported by RMA software. It cannot accommodate retention periods based on designated events such as the termination of a project. It does not permit detailed, customer-defined metadata at the folder and subfolder level. It does not support version control or provide multiformat viewing software for attachments where the originating application is not available. Generally, these shortcomings are less significant for email than for other types of digital documents. Email messages are rarely subject to version control, for example, and as long as email client software is available, users have little need for a multiformat document viewer to read messages.

SUMMARY OF MAJOR POINTS

☑ A digital document is a computer-processable record created for purposes that would otherwise be served by a paper document or photographic record. If a digital document did not exist, the same information could be created in nondigital form. Digital documents can be printed to produce paper or photographic documents of comparable content, appearance, and functionality. These characteristics apply to documents that are "born digital," such as word processing files and computer-aided design drawings, as well as to digital images created from paper or microfilm records.

☑ Compared to paper filing systems, digital document technologies can simplify records management operations and facilitate the execution and completion of information-dependent business processes, transactions, and tasks. As their principal advantage over paper recordkeeping, digital document technologies provide fast online access to documents. They also provide effective functionality for document distribution, storage, version control, and security.

☑ While digital documents can be arranged in folders and subfolders based on a predetermined file plan, indexing provides a more effective method of categorizing digital documents for retrieval. As an alternative to browsing through folders and subfolders, an index search can quickly identify and display digital documents with specific characteristics, but the successful implementation and distinctive capabilities of digital document technologies depend on the characteristics and effectiveness of indexing concepts and procedures applied to specific document collections. If documents are not indexed accurately, they cannot be retrieved reliably.

☑ A document management system, also known as an *electronic document management system (EDMS)*, is a computer application that creates and maintains organized, searchable repositories of digital documents. Documents in different formats from a variety of sources can be comingled within a given repository, and multiple repositories can be established for specific organizational units, document collections, or business processes. Within a repository, document management software supports folder-oriented document organization as well as indexing methodologies. Digital documents needed for a given purpose can be identified by browsing through folders and subfolders; by searching metadata associated with specific folders, subfolders, and documents; or by the words or phrases contained in documents, assuming that full-text indexing is utilized.

☑ While document management systems are principally intended for actively referenced digital documents, records management application (RMA) software provides a reliable repository for retention of digital documents in the inactive phase of the information life cycle. RMA software can identify digital documents eligible for destruction in conformity with an organization's retention policies. Digital documents transferred to an RMA repository are considered official copies. They cannot be edited, deleted, or replaced until their retention periods elapse. If revised documents are added to closed files, they are treated as unique records rather than as replacements for older versions.

☑ Email archiving software creates and maintains organized, searchable repositories for retention of messages and their associated attachments. When combined with comprehensive policy guidance, an email archiving solution will ensure that messages and attachments are retained for the periods of time required to satisfy all legal, operational, and scholarly requirements to which the messages and attachments are subject. Archived messages and attachments cannot be deleted until their retention periods elapse. Archived messages and attachments remain accessible online by mailbox owners or other authorized persons.

Glossary

The following list contains brief definitions of selected terms used in this book. Except for a few grammatical changes, the definitions are identical to those presented in the chapters where the terms are introduced. The relevant portions of individual chapters should be consulted for a fuller explanation and discussion of specific terms.

This glossary is provided for the reader's convenience. It is not a comprehensive list of records management terms nor is it intended as a substitute for other general or specialized glossaries such as ARMA TR 22, *Glossary of Records and Information Management Terms*, published by ARMA International; *Glossary of Terms*, published by the International Records Management Trust; ISO/IEC 2382 ISO 5127, *Information and Documentation—Vocabulary*; ISO 6196, *Micrographics—Vocabulary*; ISO 12651, *Electronic Document Management—Vocabulary*; or ISO 18913, *Imaging Materials—Permanence—Vocabulary*.

A – B

active record. A record consulted frequently and must be conveniently available for that purpose.

administrative retention criteria. Retention criteria based on an organization's operational requirements.

aperture card. A tabulating-size card with an opening that contains one frame of 35mm microfilm.

archival agencies. Agencies principally concerned with the preservation of records of scholarly, long-term policy, or administrative value.

arrangement. The physical sequence of records or groups of records within a records series.

automatic categorization. A form of automatic indexing in which software analyzes digital documents and assigns them to categories in a predefined file plan or indexing scheme.

best practices. The most advisable courses of action for particular recordkeeping problems or processes.

breaking files. The practice of subdividing a records series chronologically to simplify the identification of records eligible for retention actions.

C – D

categorization software. These products employ synonym lists, pattern matching algorithms, word clustering, word frequencies, word proximities, and other lexical and statistical concepts and tools to analyze a document's content and identify key words or phrases for indexing purposes.

central file. A collection of records consolidated for storage in a single location where authorized persons can access them.

certificate of destruction. A record that documents the disposal of specific records in conformity with an organization's formally established retention policies and schedules.

cloud computing. Web-based access to computing services, including storage of databases, digital documents, and other electronic records.

color-coding. The use of color to identify file folders or records with specific attributes.

COM recorder. A device that produces computer-output microfilm.

computer-output microfilm (COM). Microforms produced from computer-processable information.

cubic foot. When measuring the quantity of records, the contents of a container with interior dimensions of 10 inches high by 12 inches wide by 15 inches deep.

data migration. The process of periodically converting electronic records to new file formats and/or new storage media to satisfy long retention requirements.

departmental retention schedule. A retention schedule prepared for a specific department or other program unit and that is limited to a records series held by that program unit.

digital document. A computer-processable version of documents in text or image formats created for purposes that would otherwise be served by a physical document or photographic record.

digital document imaging. Images produced by document scanners and recorded onto computer storage media for retrieval, distribution, or other purposes.

document management system. A type of software product that automates the preparation, organization, tracking, and distribution of digital documents.

E – G

electronic records. Records that contain machine-readable information that is electronically encoded; examples include computer records, audio recordings, and video recordings.

field-based indexing. A list of words limited to significant names and major subject concepts.

filing. The process of organizing information by placing logically related records in close physical proximity to one another.

filing system. The combination of policies, procedures, labor, equipment, supplies, facilities, and other resources that relate to the organization of records.

full-text indexing. An indexing method that permits retrieval of documents by the words contained in them.

functional retention schedule. A retention schedule that categorizes records series by the business functions to which they pertain as to the program units where they are kept.

Generally Accepted Recordkeeping Principles® (the principles). A set of eight recordkeeping principals issued by ARMA International in 2009 to foster general awareness of records management systems and standards and to assist organizations in developing effective programs for records management programs and information governance.

I – L

inactive record. A record that is not consulted frequently but must be retained for legal, operational, or scholarly reasons.

index. A set of descriptive words or phrases that applies to specific records and that facilitates the retrieval of such records.

indexing depth. The number of index terms per document.

indexing parameter. A category of information by which records are indexed for retrieval.

information life cycle. The concept that information is subject to changing requirements for storage, retrieval, and distribution from its creation or receipt through destruction or permanent retention.

inverted index. A computer file that contains a list of words with pointers to the digital documents in which they appear.

knowledge management. A multifaceted discipline concerned with the systematic management, utilization, and exploitation of an organization's knowledge resources.

legal retention criteria. Retention criteria based on recordkeeping requirements specified in laws and regulations or on the need to keep records for possible use in legal proceedings.

litigation hold. Temporary suspension of destruction for records that may be relevant for litigation or government investigations.

M – N

microfiche. A sheet of film that contains miniaturized document images in a two-dimensional grid of rows and columns.

microfilm camera. A camera that produces highly miniaturized reproductions of paper documents.

microfilm duplicator. A device that produces copies of microforms.

microfilm jacket. A transparent carrier with sleeves or channels for insertion of strips of 16mm or 35mm microfilm.

microfilm processor. A device that develops microfilm images following exposure.

microform. A photographic information carrier that contains highly miniaturized document images; types of microforms include roll microfilm, microfilm cartridges, microfiche, microfilm jackets, and aperture cards.

microform reader. A device that magnifies microimages for viewing.

microform reader/printer. A device that magnifies microimages for viewing or printing.

microform scanner. A device that produces digital images from microimages.

micrographics. A document imaging technology concerned with the creation and use of microforms as storage media for recorded information; also known as *film-based imaging.*

microimages. Highly miniaturized document images that consequently require magnification for viewing or printing.

mission-critical operation. A business operation that an organization must perform.

nonrecords. Information-bearing objects that are excluded from the scope and authority of an organization's records management program.

O – P

obsolete records. Records no longer needed for any purpose.

office of record. An office designated as being responsible for retaining the official copies of a specific records series for the complete designated time period.

official copy. The copy of a record designated to satisfy an organization's retention requirements for information that exists in multiple copies; also known as the *record copy*.

operational retention criteria. Criteria concerned with the availability of records for long-term administrative consistency and continuity, as well as for the day-to-day operations of individual program units.

operational retention parameters. Retention limits determined by the operational requirements of employees who rely on recorded information to support an organization's daily business activities or long-term goals.

operational risk. A danger of damage or loss to an organization resulting from inadequate internal processes, including inadequate information management practices, or from external events.

physical (paper) documents. Records in paper form such as records stored in office file folders and file cabinets, business forms, engineering drawings, charts, maps, and computer printouts.

photographic records. Records composed of photographic films, including photographic negatives and slides, motion picture films, filmstrips, and microforms.

pretrial discovery. The investigative phase of litigation when the opposing party can obtain access to recorded information believed relevant to its case.

program unit. A division, department, section, or other administrative unit that maintains recorded information.

program-specific retention schedule. A retention schedule that is limited to records series held by a specific department. (See **departmental retention schedule**.)

R – Z

record. An information-bearing object, regardless of physical medium or format, that comes within the scope and authority of an organization's records management program.

record copy. The copy of a record designated to satisfy an organization's retention requirements for information that exists in multiple copies; also known as the *official copy*.

recorded information. Any and all information created, received, maintained, or used by an organization pursuant to its mission, operations, and activities.

recordkeeping. The creation, organization, storage, retrieval, and use of recorded information.

recordkeeping requirements. Records retention requirements specified in laws and government regulations.

records center. A specially designed, warehouse-type facility that provides safe, economical, high-density storage for records consulted infrequently but must be retained for legal or operational reasons.

records inventory. A fact-finding survey that identifies and describes records maintained by all or part of an organization.

records management. A specialized business discipline concerned with the systematic analysis and control of recorded information.

records series. A group of logically related records that support a specific business or administrative operation and that are filed, indexed, and/or used together.

records retention. An aspect of records management work that determines how long records need to be kept.

records retention audit. A sampling of records in one or more series may be examined for compliance with organizational policies and procedures by the records management department or by a compliance-oriented organizational unit such as an internal audit or quality assurance department. In addition to conformity with retention schedules, an audit may consider the security of records, appropriate methods for destroying confidential information, backup protection for vital records, efficient use of available storage space, or other matters.

records retention schedule. A list of records series maintained by all or part of an organization together with the period of time that each records series is to be kept.

reduction. A measure of the number of times a given linear dimension of a document is reduced through microphotography.

reference activity. The frequency with which a given records series is consulted for business or other purposes.

resolution. A measure of the ability of microfilm equipment and photographic materials to render fine detail visible within a microimage—image sharpness. Resolution is measured by examining a microimage of a specially designed test target that is recorded on a roll of microfilm or microfiche.

risk analysis. The process of evaluating the exposure of vital records to specific risks.

scanner. A computer input device that produces digitized images from paper documents or microfilm.

scholarly retention criteria. Criteria based on information of interest to historians, political scientists, sociologists, economists, demographers, or other scholars.

source document microfilming. The production of microforms from paper documents.

spoliation. Destruction of evidence, including records that an organization knows or reasonably should know are relevant to impending or ongoing litigation or government investigations.

statute of limitations. The period of time during which legal action can be taken pertaining to some matter.

vital record. A record that is indispensable to a mission-critical operation.

[This page intentionally left blank]

Suggestions for Further Study and Research

A large and growing number of books, articles, conference papers, and other publications contain more detailed or otherwise different treatments of topics covered in this book. While a comprehensive bibliography is beyond the purpose and scope of this book, this appendix provides some suggestions for further reading and research, with citations for illustrative English-language titles where applicable.

Library catalogs, which are searchable at library websites, are the best resources for citations to books and monographs about records management. Large national and academic libraries are likely to have the most complete holdings. The Library of Congress Online Catalog and the OCLC WorldCat database, which combines the holdings of thousands of libraries, are good starting points. "Records Management" is a Library of Congress subject heading. Other useful headings include "Records," "Business Records," "Public Records," "Electronic Records," "Records Retention," "Filing Systems," "Indexing," "Electronic Filing Systems," "Document Imaging Systems," "Micrographics," and "Archives."

Various business indexes and databases contain citations to articles about electronic records in professional journals, popular periodicals, and newspapers. Examples of online databases likely to be available in many medium-size and larger academic and public libraries include ABI Inform, EBSCO Business Sources Complete, and Factiva. Records management publications are also indexed in library science and technical databases, including Library, Information Science and Technology Abstracts (LISTA), Library and Information Science Abstracts (LISA), Ei Compendex, Inspec, Web of Science, and Scopus. Articles indexed in these databases range from brief overviews of recordkeeping issues and concerns to detailed case studies that describe records management practices in specific companies or government agencies. Bibliographic and ordering information for standards cited in this book is available online from their publishers' websites. Most countries provide online access to laws and regulations that contain recordkeeping requirements.

English-language periodicals that deal principally or exclusively with records management, or related topics, such as archival administration, include *Information*

Management, published by ARMA International; *Records Management Journal and Journal of Documentation*, both published in the United Kingdom by Emerald Group Publishing; IRMS Bulletin, published in the United Kingdom by the Information and Records Management Society; *IQ—The RIM Professionals Australasia Quarterly*, published by the Records and Information Management Professionals Australasia; *American Archivist*, published by the Society of American Archivists; Archivaria, the journal of the Association of Canadian Archivists; *Archives*, published by the British Records Association; *Archival Science*, published by Springer; *Journal of Archival Organization*, published by Routledge; *Comma: International Journal on Archives*, published by the International Council on Archives; *Prologue*, published quarterly by the U.S. National Archives and Records Administration; *ACARM Newsletter*, published in the United Kingdom by the Association of Commonwealth Archivists and Records Managers; and *Archives and Manuscripts*, published by the Australian Society of Archivists.

Thousands of web pages feature records management policies and procedures, samples of records retention schedules, descriptions of recordkeeping products and technologies, position papers, and other useful items that would have previously required an impractical level of effort to identify and collect. Google and other web search engines are obvious starting points to locate pertinent websites about records management topics, but the voluminous results they deliver can require time-consuming browsing. At the time of this writing, for example, a Google search for web pages containing the phrase "records management" retrieved over 6.4 million items covering policies, procedures, practices, issues, and problems in varying levels of detail and with varying degrees of reliability and usefulness. (When the previous edition of this book was written, the same Google search retrieved about 4.5 million items.) When searches are narrowed to focus on specific topics, fewer items are retrieved, but the results are still unwieldy. For example, a Google search for "records management" and "vital records" retrieved over 83,000 items, and a search for "records management" and "record retention" retrieved over 59,600 items. A search for "record retention" retrieved 748,000 items. A search for "document retention" retrieved 397,000 items. Narrowed further to "record retention schedule," a search retrieved 52,900 items, while a search for "document retention schedule" retrieved 375,000 items. Quantity aside, many of these items are highly informative.

The websites of national, state, and provincial archival agencies contain much useful information about electronic records, including policies, procedures, regulations, and position papers. Examples include the websites of the U.S. National Archives, Library and Archives of Canada, National Archives of Australia, and British National Archives. Vendor websites are good starting points for technical specifications, case studies, white papers, and other information about records management products, including filing equipment and supplies, document scanners, microfilm equipment, document management systems, records management application software, and email archiving software.

As might be expected, the websites of professional records management and archival associations are valuable sources of information about many of the topics discussed in this book. Examples include the websites of ARMA International, the National Association of Government Archives and Records Administrators (NAGARA), the Records Management Society of Great Britain, Records and Information Management Professionals Australasia, PRISM International, the Information and Records Management Society (IRMS), the Society of American Archivists, AIIM, ASLIB, the Association for Information Science & Technology, the Association of Canadian Archivists, the Australian Society of Archivists, the Archives and Records Association of New Zealand (ARANZ), the International Council on Archives, and the Association of Commonwealth Archivists and Records Managers. The International Records Management Trust emphasizes the problems of managing public records in developing countries, but much of the information available at its website is applicable to records management practice in other settings. Examples of organizations that focus on sector-specific records management issues include the Nuclear Information and Records Management Association (NIRMA), the Pharmaceutical Records and Information Management Organization (PRIMO), and the American Health Information Management Association (AHIMA).

[This page intentionally left blank]

Index

S – W

[This page intentionally left blank]

About the Author

William Saffady, Ph.D., is a records and information management specialist based in New York City. He is the author of over three dozen books and many articles on electronic records retention, digital document management, storage and preservation of recorded information, and other information management topics. Recent books published by ARMA International include *Legal Requirements for Electronic Records Retention in Western Europe, Legal Requirements for Electronic Records Retention in Eastern Europe, E-Mail Retention and Archiving: Issues and Guidance for Compliance and Discovery, Records and Information Management: Fundamentals of Professional Practice*, 2nd edition, and *Cost Analysis Concepts and Methods for Records Management Projects*, 2nd edition. In addition to research and writing, Dr. Saffady serves as an information management consultant, providing analytical services and training to corporations, government agencies, not-for-profit entities, cultural institutions, and other organizations.

[This page intentionally left blank]

About ARMA International

ARMA International is a not-for-profit professional association and the authority on governing information as a strategic asset. Established in 1955, the association's approximate 27,000+ members include information governance professionals, archivists, corporate librarians, imaging specialists, legal professionals, IT managers, consultants, and educators, all of whom work in a variety of industries, including government, legal, healthcare, financial services, and petroleum in the United States, Canada, and more than 30 countries around the globe.

ARMA International's mission is to provide informational professionals the resources, tools, and training they need to effectively manage records and information within an established information governance framework.

The ARMA International headquarters office is located in Overland Park, Kansas, in the Kansas City metropolitan area. Office hours are 8:30 a.m. to 5:00 p.m. (CT), Monday through Friday.

ARMA International
11880 College Blvd., Suite 450
Overland Park, KS 66210
913.341.3808
Fax: 913.341.3742

headquarters@armaintl.org
www.arma.org

Made in the USA
Coppell, TX
05 January 2021